# NOW I SPEAK

## BY
## ANNA NASSET

Ballast Books, LLC
www.ballastbooks.com

ISBN: 978-1-955026-86-4

Printed in the United States of America

Published by Ballast Books
www.ballastbooks.com

For more information, bulk orders, appearances, or speaking requests,
please email: info@ballastbooks.com

**Author's Note:** This memoir has been written using timelines, court documents, evidence, Facebook messages, emails, photographs, and conversations. The names of many people have been changed. Eight years have been condensed for this book; therefore, the timeline will be condensed as well. Conversations, if not from court records, are how I, the author, remember them. Many of the messages from Jeffrey have been cut down to protect innocent parties, because of violent content, or for length. These messages, along with my victim impact statement and emails, contain typos and punctuation errors because they are shown as received or written.

This is my story, recalled with great care to detail and truth, taking into account over a decade of psychological trauma in the form of stalking and nearly a lifetime of gender-based and sexual violence at the hands of various men.

For the millions of stalking victims
who cannot speak, and to Erica and
the others who did.

# Table of Contents

# Introduction

Fur-lined hats, scarves, and jackets adorned the coat rack and backs of chairs in the pub at the inn. The fireplace, barnwood walls, and cozy atmosphere warmed each guest after their day on the slopes. Through piles of snow and down a steep flight of stairs, diners gathered, eager for sustenance or attention. Wine and water glasses stayed filled as people feasted on steaks from cows raised just down the road. Rosy cheeks, laughter, and cheer filled every ounce of the pub.

To quote Bing Crosby in *White Christmas*, "Oh, well, that sounds very *Vermonty*." And indeed, it was to everyone—except for me.

An hour earlier, a stack of folded cloth napkins towered to the right of me as I focused on the square of fabric in front. The material slipped through my fingers as I made three folds and placed it on top, then watched the tower wobble like a game of Jenga. I relished the feel of the fabric; fiber has always soothed my soul and comforted me.

Matched with the quietness of the empty pub, I could breathe into the stillness, sit in my sadness, and steel myself for the evening ahead. Tying the apron around my waist was more akin to putting on a disguise than a uniform. I looked at the chairs I used to sit in and now served, selected the stories I would tell that evening, and got to work.

The first table I was assigned: an educated family of five on a ski holiday from Connecticut. As I refilled their water glasses, they began the line of questioning...

"Are you from here?"

"No."

"Oh, why did you move here?"

Story A: "I moved here for a job with a non-profit, but they lost their funding, so here I am serving you."

Five minutes later...

The second table: a sixty-year-old couple celebrating their anniversary.

Story B: "I moved here after my father died to be closer to family."

Three minutes later... *Keep the smile on your face. Don't let them see the cracks. Just keep smiling as you weave through the crowded pub with your tray of drinks. Three more hours, and you'll be home. You've got this, Anna. You're not going down tonight. Keep smiling.*

The third table, the dreaded table: wealthy middle-aged men from Boston. They'd probably had more beers than ski runs that day.

Story C: "I just really love cheese, so I moved to Vermont."

That's the one that always got the biggest laughs. I told the truth in each story, but they covered up the actual reason. Nobody wanted to hear my story; they were on vacation, after all, and I was just playing my part. Night after night, it was the same, every table asking a series of personal questions that they viewed as polite and I viewed as horribly invasive. They asked, assuming I would share my ideal Vermont life, so I gave them what they wanted. I give everyone what they want. Nobody knew my hidden truth—not my coworkers, bosses, friends. *If it stays tucked away, I'll be safe.*

The noise in the pub grew loud and rattled in my head. I navigated around the tables in a frantic series of dance moves, the tray of drinks lifted high above me. I glided across the floor as I played Dr. Dre songs in my head to keep my sanity and rhythm. It would get me through, and no one could hear me as I sang under my breath; no one wanted to listen to what I had to say anyway. But each one of those stories I told traveled with me and stuck in my brain; they fought for space along with the list of drinks and orders I was trying to remember.

Gin and tonic, Coke, Fiddlehead, *I miss my dad*, martini Grey Goose extra dry with a twist.

The burger rare with bacon and cheddar. *Who would move someplace for cheese?* Gnocchi, halibut, chicken dinner. *Am I safe here?*

Get water for table fourteen, bring a steak knife to table nineteen, *remember when you trained to knife fight?* Grab bread for twenty-two. *Try not to punch the drunk middle-aged men hitting on you when you check on them. You need a big tip, and you need this job.*

My brain gave itself a pep talk: *Don't crack now. Never let them see you falling. Just keep smiling, even though all you want to do is lie down and die.*

I wanted to go back to the ocean. I wanted to fail with triumph and win like a warrior. The results would have been the same, but I wanted a chance to experience it all differently.

Walking back to the table of men, I could smell the beer, money, and dark secrets they most likely kept. Their leering eyes and the occasional unwelcome physical contact on my elbow or hand greeted me as they asked more questions about my life, prying at me like an oyster knife, hoping that they could open me up fully and suck me right out of my shell. I was just a waitress—I was there to serve them, to entertain them, to work for my tip.

My withering smile was lost on them as I tried to answer questions politely. I failed with my initial story for why I moved here, and they pressed further. One of the men grabbed my wrist to keep me at the table—just a gentle grab but an unwanted and unpermitted touch.

"Oh, I bet it's a man. I bet she moved here for a man."

"But it didn't work out. It never works out for a woman when she moves for a man."

"Was it...did you move here for a guy?"

The withering smile disappeared from my lips. My face went stone cold, and the bright eyes of mine that they had just complimented me on became daggers of light, cutting each man off as I slammed both hands on the table they were sitting around. I leaned in close. I smelled the faint scent of fear mixed in with their toxic privilege, and I spoke.

"Yes, it was a man. You win—you guessed it. Do you want to know the truth? The man I moved to escape has stalked me for years. He thinks we are married and wants to murder me. I'm terrified every moment of the day. My life and world collapsed from success to a pile of rubble due to his obsession. But a big round of applause to you fuckers—you win."

With silence, I straightened myself up, swiftly turned around, and walked away. I didn't want their apologies, I didn't want their pity, and I certainly didn't want any more questions. I wanted their silence. I wanted them to feel how I live. I live in silence.

Flash back to reality, that last man's words still echoing in my ears—"Did you move here for a guy?" I steeled myself. My smile didn't falter. I didn't falter. "Yes, it was a man. You win—you guessed it." Then, I turned on my heel and pushed my way back through the crowd, eyes stinging, smile cracking, listening to the satisfied laughter of those men rise behind me. They didn't want my reality, and they didn't want my story, anger, or disgust. They wanted me to fill their water glasses, bring them food, and tell them how bucolic my life was in Vermont. Ski slopes and maple syrup. No one wants the truth of the lives of the people standing right in front of them.

---

Now I speak. Now I give over the words. It's not that there is anything particularly significant about my life. I've experienced what countless others have experienced—a lifetime of gender-based violence, which, for me, happened to be at the hands of men. I'm not special; I'm not unique. I am set apart in that I have the privilege to share my story when millions of others cannot. My only hope is that my words will allow others to not only have a voice but have a life.

Gender-based violence is a general term used to capture any type of violence that is rooted in exploiting unequal power relationships between genders. This can include gender norms and role expectations specific to a society as well as situational power imbalances and inequities. Gender-based violence can impact anyone and can include intimate partner and family violence, elder abuse, sexual violence, stalking, and human trafficking.[1]

# PART ONE

# FREEZE

# CHAPTER ONE

# November 4, 2011

The Office of Violence Against Women (funded by The United States Department of Justice) defines stalking as, "engaging in a course of conduct directed at a specific person that would cause a reasonable person to fear for his or her safety or the safety of others or suffer substantial emotional distress."

K nowing I would soon be dangling off a ladder, I wore hand-me-down jeans, the kind with a well-placed bleach stain or two; a sheer gray blouse purchased on discount at a Seattle boutique; and tall vintage boots. As I rushed out the door, I selected my perfect pair of white sunglasses to match the day. The cheap plastic was smooth to the touch as I fingered my way through the pile of sunglasses on the dresser and selected an oversized pair that threw back to the 1970s.

The salt air caught me as I floated down the stairs of my studio apartment at North Beach. I hopped in my car and headed to Port Townsend, Washington. The ten-minute commute wove along the water's edge, dipped and turned through lush evergreen forests, and burst with vivid color in every wheel rotation as fall settled in. Past Fort Worden, up the cliffs, through the open vistas of the Strait of Juan de Fuca, and around the bend to the uptown area with its quirky houses and gardens. After a quick jaunt down the hill after braking for a deer or two, I was at MY gallery.

Tucked in among Victorian buildings of historic downtown Port Townsend, my gallery was my dream, my little jewel box, my heart in four walls. The turn of the bronze key in the worn door unlocked my world, and the click of my heels on the whitewashed wood floor brought me joy. A jumble of paperwork, hardware supplies, and sunglasses tumbled from my arms onto my desk as I set about checking emails, sweeping the floor, and relishing in the mundane busywork of owning my own business.

●　　●　　●

*In 2000, I visited my parents when I was on break from college. I was on a mission, peering into my past to make sense of my life. I noted that on my parents' dining room wall hung a collage of pictures featuring my sister, Carrie, and me. Taped onto the brown matte, each photo was oval and trimmed with a gold decorative flourish. Me, three years old, wearing a red and white jumper. My sister, five years old in an ET-themed swimsuit, smiling shyly at the camera. In my hand, I clutch a white pair of sunglasses.*

*The pair of us linked in our differences, she was, and is, one of my biggest champions and dearest friends. Our parents, loving and fierce protectors, raised two unique daughters, and our lives have followed vastly different paths. Regardless, she is the string, and I am the balloon. There is a video of us as children; she is standing still, grinning and waving. I am running in circles around her. We need string, and we need balloons. I surround myself with string; spools of thread, yarn, cords, and quilts fill my home. It keeps my feet tethered to this earth. If not for it, I would drift away.*

●　　●　　●

Once a burgeoning seaport, Port Townsend is a town of dreamers, sailors, artists, and misfits, surrounded on three sides by the Puget Sound. The towering houses of the uptown district held captains' wives who would watch for the ships to come home, while the downtown housed prostitutes and sailors, eager to make a wage however they could. In the mid-eighteenth century, Port Townsend was on track to be the largest city and harbor in the Pacific Northwest. With the Great Depression, the railroads never made their way to town, and the bustle turned quiet. The merchants and seamen left, and the city was held together by the paper mill. Its plumes of smoke and stench linger in the air to this day.

In the late 1960s and 1970s, hippies and sailors began to flock to the peninsula and rebuild the community, filling it with eclectic characters, festivals, art, wooden boats, and curiosity. They took over what remained—the rich history of possibilities in the form of grand buildings that once housed brothels and bars, a series of underground tunnels, abandoned captains' homes—and turned it into the Port Townsend I know and love.

Port Townsend's history hung in the streets. In the mornings, as the fog rolled out to sea, the air filled with the smells of cupcakes baking next door and roasted garlic from across the street. The faint scent of pizza dough creeping down the block teased me as I sashayed across the road and headed down into the tunnels. Wafting up from the passageway was the unmistakable scent of coffee from The Undertown Coffee Shop, part of a series of tunnels under the downtown, created the underground heart in the community. Each step into the brick-lined abyss evoked a twinge of embarrassment when I thought of descending those very stairs eighteen months prior to my wedding reception, on the arm of my new (now ex) husband, Carson.

That November morning, pushing failure aside, I flung open the door. Baristas with their matching shaved heads and unmatched love for one another poured coffees at the counter. Shipwrights, gutter punks, and an occasional suit or executive occupied the couches and tables. Grabbing her latte with the other regulars, wearing paint-streaked clothes and the always present beanie on her head, Ellen stood in all her glory. The sea of people parted, knowing that Ell and I required more space and air than the room could provide. The combination of her Irish accent and my Midwest dialect collide into a language that only we can understand. Our friendship, just a year old, had already reached the greatest depths of any I've known.

Hot coffees in hand, we ascended from the earth, our words and bodies tumbling out onto the street. We headed straight, marching onto the wooden dock in the middle of town. The dock where I had given my wedding vows, where J. Lo had filmed *Enough*, where high schoolers smoked pot, and from which I had jumped onto sailboats. It held the stories of me and countless others in its worn wood planks.

Ellen and I created our history and story while walking our chosen path. Discussions varied from the upcoming gallery show, my new relationship with Dave and her wary attitude toward it, her latest crush, our weekend plans. The simplicity of our conversation's routine and depth set the tone as we bid farewell and went forward to rule our empires.

With the monthly gallery walk looming the next day, that Friday in November found me scurrying about, climbing up a ladder, reconfiguring the entire space, and hanging the show. I had named it "You, Me, and Geometry," and it would feature three Pacific Northwest artists who worked with geometric shapes in their 2-D and 3-D pieces. I knew that gallery walk would be a blowout party. Owning what had been branded the "Hottest Gallery on the Olympic Peninsula" was a role I took very seriously—as seriously as I took my white sunglasses collection.

---

I had gotten a divorce six months earlier and moved my gallery to Water Street just two months prior. My confidence was growing in each decision because these choices were solely mine. For the first time in my life, I felt in control of my future.

The Friday rolled on, and I turned my attention to my favorite part of getting the gallery ready for a new show: the windows. My windows—hot damn, could I design a window. They were the cherry on top of each show I launched, and I labored over them with love and attention.

Designing and building the window displays allowed me to be creative, to tap back into my artistry and present something beautiful for the community. Had I once dumped half a ton of sand in a window? Yes. Was there a time I used five hundred newspapers to create a visual feast? Of course. Did I suspend a log and make hundreds of feet of paper chains for a display? You bet! I did not create alone; the displays were a community affair, with friends stopping on their errands or taking a break from shopping to help me create visual masterpieces to lure in new customers.

There were two windows to the gallery, with the door to enter between them and slightly set back. Each window sat a few feet off the ground and had a base perfect for building large-scale displays. I had finished one window the evening before, placing a large neon piece by an artist atop a long white bench with fabric behind to create a glowing street view.

Dave, my new boyfriend, came down to the gallery to assist in the endeavor. I had learned from experience with Carson that mixing romantic relationships with art hanging was a recipe for disaster, fights, and tears. But Dave, the handsome, down-to-earth landscape company owner, showed up in his dirty Carhartts and dutifully did as I instructed. The relationship was only a month old. I "knew" he was different than the others. All signs were pointing toward LOVE, except, of course, the obvious signs that weren't. I just couldn't see them at the time.

The art on the walls served as inspiration for the empty window. I often created dresses out of various materials, a practice I began in college, and I leaned into that skill as I sketched my ideas down. Standing outside of the gallery, I thought of building a geometric dress out of cardboard, keeping in mind that my monthly window budget was free to basically nothing, and cardboard could be found for free! By scoring the cardboard and "cracking" it into shapes and angles, I could create a modern three-dimensional dress to display jewelry.

After scavenging through the back room, peering around paint cans, backstock, files, and dishes, I finally resigned myself to the fact I had no cardboard. Luckily, I passionately believe you can solve all of life's problems with a visit to the hardware store. At that moment, getting cardboard was my only problem. Little did I know, within a few hours, it would be the cardboard that revealed the most prominent problem in my life.

Since it was already late in the day, I flipped the sign to CLOSED, locked up, and headed to the hardware store near the town's entrance. After a quick chat with my local hardware helpers, who shook their heads and chuckled over my idea, followed by a dive into their recycling dumpster, I had a collection of white cardboard and was ready to tackle the dress. However, there was one problem. The hardware store was across the street from the Port Townsend Brewery, and it was Friday after all. Everyone would be at the brewery, just as they had been every other Friday for as long as I had lived there. The window creation could wait for an hour. I wanted to see my people.

Megan stood behind the bar, pouring beers and wines as she greeted each person with her melodic voice and joyful disposition. In the noisy, crowded room, Megan's eyes locked with mine, and we shared our love and history in a glance as she handed me a glass of white wine. Weaving through the people, I toasted The Edensaw Woods crew, sailors turned lumberjacks holding court in the corner. I chatted with other friends, talking about the weekend, the gallery opening, Sunday's football game.

Ellen flew into the brewery with her usual exuberance. We had parted only hours earlier and now recounted our days while attempting to keep Megan in the conversation. The hour rolled on, and Dave showed up. We still had the new relationship butterflies you get when you see your person in public. Not long after, Megan's boyfriend came along, just off work as a welder in the boatyard, covered in tiny metal particles. Everyone was gathered together in that small warm room, voices bouncing out the door into the dark waters.

Had I known then what was to unfold, I wonder what I would have done. Maybe I would have rung the bell and bought the bar a round; stood on top of a chair and given an impassioned speech as I toasted the life I knew goodbye; had a conga line, a ticker-tape parade, a marching band escort me out... But we don't get to know when our life is going to end. I cannot say I wish I never went back to the gallery that night because it does not matter; the putsch had been put into motion long before, and what would happen was inevitable. There was no avoiding the path I would walk down; he, whom I did not know, had paved it.

I know this—I would have hugged every person in the brewery that night. I would have squeezed everyone so tight, and I would have told them I love them, said I'm sorry for what is going to happen and how it's going to affect you. I would have held on to each person for dear life because the reality is that I *would* end up clinging to each one of them for my life. But instead, I waved goodbye and headed out the door into the November evening air.

The evening was my favorite time to work at the gallery. The darkness of the Pacific Northwest that time of year contrasted with the lights of my idyllic town as I scurried about creating my window. Friends on their way out to dinner would perhaps stop by to say hello; occasionally, a tourist would stroll by, and I'd let them in to make a sale. That morning, day, and evening were a simple example of the contentment I had fought to create in my quirky community. I threw on my tunes, danced my jigs, and delighted in an evening well spent.

I studied my failed attempts to create the cardboard dress from outside the gallery and spotted an armful of clothing moving toward me. My friend traveled to Paris each year and would pick up the most delicious materials that she would turn into shirts, dresses, shawls, and more. In turn, I would sell the clothing. We quickly set to work looking over each piece, ohhhhhing and ahhhing as we worked on the display. The warm wood gallery floor and bright spotlights above were the perfect backdrops for our impromptu fashion show. I "needed" the last piece I tried on, a black wool blend poncho with gold threads running through the fabric. The generous cowl neck and warm, soft fabric gave a glamorous hug to my body. If I'd had a beret, I would have thrown it in the air "á la Mary Tyler Moore" and done a spin. I threw on my white sunglasses, and my friend snapped a few photos of me modeling the wares in the window before she headed into the evening and I got back to creating.

I was a woman in a window, on display, shining in the spotlight of the dark night descending upon me. Society says that women in windows are objects, possessions, there to fulfill your desires—and unbeknownst to me, that is precisely what I was at that moment. I was someone's "woman in the window." My autonomy and humanness were stripped from me without my knowledge or permission.

Focus and frustration filled the window as the cardboard creation collapsed yet again. Surprise interrupted my distracted state when I looked down from my perch and saw a man a few feet from me in the doorway, just the pane of glass separating us. Our eyes met, and with his empty hand, he motioned for me to open the door. In his other hand was a small package. Looking him over as I hopped down, I thought there was nothing of note about the guy. Around my age, Caucasian, receding hairline, metal glasses, strange, eerie smile, a little plump, average height. Average in every aspect. I unlocked the door, the door that held my bright future behind it, letting the chilly air in.

The years of my mother lecturing me on "stranger danger" kicked into my psyche as I made an unconscious decision. My mother raised me to check under my car before getting in, always lock my doors, not walk down dark streets alone, carry my purse across my chest. She even sent articles to me about parking lot kidnappings and scams. I, in turn, dismissed her warnings, despite my history experiencing violence at the hands of men. I walked with freedom, confident of my future of safety. Like most people in Port Townsend, I didn't even lock my car and usually left my keys in the ignition. But damn it, she had been right all along.

I instinctively only opened the door partially, maybe a quarter of the way, and placed my foot behind it.

The man introduced himself. "Hi, I'm Jeffrey." Then, he thrust the package at me, and I discovered it was a small painting that, as he explained, he had made for me. I glanced at its murky layers of ocean green paint broken up with splashes of magenta and put the gift on my desk while I muttered, "Thank you."

Jeffrey continued, saying he wanted to show his artwork at my gallery. Inwardly, my eyes rolled.

Nearly every day, artists approached me, wanting to show at the gallery. They would stop in with an armful of paintings, interrupt me while I tried to make a sale, call and invite me to their studios in the middle of nowhere. The daily disruptions rarely led to the artist showing at the gallery. I would politely repeat my memorized script: "Thank you so much for showing interest in the gallery, but it is challenging to give you proper consideration when I'm open for business. Please take my business card and email images of your work along with your bio." I would hand the artist my card, and that would be that. I could deliver the spiel in my sleep because I had done it so many times.

I recounted a version of my script to Jeffrey and handed him a business card to submit images and his bio. The only difference in my interaction with him versus any other artist was that he gave me a painting, along with a slightly odd feeling, which I brushed aside. Artists don't usually give away their work; it was a bold gesture. Jeffrey took my business card, said goodbye, and walked back into the inky Pacific Northwest evening. Pulling the heavy door closed, I brushed the encounter out of my mind and locked my world safely away for the evening.

The interaction with Jeffrey had only lasted five minutes. That five minutes would change the course of my life.

# CHAPTER TWO

# November 5 – 10, 2011

Stalkers use many tactics, including:

- Making unwanted phone calls.
- Approaching the victim or showing up in places when the victim does not want them to.
- Following and watching the victim.
- Sending unwanted texts, photos, emails, and messages through social media.
- Sending unwanted gifts.
- Using technology to monitor, track, and/or spy on the victim.[2]

The following day felt like Christmas as I bounded down the small spiral staircase of my lofted bedroom. It was gallery walk day, my day to shine and give my gift to the community in the form of art. Much like parents on Christmas morning, I was already exhausted and driven by the joy of giving to others. I put on a soft, threadbare, black and white flannel shirt and another pair of hand-me-down designer jeans and selected white Ray-Bans from the collection. They were the only expensive pair of sunnies I owned, and gallery walk day required a little extra flair.

Rachel, my faithful gallery employee, greeted me at the shop's door with camera in hand, snapping pictures of me and the works on the walls. A true child of the West Coast hippie movement, Rachel radiated quirk and delight. Her shock of red hair with its ever-present red rose pinned in matched my caffeinated buzz of enthusiasm.

Being a popular destination on the gallery walk required throwing a damn good party, and the list to accomplish before the opening was long. Help the DJ unload his speakers. Climb on top of the door frame to install a projection system, which I would later use to simulcast a gallery opening in Seattle. Pull together the cardboard dress I had abandoned in frustration the evening before. Set up the wine station. Get the wine. *Do I have enough plastic cups? What am I wearing tonight?* The list was never-ending. The previous owner, who'd entrusted me to take the helm, had turned the gallery into the hotspot it was. I worked my ass off to live up to this obligation, pressure, and standard and then make it more prominent than anyone could have ever imagined.

I was perched on the gallery's door frame, completing the projector task. A reporter from the *Peninsula Daily News* popped in and asked me to come down from my perch. I wiggled my body off the ledge and down the ladder, back to the sacred earth of my gallery. He presented me with a piece of paper, and I beamed as I read the certificate. My eyes misted over the faintest bit. I had won Best Gallery on the Olympic Peninsula. I was crushing it!

●　　●　　●

*The summer of 2009 found me hunched over a table in the guest bedroom riddled with Carson's clutter as I went about the daunting task of writing the business plan for my gallery. Every time I tried to tidy and organize the room, he would bring in more outdoor gear, yard sale scores, and junk. I rode high on our engagement, only a few months old, and turned my back to the apparent lack of support as he packed his belongings around my tiny corner while I tried to write my future.*

*Carson traveled regularly, and I found peace in the daytime when he was gone, leading wilderness trips for a drug and alcohol treatment facility. At night, I slept with a heavy metal lemon squeezer under the pillow, ready for combat. I respected and supported Carson's work, but as his newest sponsees, days or weeks fresh into their sobriety, knew where we lived and that I was alone, I feared for my safety.*

*No bank was going to give me a loan, and with the very meager funds in my bank account, I needed a private investor to purchase the gallery. It took nearly two months to research and write the business plan and secure an investor; it took two days to plan the wedding. \*

*We had fought over owning the business together; it was mine, and I was very protective, triggered by the men in my past who had taken what was mine so many times before. Eventually, I caved, and on the day of ownership, he beamed beside me as our pens hit the paperwork.*

*His good-natured public side masked the deeper issues that I'd become accustomed to experiencing. I seek out the companionship of men who wear masks, the ones who draw people in with their charisma but reveal control, manipulation, and judgment behind the closed doors of our relationship. I flee, pass over, and run from those who carry the traits I crave—understanding, listening, empathy, and strength—in favor of the "street angel/house devil."*

*Before Carson and I ever hit the wedding aisle—or dock, in our case—our relationship was teetering between my fear of our future and our shared drive not to disappoint Midwest families and the Port Townsend community. After therapy, shouting, blaming, and crying, I asked to postpone the wedding.*

*One battle led to Carson bursting into the gallery, shouting, "What the fuck do you want to do? Do you want to break up?!"*

*In tears, I responded in fear. "No! I love you so much, I'd marry you tomorrow!"*

*I in jeans and a white lace top, he in a cowboy hat, we eloped three days later on the dock with a small group of friends. The hastily planned ceremony was followed by coffee and treats at the Undertown. A cautionary note: If you want to postpone a wedding or not go through with it, do not marry that person instead.*

*Within the year, our battle to survive ended. White flags were flown as the fiber of our marriage disintegrated. Carson played "99 Problems" by Jay-Z on repeat at the house while I packed up my belongings. His statement was clear, though it hurt, and the sense of relief washing over me felt like an ocean cleansing me.*

*Despite the relief I felt in divorcing Carson, when I discovered he'd replaced me immediately with a younger woman and impregnated her before our divorce was finalized, I sobbed in the back room of the gallery. The magnitude of the decision to marry and the divorce stayed with me, and I never imagined I could be erased and replaced that quickly or permanently.*

*With the heartache of losing a life I didn't want, I walked to the shores of North Beach each evening, tossing a rock into the moving water, letting go. My failure visually turned into taller heels, bigger hair, sophisticated outfits, and edgier shows at the gallery. I will make myself irreplaceable, I thought.*

●   ●   ●

The few months that had passed since my divorce had been the best, hard in growth, but deeply satisfying in all that I had accomplished. I looked around my world, from where I had come, and felt awe and excitement for what the future held. I would challenge myself to accept the future and remind myself of the feelings I had never known before after years of depression and anxiety.

The first Saturday of the month was my marathon, and I always came in first. Texts, emails, and phone calls of instructions, directions, sales, and questions filled every moment, adding to the frenzy in which I thrived. During one scroll through the emails, I noted that, indeed, Jeffrey had submitted his portfolio and bio in hopes of being accepted to the gallery. I ignored it; I'd reply to him on Monday. I had a party to throw.

And a party I did throw. I wore a black and white striped asymmetrical sweater with a black belt around my waist, black skirt, and towering high-heeled boots, and my geometric haircut matched the show perfectly. Friends poured wine for the guests, and Rachel made the sales. I weaved in and out of the crowds, chatting and schmoozing. The simulcast to Ghost Gallery in Seattle kept the party going across the Puget Sound. Techno and house music filled the gallery and drifted down the street while the DJ spun tunes. With the music thumping, people danced and followed the sound onto the street, bodies bouncing up and down in front of the gallery.

The cops arrived after a noise complaint was called in, and I sheepishly met them outside. Instead of shutting the music off, the officer on duty said we had to turn it off by 10 p.m. With that, I slid my way back into the buzzing four walls and continued to drink in every damn second of the night. Not wanting the evening to be over at our ten o'clock cutoff, I went with the artists and danced into the night at the local dive bar.

Foggy-brained the following day, I sipped on my mimosa on the deck of an expansive house near the water, enjoying a private brunch with the artists before they headed back to Seattle. I could not have been more content with my life, and it was the best farewell party I never knew I had.

Content as I was in my celebratory haze of a party well-executed, Monday rolled around with its regular routines. Pay the bills, answer emails, visit artists, work on bookkeeping—the ordinary things. Among the tasks was to shoot off a quick email to Jeffrey, politely declining to show his artwork.

I looked through the email message and attached images of paintings. They felt familiar, and I realized Jeffrey had sent me an email of his work the previous year. He had been in the gallery before—several times in fact. I had never answered his original email and had not recognized him when he'd approached me a few evenings earlier. With people coming in and out of the business it wasn't strange that I didn't recall him during our evening conversation. However, it was out of the ordinary for me that I didn't respond to his email. Looking through the works, I knew why I hadn't answered the year prior. I didn't have words for the strange blobs of color, slashes, and shapes and had chosen to simply ignore him.

I replied to Jeffrey with an email stating something like, "Thank you very much for submitting your artwork to AOT Gallery. I am not interested at this time but will keep you on file for future reference." Simple, to the point. I crossed it off my list of things to do and hit "send." Most of the time, I would write an additional personal note, suggesting other venues, artists to study with, or a bit of encouragement. However, there was no reason to add anything else to the communication with Jeffrey. I had no advice to give him other than maybe find a different career.

Sunglasses, drive, park, drop off armful of files, coffee, Ellen, open gallery. I flipped the sign to OPEN with a flair. A well-oiled machine of gallerista management—that's what I was. Towering piles of dishes and empty wine bottles filled the back room, still a hot mess from Saturday's gallery walk, and I tackled cleanup.

Blinking up at me from the voicemail was the number "1," one new message. I hit play on the machine while scrubbing dishes. My body paused as Jeffrey's squeaky male voice filled the cramped back room. He wanted to make sure I had gotten his email, invited me to his studio to view his work in person, and encouraged me to have a nice day and call him back. Hitting "delete," I listened as his voice dissipated and disappeared. *He's an eager beaver, I'll give him that. He probably hasn't gotten the email I sent him. The poor guy will probably feel foolish he left the message.* Back to the dishes I went.

The weekend event's frenzy had given way to most days' normalcy at the gallery. Customers came in, and I assisted them in selecting the perfect piece of jewelry for an anniversary. Community members stopped by to view the show. Friends popped by to chat. In the space between customers and friends, there was the quiet when I wrote emails, caught up on sales input, and organized jewelry cases. As glamorous as people perceived my work to be, it was often a mundane routine.

Rachel, my trusty part-time gallery worker, was also a photographer, and I needed to upload the images of the show to the Facebook page. The blue message icon in the top right corner of my Facebook page was on, and I clicked it to read the incoming message.

"Dear Anna, I left a message the other day on the store phone. I don't know if that is what you meant for me to do when you gave me your card. I've sent images over email in the past but you did not respond. I don't think that is really the ideal way to see art unless you have to do that. My studio/garage/living space is uptown. Part of me wants to give away my art but I thought you could take a look at it and see if you could make any money off of it. Oh, and I should say that the name of the painting I gave you was called "Marry Me," which doesn't mean that I want to marry you, as I don't really know you, but it was the first thing that popped into my head when I went about naming it. It could mean many things. Anyhow it would be cool to be your friend on Facebook too if you should so like. The show was nice the last weekend. You are hella hot. OK, I'll talk to you later."

CLANG, CLANG, CLANG, the alarm bells in my head pounded. I read the message several times over as my nerve endings tingled. Working to calm my breathing and silence the continuing "clangs," I thought, *Okay, I'm an asshole. I never responded last year to the request to show his shitty art; that was unprofessional, and I'm sorry.*

The rational thinking didn't help, and I lingered over the words "Marry Me." My brain stuttered. *Why, why, why would anyone give a stranger a painting called* Marry Me? The clarification of the title with a bizarre justification of not knowing me didn't soothe my nerves. I didn't recall Jeffrey coming into the gallery; how did he know the show was "nice"? Or maybe he had been there, and I just hadn't noticed?! *I still remember the drink orders of people I waited on twelve years ago, and I damn sure remember every face at a gallery walk. The dude wasn't there, but then again, I hadn't remembered he had come in before.*

My thoughts were flipping and tripping over one another. *What the flying fuck does my appearance have to do with anything?* I screamed into the tunnels of my mind. Most importantly, *I most certainly am not going to this stranger's studio/garage/living space or speaking to him later!*

Not wanting to overreact, as I have been accused of by almost every man I have ever dated, I didn't respond. I needed to sit with it. Sinking into the soft olive chair under a neon painting, I gauged whether I was responding to past traumas or had legitimate concerns. The therapist in Indiana had taught me this trick years ago allowing myself to sit with the current fear and let past traumas resurface to navigate why the fear was there. After the exercise, I chalked it up to Jeffrey being a bit too eager, breathed deeply, and regained my composure.

While cooking spaghetti in the country at Dave's home that evening, I brought up Jeffrey's strange messaging, showed Dave the message, and explained my anxiety. The faint smell of leaves and gasoline filled my nose and brought me calmness as Dave leaned over me and read the message. He chuckled at the "hella hot" comment and noted that Jeffrey wasn't wrong, then, shocker of all shockers, told me I was overreacting. We did agree I should send a clarifying message that was simple and to the point, reinforcing that I wasn't interested in displaying Jeffrey's artwork. Dave encouraged me to use the format I would use for any other artist and not give it any more thought. That night, I snuggled into the security and safety of Dave's arms. I'd write Jeffrey tomorrow.

Flip, flop went my stomach as I drove to town from Dave's house in Chimacum on a gray morning the next day. The Olympic and Cascade

Mountains didn't even evoke my usual gasp as I crested the hill that dropped down into town. My gut works as a barometer, measuring the pressure I am under, and responds in such a way that I should own stock in Pepto-Bismol. We are told to trust our gut, and while mine betrays me, it knows when I require concern before I know. It churned like the ocean that morning. The bronze key clicked the lock in the door, opening up the enchanting world in front of me. I ran past all of the beauty to the bathroom.

My stomach emptied, coffee and croissant procured, chat with Ellen complete, I sat down to respond to Jeffrey. We were not friends on Facebook, but it was as easy as transmitting an email to send a message to a "non-friend" back then; therefore, I replied by Facebook. I repeated my rejection, hoping it would make my point clear.

"Jeffrey-

Once again thank you for the painting, that was very kind of you. At this time I am booked for shows for the next year, I will keep you on file for future reference.

Best of luck,

Anna"

One minute passed, two minutes passed, three minutes passed. The message icon turned blue.

"Well, Anna, if you ever need some "Christian Paintings," or "Port Townsend Paintings," or "Russian Paintings," or "New Jersey Paintings," or even "Psychiatric Paintings," to sell, then feel free to give me a call or message. It was nice to see you today..."

He trailed on, asking me several gallery-related questions.

"IS THIS MAN WATCHING ME?" I yelled into the empty room. The paintings, the jewelry, the space, the artists, the customers, the very essence of the gallery, the world I had clawed to create, changed at that moment. It was now a fishbowl, and I was the fish. Simultaneously stone-like and crumbling, I couldn't move from my desk, my eyes fixed on the phrase, "It was nice to see you today." I replayed my movements that morning in my head. I had parked the car in the same spot I always did, walked to the Undertown as I did daily, and meandered with Ellen, all in a two-block radius. My body broke out of its frozen state, and I found myself standing in front of the locked door, scanning the street with my eyes. *Where is he?*

I'd been watched before, and I was as angry as I was scared.

# CHAPTER THREE

# November 10 – 11, 2011

**Less than a third of all stalking victims reported the victimization to police in 2019. Crime victims chose not to report their victimization to police for a variety of reasons. One of the most common reasons was feeling that the victimization was not important enough to report to police.[3]**

Pacing the gallery floor, my eyes to the door and the windows, I wondered whether Jeffrey was out there, and my mind couldn't focus on anything else. *Could he harm me? Would he rape me? Why is he watching me? How long has he been watching me? Remember last year when someone spit on the windows several days in a row? Come on, Anna, you know it was cum; you just told yourself it was spit while you cleaned it... Was that Jeffrey?*

I grabbed a tin whistle made by a local artist and put it around my neck. It was the coolest rape whistle there ever was. The words rang in my brain—just seven words that had changed everything: "It was nice to see you today."

Tiny cracks in my foundation began to form by the late afternoon as I grew smaller, sitting transfixed at my desk. Subconsciously, my fingers fell on the keyboard, navigating to the Google bar. I typed Jeffrey's full name, Jeffrey Bradford, and was not prepared for what I found. His vacant eyes gazed at me from the screen. Image after image of a face I didn't know clawed into my brain. I looked back at it, trying to find the answers that only that haunting face knew.

After scrolling, I found social media and YouTube accounts, plus a blog about running for president in 2020. Toward the bottom of the first page, my breath caught when I saw court cases. "Click," went my cursor, revealing more of the unraveling situation I was only just now discovering I was a part of. I read the unpublished opinion of a court case, and my blood turned cold.

"The trial court found that (1) [Bradford's] comments were threats expressing an intent to harm because the probation officers, deputies, and employees at Jefferson County Mental Health believed he would carry out the threats; and (2) it was reasonable for Jefferson County Mental Health employees to fear their death as a result of [Bradford's] threats because of the long-standing animosity and tumultuous relationship between [Bradford] and Jefferson County Mental Health. Based on these findings, the trial court determined that a reasonable person in [Bradford's] position would have foreseen that his statements would be taken 'as a serious expression of intent to take the life of another individual.' RP (Dec. 7, 2009) at 155. Accordingly, the trial court entered a guilty verdict for the crime of felony harassment (threats to kill) and sentenced [Bradford] to serve 60 days in jail. The trial court also entered no-contact orders preventing [Bradford] from contact with Jefferson County Mental Health and any of its employees. [Bradford] timely appeals."[4]

*Click, click, click, click.* Each open program on my computer shut off. *Click* went the lock on the door. The heels of my shoes clicked swiftly on the wood floor as I threw my belongings in my purse, scribbled out "sorry, we are closing early today" on a Post-it, slapped it on the door, tossed my white sunglasses on my face, and speedwalked to my car.

●     ●     ●

**Six-year-old me noticed the bright and cheery walls. Studies have shown that medical buildings should never use the colors red, orange, black, or**

*brown, as they don't bring comfort. Accordingly, the walls of the extensive medical waiting room were painted buttercup yellow. Rows of waiting room chairs sat by themselves, empty of patients, only my mother and a few others filling them.*

*Carrie and I played with the blocks and books in the kids' area that jutted out from the otherwise rectangular room. I never minded a visit to the doctor, of which there were many; there were always new toys to play with, a different selection from the My Little Ponies, Cabbage Patch Kids, and Rainbow Brite at home. I was a curious child. I enjoyed looking at the world around me and learning from it; my attention was held easily.*

*I looked up from my play. Carrie was engrossed in her activity; Mom, reading a magazine. Scanning the room, I saw a man far behind Mom, and he locked eyes with me. Partially behind a tall plant, he held my gaze. I wanted to look away, but he wouldn't let me. He kept me captive while he unzipped his pants and began to tug on his dick. I'd never seen a man's penis; I was only six years old. I broke his hold on me and looked down; I couldn't compute what he was doing, only that it felt wrong, and I was frightened.*

*Carrie continued to play, Mom turned a magazine page, and I said nothing as I looked back at him. He smiled because he had me—he'd caught me. He tugged away, his face contorting into painful ecstasy. Breaking free of him, I frantically looked around; nobody knew, no one saw, just me, and shame washed over me. I looked to the plant once more, and he was gone.*

●    ●    ●

The facts rolled in my brain as I drove out to stay at Dave's in Chimacum because there was no way in hell I was spending the night alone at my apartment! *He thinks you are hella hot. He saw you today. He has a mental health condition. He has threatened to kill people. He has harassment convictions. Fuck me! This has turned into a very, very shitty day.*

I needed the safety of my new boyfriend. My fear drove the car. That day, I unknowingly turned into Anna the Investigator, Anna the

Advocate, Anna "You Picked the Wrong Woman" Nasset, though I wouldn't fully meet her for years.

Fragile and small, I slumped over the kitchen table and talked in quiet tones with Dave that evening. His son was playing in the next room, and I didn't want him to hear what we were saying.

Dave still thought I was overreacting but agreed that maybe if Jeffrey knew I was in a relationship, he would leave me alone. Noting that Jeffrey communicated with me through Facebook, we decided to use that mode as my announcement. I couldn't give two shits about setting my relationship status on Facebook; after my divorce, I had turned off that bit of personal information. However, in the late evening, I turned my status to "in a relationship" and was met with a flurry of thumbs ups and "congratulations." No one who was celebrating my life victory knew why I had made the public announcement. But my friends weren't the only people who saw the grand information that night.

Foggy-headed and confused, I drove to town, my mind tripping over itself. *Jeffrey hasn't done anything wrong, has he? He sent me messages, but he talked so personally, as if he knows me, and commented on my appearance, giving hints that he was watching me. I read yesterday there seemed to be a mental health component from the court case. I know that having a mental health condition doesn't make someone dangerous, although Hollywood and media like to paint a different picture. So what if this guy has a mental health condition? That accounts for nothing. I've dealt with my fair share of depression and anxiety.*

Arriving at the edge of town, I thought of the one person who would set me straight, tell me I was overreacting, and put my fears to rest. I knew exactly who I needed to call.

I swung a right-hand turn at the town entrance, pulling into the large commercial boatyard that welcomes everyone to Port Townsend. The boatyard felt like home, and I felt safe winding down the dirt roads, between boats on stilts and clusters of buildings. Large metal structures, humble shacks, and tarps supported the luxury yachts and fishing vessels.

I pulled into "my" spot facing the water with the rough and modest wooden boat empire at my back. For years, I had sat in the boatyard when I had a few minutes to kill, making phone calls, answering emails, or staring out at my beloved bay of churning water. Now, I searched my phone for Ford's number and then hesitated before dialing.

Ford was Carson's best friend and mentor. He had been supportive through the divorce, but I didn't know if he would answer. Once the paperwork had been signed and the divorce had been finalized, I assumed that my friendships with Carson's "side of the family" had ended as well. But, at that moment, Ford was who I needed. He owned and ran the local alcohol treatment recovery center, was a retired Marine, volunteered in the jail, and knew every cop in town. Along with that, he knew everyone who got into any trouble.

I shouldn't have been surprised at all that Ford picked up on the second ring, but I was. "How ya doing, darling?" he asked in his deep, slow voice.

I thanked him for his service—it was Veterans Day, after all—and stammered that I needed his advice. "I'm probably overreacting, but have you heard of this guy, Jeffrey Brad...?"

Ford interrupted me before I could get out Jeffrey's full name, saying, "Go to the police right now."

This was not the reaction Ford was supposed to give me. He was meant to laugh at me, tell me I was being dramatic, and send my silly overthinking brain back to work. I protested, I pleaded, and he stood firm: go to the police. My argument ceased as the gravity of the situation washed over me. If Ford tells you to go to the cops, you go to the cops. My beautiful boatyard shattered around me; my dear dirt-streaked life of safety began to crumble.

Hanging up the phone, alone in my car, I screamed over and over the word "NO" while I bashed my fists on my dashboard. I clung to the steering wheel, rocking forward and back, my screams giving way to sobs and whimpers.

Glancing in my rearview mirror, I realized my bright eyes had turned dull and puffy. Gathering my composure, I did my best to repair the damage with my compact and lipstick. I had breakfast plans with a friend who was waiting at the Blue Moose, located just behind me in the boatyard.

I put off Ford's direct instructions and pushed eggs around my plate, mindlessly gulping coffee. Our breakfast catch-up turned into me recounting what was happening and asking my friend to go to the police station with me. With no hesitation, she escorted me up the hill to the Port Townsend Police Department (PTPD).

---

The emotional backpack I wore weighed me down as I climbed the steps of the police station, located in the town's former middle school. The criminal justice system is set up to protect people like me, young, attractive white women; even so, I was still frightened entering the building. The tap of my brakes when I passed a cop created a rush of anxiety; the guns on their hips made me shudder; the sight of uniforms and badges pulled my shoulders back. A system designed to uphold justice instilled fear.

The police department doors swung open, and I stepped into the unknown.

"I'm Officer Corrigan. How can I help you?" His gentle yet firm voice filled the air. The slightest ease came over my tense frame. Officer Corrigan's presence felt protective and kind. An Air Force veteran turned police officer, Corrigan, as I call him, in his mid-fifties with a fit frame and shock of silver hair, met me, saw me, and heard me in that instant.

*I don't know what to say. I don't know what is wrong.* My head worked on overdrive, trying to find words. "This guy Jeffrey has been sending me messages. He gave me a painting. I don't know what's going on. Ford told me to come here. Do you know Ford? Of course, you know Ford. Well, he told me to come here and tell you about Jeffrey, so I'm here. Why am I here?"

Officer Corrigan nodded his head and invited us down the hallway to talk. In the room where we sat, a former classroom rid of its days of learning, I sank into a folding chair and absorbed what was happening to my life.

Corrigan shared that Jeffrey was from Port Townsend and was just a year or two younger than me. I found out that he did indeed have a mental health condition, most likely a rare form of schizophrenia, and that he preferred not to receive treatment or take medication. Jeffrey came from a caring and well-off family who would do anything to get him the help he needed, but he fought their assistance and treatment options. I learned that he was known to stalk people (not just women) in the community for short periods, and as gently as he could, Corrigan said that I appeared to be his next target.

I shook my head back and forth, letting the information sink into my pores. I found myself apologizing over and over for probably over-reacting and taking up his time. Corrigan stopped me and reassured me I had done the right thing by coming in. He didn't offer hope or false safety; he explained that if this followed Jeffrey's pattern, he'd move on after a short time. *Well, that's unsettling to the next poor person he sets his sights on, but at least this will be over soon.*

Corrigan then began to share tactics I could implement to keep myself safe. "Break up your routine," he urged.

*Wait—what? I like my routine; my life is a routine. I don't want to park my car in different spots, and there are only two ways I can walk to the gallery. Plus, I need my coffee!*

"Keep a log," he explained.

*Nope, nope, nope. I do not want to document every time he contacts me or calls me. Isn't that the police's job?*

"Consider carrying Mace."

*Okay, you have to be joking with me. My mom and her friends carry Mace. I am not sixty. I don't need Mace.*

"Think about creating a safety plan, keep in mind distractions, carry your keys in your fist," he continued.

*This is just nuts. Two hours ago, my life was mine, and now this—all of this.*

"You need to think about a protection order. Do you know how to pursue that?" asked Corrigan.

*No, Corrigan. No, I fucking don't know how to do that.* But instead of voicing my thoughts, I simply whispered, "No."

He went on to walk me through the steps. I would need to communicate with Jeffrey that he could not contact me or come to my gallery.

*Let's put that on the back burner.*

I learned if I decided to take that course of action, once he did contact me again, I would go fill out paperwork at the courthouse. According to Corrigan, there would be a court date where both Jeffrey and I would appear NEXT TO EACH OTHER in front of the judge and plead our cases.

*This step isn't even on the back burner; I'll take that pot full of bullshit and throw it straight out the window.*

"Do not respond to Jeffrey," he firmly said.

*No problem with that advice, Corrigan.*

"Think about taking a self-defense course."

*Okay, that sounds badass.*

Corrigan handed me a blank police report and pen. With a shaking hand, I filled it out and signed it at 10:32 a.m. on November 11, 2011. Then, out into the world I went.

White sunglasses hiding the fear in my eyes, I scanned the landscape around me. Even in my terror, I took with me the kindness of Corrigan, grateful that from my first step into the police station, he'd simply started by believing me. Did that happen for everyone? I certainly hoped so, but I began to think about the fact that I had a lot of privilege, even in this unwanted and terrifying situation. I was known in my community in a positive light, Jeffrey was known in a negative way, I didn't know Jeffrey, I hadn't dated him, and I had Ford's name to use to my advantage. What happened to the people who didn't have these advantages?

*Before*, I opened my gallery at 10 a.m. every day. Now, Jeffrey was breaking into my life and stealing my time. I didn't rush to work that morning; I felt stunned and small. I hoped he would never bother me again. In fact, I was sure that he wouldn't, but how dare he take my time and energy? Eventually, I unlocked the door, and my phone chimed with a notification. There was the next scratch at my life from Jeffrey.

"Well, I was going to ask you if you were married, but it seems you are officially in a relationship. I was going to ask you if you wanted to go to a movie. Maybe you still do?"

The idea that changing my relationship status would stop Jeffrey's behavior backfired quickly.

# CHAPTER FOUR

# November 12 – 21, 2011

**Stalking victims suffer much higher rates of depression, anxiety, insomnia, and social dysfunction than people in the general population.**[5]

**D**ave gave me a taser because if other men took the situation seriously, so would he. I whispered what was happening in quiet conversations with Megan and Ellen over drinks at the brewery. I began to forget where I parked my car, forget to return calls, and forget what I was making for dinner. I'd become a timid automaton building a new routine based on receding from the public persona I had worked my ass off to create.

The days grew shorter, and darkness crept in a few minutes earlier each late afternoon. Petrified, I hid, a "sitting duck," in my bright gallery. The wild winds that whip the air of the Pacific Northwest toyed with me as I nervously walked to my car night after night, pretending to be on the phone, keys in my fist.

"Hellooooo, Anna." My mom's voice emanated from my phone, conveying her excitement to catch up on the week's happenings. Although I left the Christian faith while in college, we made it a point to keep the closeness with my family intact. They may have thought I was going to Hell, but at least they knew how much I loved them.

"Hi, Mom," I responded in a taut voice.

"What's wrong?" she inquired. Mothers always know. Despite the miles between, despite the hurt you've caused them, they always know.

I fell into the nonsensical recounting of Jeffrey's presence in my life, tripping and stumbling, trying to allow my sharing to help me make sense of it all. She listened. I could picture her in the living room, sitting in the pastel flecked armchair, taking it in and processing. She held my words and my fears but also snapped into mom mode.

"Don't give him any attention. Just put him out of your mind, lock your doors, lock your house, be aware. Did I send you that article about people breaking wiper blades in parking lots to kidnap people? I'm going to send it to you now!"

My head felt dizzy with support and advice. My mom asked if she could pray with me; she always asked as if she were treading on thin ice. I responded, "Of course!" I may not believe in Jesus, but I have nothing against the words one offers up to the earth. She prayed that Jeffrey would stop his behavior and get the help he needed. I couldn't argue with that prayer.

●　　●　　●

*By winter break my junior year of high school, I had secured the most popular boy as my boyfriend, had been elected to homecoming court, and was excited for a holiday break full of sleepovers and presents. The first sleepover took place at Tina's after the big basketball game, where we cheered on our boyfriends with glee. When we returned after the game, Tina's mom met us at the door to tell me that my parents were on their way to get me. There had been an accident.*

*On the car ride home, I would learn there was no accident. There had been a choice. My grandfather, my dear Paw-Paw, had killed himself, leaving my Maw-Maw and the rest of the family to bury him on Christmas Eve.*

*I picked out my dress for homecoming court at the mall in Toledo, Ohio, as my dad returned the Christmas gifts Maw-Maw had bought for Paw-Paw. There is an unfairness in death, and I hadn't experienced the loss of anyone close before this point. In my selfish sadness, I felt angry. I couldn't understand. I couldn't grasp the cruelty of life and the fact that, often, you don't get a break. Those few months of freedom at Delaware Christian School felt far away as I stared into the pit of grief.*

*I didn't have the ability or tools to process Paw-Paw's death or what had happened to me at my former school. On occasion, I would burst into tears in the classroom if a book mentioned suicide or someone made a comment that triggered me. I found solace in the art room with Mrs. Price and in having conversations with Mrs. Schrader. It made a difference, but I needed professional help.*

*Instead, I shrank again. I barely ate. I would do crunches in the middle of the night, yearning to be as skinny as the women in the magazines, but also because I wanted to disappear from the world. Depression and harm filled my head, and though I was living with the effects of suicide, I thought about killing myself on more than one occasion. Instead, I chose to take out my pain with a small razor on my arms. That pain was made tangible when small trickles of blood appeared to show I was alive.*

•   •   •

As I dragged my body to work the next day, my shoulders carried the fear's weight. Tension filled my muscles with the shop's door unlocking. I headed to the back room, and once again, the message light flashing on the answering machine crippled me as I heard Jeffrey's voice inviting me to his studio.

*Collect your evidence.*

I jotted down the call time, pushed my stomach out of my throat, and documented before deleting the message. I chided myself and beat myself up immediately afterward; it was, after all, evidence. I had wanted the message to disappear and had forgotten Corrigan's advice to keep everything, not just document it.

The *Port Townsend Leader*, the town newspaper, came out once a week on Thursdays. Since it was a small-town newspaper, one of the best sections was the police/crime log. Reports of chickens on lawns, a found pair of dentures at the beach, a stolen traffic cone—these trivial "crimes" filled the log.

After my initial report to the police department, I picked up a copy of the *Port Townsend Leader* and scanned the articles that Thursday. Settling on the police/crime log, I was ready for a good laugh. The problem is I was the punchline that week. It read something to the effect of, "Young female gallery owner felt threatened by the gift of a painting titled *Marry Me*."

The paper slipped from my hands and fell onto the floor, along with the few shreds of privacy I had left. *You stupid idiot. Why did you listen to Ford? Why did they include this bullshit account of my report in the paper? Why is any of this happening?* If Jeffrey didn't know I was onto his bullshit, he certainly did now, along with the whole town.

Since I was the only young female gallery owner around, I immediately had friends and acquaintances messaging me. I was humiliated and pissed. I didn't realize that you have to request for police reports to be confidential, something Corrigan very well may have mentioned. At the station the week prior, I, in such a state of shock, couldn't compute the criminal justice system being laid out in front of me or make decisions in my best interest.

That day taught me to be private because, as people inquired about the police report and nudged into my personal life, I wanted quietness. I had already publicly gone through a divorce and was a prominent business owner. I needed some space to breathe, and I did not want to be blamed for Jeffrey's actions. Every accusatory voice filled my head with "this must be my fault."

Being a reasonable person, I had safety planned for myself and my circle. I was a public figure, and if I was in real danger, then those around me were as well. Additionally, if Jeffrey was out there lurking around, fitting the definition of everything I knew about stalkers, I needed to be protective of my community.

With another simple Google search, I found a picture of him online, and his smile leered out of the screen at me. I printed it out and showed it to my neighbor at North Beach, a sixty-something retired Marine who was in better shape than I'll ever be. He was ready to be on safety patrol.

Then, I turned my attention to the business. Rachel was only there two days a week, but I needed to alert her. I did so with all the ease one can muster when they are terrified. Trying to downplay the situation a bit, I used language like, "Don't be alarmed," "You have nothing to be scared of," "I'm not scared—I'm sure he will leave me alone," and "If you see him, please let me know immediately." I felt protective for each person's peace of mind as well as for their physical safety. With her red rose pinned in her hair, Rachel joined me, the two of us becoming investigators in arms.

The following Sunday, November 20, Jeffrey appeared outside the gallery twice. He loitered outside, peering in the windows. I was completely oblivious as I wasn't present that day.

Rachel would regularly call on my days off to ask questions. When my cellphone rang, I thought nothing of it. However, waves of grief washed over me as she informed me of Jeffrey's presence. Immediately, I logged the incident in the file I was keeping. The puzzle in front of me grew.

*Would he target Rachel after he stopped targeting me? I can't go to the gallery to comfort her because he is downtown. How do I stop this?* Paralyzed by my lack of options, I knew Monday would land me on the steps of the PTPD once again.

Corrigan looked over the police report I had filled out. The short statement listed off the messaging, call, and loitering. He pointed at the bottom, stating, "Write that this statement is confidential." I signed the document on November 21, 2011, at 9:50 a.m.

The sun hit my face when I left the station, and I pushed my white sunglasses onto my face. The list of gallery business and errands was long that Monday, but I needed to first follow Corrigan's instructions and politely tell Jeffrey to fuck off.

Down the steps of failure, I descended with my laptop into the Undertown. The loneliness in my bones needed the noise and bodies of others, and it felt safer there. With my coffee cup fueling my already frayed nerves, I wrote and erased the simple message repeatedly. Questions and fears bubbled in my throat.

*I've ignored him, hoping he would go away, and maybe he still will if I stay silent. Will this message anger him? What will he do with his wrath? Is he going to kidnap, rape, and murder me? What if he messages me again? Will I have to stand next to him in court to get a protection order? WHY ME? I just want him to get the help he needs and stop this.*

Despite my reservations, Corrigan had told me I needed to send the message, and I would follow his orders. After approximately one trillion attempts, I was as satisfied as I could be.

"Jeffrey – Do not contact me via any means and do not come into my gallery or outside my gallery anymore. – Anna"

I hit send. That would be the last time I ever responded to his messages.

# CHAPTER FIVE

# Late November 2011 – December 2011

**Two out of three stalkers pursue their victims at least once per week, many daily, using more than one method.**[6]

I worked to have as much anonymity as possible. In addition, I spent most nights at Dave's; I felt safer there. However, the stress of the situation seeped into our relationship. I became anxious and short-fused, and I started drinking. He kept pouring glasses of whiskey as I sank into depression.

Less than twenty-four hours after I'd sent Jeffrey the message to not contact me anymore, the Facebook Messenger app lit up once again:

"Anna, I understand your point of view. I don't know why I was talking in that sort of way. You seem like a very proud woman and I like that. I hope you wouldn't mind me coming into your shop once in a while. It is nice to see new art."

He went on to talk about another woman he may want to marry but stated that he could change his mind. He needled at me for the message that I had written, compared me to a man he knows, and wrote about Officer Corrigan visiting him to tell him to leave me alone. Then, he talked about the painting he had given me and finished with this:

"Is there anything I can do for you? I felt a little bad that I didn't ask you if you wanted any help the other day when I came by. Anyway, I can certainly not come by your gallery. I hope you don't mind if I walk by it though, as it is a little hard to avoid when walking down the street."

In the space of this message, he went from asking me if he could come to the gallery to saying he would not enter it five different times. *This can't be the way I live. I can't do this.*

---

The ringing of the gallery phone jostled my nerves the next day. The caller ID informed me it was Jeffrey. Pushing my seizing muscles into action, resisting the urge to chuck the phone into the sea, I grabbed my cell and took a picture of the caller ID. The ringing stopped, and my body started to release. Mid-release, the ringing started again with the same number but no name attached to it. *Jeffrey, I'm not an idiot. I know it's you.* Every muscle contracted again, but I pushed through and took another picture. He left no message on the answering machine, but the unstated message was clear. He wasn't going to leave my life quietly.

Since that day, I will not answer numbers I don't know. I am sure I have lost business, screwed up opportunities, and simply let people down. But I will forever be scared of who is on the other end of the line.

If I had followed Corrigan's instructions, I would have put the CLOSED sign on the gallery window and marched myself up to the courthouse to file a protection order. Let's step back—if I had indeed followed his orders, I would have gone to Dove House Advocacy Services, the community's local domestic and sexual violence center, and met with an advocate. I didn't do either. My ego and self-importance left me embarrassed to access services that I desperately needed. I would protect myself alone, I decided. Advocacy centers were for others, not for me. I had hosted small fundraisers for the Dove House, and for a while, I'd sat on a board that donated money to the Dove House. I was supposed to support them, not need their support.

Choosing to go it alone, I could not fathom the protection order hearing, couldn't imagine standing in front of a judge with Jeffrey next to me to plead my case. So I documented the phone calls, put them in my file, and tried to move along with my day. He wasn't going to win my mind. But the self-talk didn't work. I couldn't move forward; he had planted a seed of fear, and it was growing deep roots.

In the next few weeks, I moved with quietly frantic motions. I didn't hear from Jeffrey, but that didn't bring a sense of relief because, with stalking, is it easier to know where the stalker is or wait for their next bite?

In the days of the impending Pacific Northwest winter, darkness fell earlier and earlier each day, the evening swallowing me whole. I kept the taser in my desk drawer, and I wore the tin and bottle cap whistle around my neck. I changed my routine the best I could, closing earlier and earlier and coming to work later and later. Each morning, my stomach began to turn against me with anxiety and fear.

---

I clung to one piece of normality: watching the Packers play every Sunday with my friends. I celebrated my team with transplant Midwesterners who would gather for the season to cheer on the green and gold at a friend's house. My buddy's home was tucked down a quiet side street in Port Townsend, and it boasted custom-made stadium seat couches and the NFL ticket.

● ● ●

*The normalcy of the Midwest girl continued as I started high school in 1994 at a small country school surrounded by cornfields. I wasn't popular, but*

*I was on the fringe of the popular kids, and when I wasn't palling around with my group of friends, I could be found in the art room or studying athletic training.*

*I have a solid aesthetic and natural ability to create, but I have another passion: football. Sunday afternoons, as the leaves fell and snow piled up, I could be found curled up with my dad, watching NFL. I love football, and more specifically, I love the Green Bay Packers. My dad, a quiet man who built up every woman he came into contact with, let me pick who "our" team would be. I loved that the Packers are owned by the community, loved their history and Midwest locale, and loved that their mascot is cheese.*

*I wanted to be part of the team, and I have a yearning deep in my bones to help people; therefore, I decided to become an athletic trainer and work for the Packers. By my sophomore year of high school, I took summer courses in athletic training and was appointed as one of the football team's student trainers. Wrapping ankles, wiping blood off uniforms, and watching practices, I was on the sidelines but part of the team, and I loved it. My future path was set; I'd be on the sidelines in Green Bay before I knew it.*

*Standing on the football field, surrounded by expansive farm fields, I felt like a brave trailblazer when Justin ran up to say hello to me. I knew him from the art room and around the school. At a small rural high school, everyone knows everyone, and he lived just up the road from the school next to my dear friend Andrea's house. We made conversation, and he managed to squeeze in asking me out on a date, to which I replied "no." I wasn't interested in him and felt no need to say yes to preserve his fragile ego.*

*The simple two-letter word "no" would be turned against me in the days and months to come. Justin made it his mission to publicly shame and violate me, enlisting his friends' and teammates' help. No place was safe; the group of boys would throw change at me in the hallways, saying the sexual acts they would do to me for a quarter. There would be groping at my locker, my skirt lifted and ass exposed. Threats and shame filled every inch of the school.*

*They took particular delight in harassing me in the art room; the place where I could create and feel safe became dreaded. Other boys in the art room joined in. I vividly remember one day when a particular boy, and former neighbor down the road, went into graphic detail about murdering me, dismembering me, and raping me on the art room table.*

*The life of a simple Midwest girl learning her worth at the hands of corn-fed boys. The knowledge I would never make it to the sidelines of the NFL sunk in. If these boys on the football team and in my classroom would treat me that way, what would NFL players and fans do?*

●　　●　　●

The savory taste of squeaky cheese filled my mouth, and friends filled my soul that Sunday in November. Chatting away, I glanced out the window from my elevated perch. My face drained of color, and I shrunk low into the couch as I whispered to the person next to me, "That guy has been watching me and following me. The police are now involved."

I hadn't learned to use the word stalking yet, nor had I accepted it. Maybe I was refusing it. My friends all peered out, and we adjusted the blinds ever so slightly to obstruct Jeffrey's ability to see in. He loitered, thirty feet away from the quiet street's edge, turning and looking at the humble ranch homes. Meanwhile, I explained to everyone what had been transpiring in my life.

A few of my friends began to express fear he would begin following them, and a few others advised that if I was ever being attacked to call them because they'd come save me. Fear and speculation flew around the room while I sat quietly with full clarity of the danger I was actually in. I began to process that I could also be considered dangerous to be around. If Jeffrey was going to cause harm to me, then that could instill fear in others that they too would be harmed. I began to learn I would have to be calm and protective in these moments.

I rationalized with everyone, insisting this had to be a coincidence. "There is no way he could know I am here; he must have been taking a walk," I reasoned with those around me. In reality, I was reasoning with myself.

He stood in the street out front for some time, fifteen to twenty minutes, before moving along. I breathed a sigh of relief and exclaimed, "How random was that?" with a smile smeared on my face. My friends exhaled but continued to ask me questions about him and his actions. I had barely told anyone what was going on at this point, and as I look back, those conversations were imperative to accepting the crime of stalking plaguing my life.

Here's the deal: There is nothing random about stalking. I know that now. The fact of the matter was my car was parked at the same house every single Sunday. By thinking he couldn't see that part of my routine or didn't know my vehicle, I had made an error. He'd known my every step long before I even knew he existed.

---

Just one month had gone by since Jeffrey had weaseled his way into my world, and it was time for the holiday window, my opus of the year. I was still spending most nights at Dave's and chose to get creative with the safety of my gallery world in order to function like a human. A team of others decided to join in the fun; their fun equaled my safety. Together, we sipped wine in the dark evening at the gallery. Previously, I had spent countless hours working into the evenings, but that had stopped abruptly due to Jeffrey's behavior.

That evening, as I cloaked myself in the safety offered by those around me, we built an eight-foot whale out of wire and paper and then suspended it in one window. The other window held a wrapping-paper-covered dinghy filled with presents. Yes, I put an actual boat in the window and then proceeded to dump so much fake snow onto the scene that I would find it everywhere for months to come.

The following day, before I flipped the sign to OPEN, I snuck into the window and tucked a camera into the whale, pointing it out to the street. Then, I poked a hole in one of the presents and placed another camera before gently arranging it back into the Christmas dinghy.

*You want to fuck with me, Jeffrey, you better believe I'll be watching.*

To say I love Christmas would be putting it mildly. I have a collection of ornaments, one for every year of my life. Back then, I hosted rigorous holiday cookie baking parties, and I still watch Hallmark holiday movies starting in October. This was my time to shine, and it was my biggest sales month and my biggest joy month. Every man in Port Townsend would come to pick out a unique piece of jewelry or art for their sweetheart. I shipped, wrapped, and smiled all month long. On Christmas Eve, when the last customer was gone, I would dance about to Florence + the Machine while sipping on champagne. Christmas morning always left me misty-eyed as I thought of the countless people unwrapping presents from my gallery and the gratitude I had for each customer.

Despite Jeffrey's presence in my life—not the Christmas present I wanted—I tried to keep pushing along, one eye on the month ahead and one eye on the gallery windows and the people passing by. I readied the gallery for the December gallery walk the best I could.

That first Saturday, just one month after meeting Jeffrey, I set out for the wine shop, just as I had every first Saturday before. The air felt festive and bright as the chill kissed my cheeks, and I walked the block to the Wine Cellar, where the proprietor would be waiting with the goods.

I was lost in my thoughts as I walked down the block. Just a few doors down from the gallery sat the famed Waterfront Pizza, and there was Jeffrey, sitting in the window eating his slice. He looked up at me, and a sick smile spread across his face. In turn, my world spun off its axis and crashed down on me in a fraction of a second.

*Him, danger, safety, Rachel, find people, there are people everywhere, go to the gallery, don't go back to the gallery, need protection, go, just go, make your fucking feet move and go.* Living the nightmare version of a "choose your own adventure" book, my body made my choice.

I chose to cross the street to have a better vantage point of his actions. My feet carried me. I began down the block, toward the gallery but on the opposite side of the street, my eyes trained on Waterfront Pizza. Blood pounded in my ears as I watched Jeffrey leave the pizza shop and begin to cross the road toward me.

*Don't go to the gallery. Rachel is alone in there. Go someplace safe, where people know you, where you can't cause danger. Go to the Undertown.*

My body rotated again, and my feet quickened their pace. Down the side street I headed, glancing frantically behind me. Jeffrey was following me—there was no denying it. I looked back one more time as I began to sprint across the parking lot toward the Undertown; he continued to accelerate his pace as well. I flung the door open. Sobbing, shaking, terrified, I grabbed a male friend and sent him outside to look for Jeffrey. I kept my eyes trained on the door, but Jeffrey didn't come in. He had vanished into the day.

That night, I wore a gray velvet jacket with fluffy fur sleeves, a sparkling top, fabulous blue-gray boots, and a fake smile. Santa came to town, the town Christmas tree was lit, a local musician played acoustic guitar during the opening, and nothing happened. By nothing, I mean Jeffrey didn't come in and attack me, and I also mean minimal sales. My entire being was focused on safety for myself and others, not generating business. As the party swirled around me, I looked at the stark painting of an iceberg on the wall, my blood colder than the frozen water I stared at.

---

Transfixed and stagnant, the month and I spun around and round. The holly jolly holidays had replaced sugar plums dancing in my head with nightmares of me being kidnapped and murdered, which kept me up night after night. As my mood plummeted, so did holiday sales.

In the darkness of a late afternoon, while trying to make a sale, I saw Jeffrey on the other side of the street, walking along and looking into the gallery. I paused the sale mid-transaction. My duty of safety for myself and others took over as I cautioned the customers of the potential danger. Understandably unnerved, they left quickly as I handed them their purchase.

I sat alone on display, shrinking myself. More and more, I heard friends and shoppers say, "We tried to stop by, but you weren't there." I heard the repeat statement, breaking me down with its criticism. I still stopped by the brewery to see Megan and Ellen on my way to stay at Dave's, but my community footprint grew smaller and smaller. Jeffrey remained silent, and I felt a false sense of hope, matched with uncertainty. I was not calling the shots; he was.

I did my best and gave my all to make it a beautiful holiday season. I poured myself into life with Dave and his son, our relationship still only a few months old. The safety of being in their life was palpable to me, and I lapped it up like a puppy.

I worked to keep the gallery on track, but I noted sales slipping lower and lower as my mental health declined. How could a man I didn't know, who had entered my life only six weeks prior, take such a toll on my world?

Each night driving out of town to Dave's, I'd mull over the miniscule sales I'd made, then turn off Business Anna as my wheels hit his driveway and attempt to transition to doting Girlfriend Anna as I walked up the steps to Dave's house.

# CHAPTER SIX

# January 2012

In 2019, about 18 percent of victims were stalked by a stranger, and 14 percent were unable to identify their relationship to the offender. Victims of traditional stalking were more likely to be stalked by a stranger (30 percent) than victims of stalking with technology (19 percent) or both types of stalking (12 percent). Victims of stalking with technology were more likely to not know their relationship to the offender (26 percent) than victims of traditional stalking (13 percent) or both stalking types (6 percent).[7]

By the time January 2012 rolled around, I hoped that I had made enough sales to carry the gallery through the winter months that lay ahead. In the quietness of a Pacific Northwest tourist town in winter, you needed strong December sales to get you through until spring. I was trying to spend more nights at my studio apartment, seeking peace in myself. Jeffrey had been quiet, and I had no listed address. He couldn't possibly know where I lived—just where I watched football, worked, got coffee, and grocery shopped.

Asleep on my futon mattress on the floor of the lofted apartment, I awoke to the sound of my phone. In the haze of my disrupted sleep, I feared a family emergency and grabbed my phone.

I was the emergency. Jeffrey had pounced again in the form of messages. They flowed in as fast as I could read them.

"You keep sending me messages through my email. I'm sure you don't know you are sending me these messages, but maybe you did? Eh? Eh? Well I don't mind. I think you're attractive. You say you are in a relationship, but I never see you with any guy, on Facebook or otherwise. Maybe that's some sort of strategy of yours to attract men. Well, it works. Hahaha."

One minute later...

"You really make me mad. I know you just want to have your own space and be a successful gallerist, but I think it's rather strange you don't email me. I guess you do, but your just talking to everyone else on your email list."

I sat frozen. I didn't know what to do. I wanted to run down the road and throw my phone into the ocean, but I was fixed sitting upright in bed, staring at the glowing screen. A short time later, I received a batch of poems Jeffrey had written for me titled "German Poems," "French Poems," "Memory Games," "Bride of Frankenstein," "Next to Love," "Sandwich Fish," "Greek Poems"—fourteen in total.
As I read, another message came in.

"I was watching a movie the other day about a bunch of French girls that look like you. But you look good. Right? Wrong? I don't know."

Before I finished reading them all, another one appeared in my inbox.
In this message, he discussed the painting he'd given me and how I could just give it back to him. He mentioned the police coming to

his house to tell him to leave me alone. He said the police must have a crush on me and indicated there was no case they could file because I emailed him back.

He finished with:

"Oh have you seen any Judd Apatow films? I think he would totally find you attractive. You'd melt him like butter. But he lives in Los Angeles."

My body and brain couldn't react until the last message finished. Terror filled my sweat-soaked head. I raced down the spiral staircase and vomited.

There would be no more sleep that night, so I jumped into action. *What can I do right now? Is he outside? It's 3 a.m. You can't call anyone. Find out how you've been messaging him. Yes, do that; you can do that.*

Immediately, I knew how I must be sending him messages; he had given me the answer in his message. He must have been on my gallery email list. When I purchased the art gallery in September 2009, the sale came with the business email list. I sent out at least one email a month about upcoming shows. I prayed and hoped that he had signed up BEFORE I owned the business and that I hadn't accidentally added him from the sign-up list I kept on the counter.

I logged onto my Mailchimp account and quickly searched his name. Sure as shit, there he was, and luckily, he had signed up for the list in March 2009. I took screenshots and made notes. I found strength in solving this riddle he had left, and I didn't realize I was building my case against him. To me, I was defending myself, quieting the voices of doubt in my mind, finding sanity when it was being stripped from me.

My eyes lingered over his comments about my relationship, once again scratching at me with his words, letting me know he was watching me. I ran to the bathroom and threw up again.

I grew sullen as I took in his words about my appearance. *Go jerk off into a handful of sandpaper to someone else, Jeffrey. You get no say in how I look.* How I look doesn't need to be justified. I feel embarrassed by sharing his comments on how I look. I hate him for forcing me to defend my appearance.

•　　•　　•

*As my fellow eighth graders whispered about the hotel we were staying at having a free porn channel, I basked in the glory of the United States of America and the cracks in its foundation that my young Midwest mind was beginning to see. The noise of my classmates interrupted the hushed awe that filled my cells as I entered the sandstone and marbled rotunda. This was the floor Anita Hill had walked on just two years prior, and now I, little Anna Nasset, was standing there.*

*An uninvited squeeze on my ass interrupted my wonderment. There stood a group of boys laughing and shrieking with joy as I wheeled around to catch them. The same boys who in choir class had tried to peer down the blouse my Paw-Paw, my grandfather, had gotten me for the first day of school. The blond one with the mullet was the ringleader. I knew he didn't come from a good home; therefore, in sympathy, I didn't want to get him in trouble.*

*I stood frozen in the rotunda, the very place where laws had been created to protect me. I felt violated. The boys laughed and jeered at the insurrection to my autonomy.*

•　　•　　•

I unabashedly love rom-com films, though I now know how prevalent stalking is, how it is romanticized, and how problematic it is in rom-com movies. *I can never watch a Judd Apatow movie again. Jeffrey just fucked up the rom-com genre for me.*

Red-eyed, sleep-deprived, I dragged myself to the police station. I knew to bring all the evidence and screenshots with me, and I had become organized in my undoing. It was the only control I could grasp. I slumped into the chair at the round table and filed my next batch of police reports.

Before going to the station, I had contacted a friend, a six-foot-tall giant with a pierced septum and broad shoulders, and asked him to return the painting to Jeffrey's house. I had planned to take it into the woods and shoot it when Jeffrey stopped harassing my life, but instead, I hoped the return might quiet him. I documented the artwork in the gallery with a picture as proof of possession, and when my friend left it at Jeffrey's door, I documented the drop-off.

I opened the gallery late once again. The four walls weren't big and beautiful anymore; they were starting to feel like a prison, and the windows to the outside seemed like prison bars as I nervously stared out at the street. I went to Facebook and blocked Jeffrey. I had waited to collect evidence; now that it was filed, I blocked him. Everything felt flat and lost.

It was the 10th of January, and I paid commissions to artists on the 10th of each month. I turned my attention to invoicing and cutting checks; at least it was busywork to keep me focused. I knew sales had slipped in the chaos of Jeffrey uprooting my spirit, but I'd be okay. I totaled up the sales for December and screamed into the gallery void. Gasping for air, I added the numbers again.

I always compared the monthly sales to the year prior. In December 2010, I earned fifty thousand in sales. In December 2011, after Jeffrey had revealed his stalking of me, I earned twenty-five thousand in sales. Things were very much not going to be okay.

# CHAPTER SEVEN

# Late January 2012 – May 2012

**Almost one in three stalkers have stalked before.**

**One in eight employed stalking victims lose time from work as a result of their victimization, and more than half lose five days of work or more.**[8]

In the early morning hours, weaving along the dark valley roads, I headed to Seattle to pick up art for the February 2012 new show. Since my car wasn't big enough for the task, I borrowed a truck from Dave and set off on this terrifying adventure. I hate driving, especially in the dark, and I was driving a truck into the city. This was a recipe for disaster to my nerves.

When I was young and filled with confidence, newly armed with my driver's license, I found myself in several car accidents—some my fault, some not. This string of accidents stuck with me as I grew into adulthood. While living in rural communities, driving was a necessity but one with a speed limit of twenty-five miles an hour, which I could manage with my anxiety. Highways and cities were a different matter. The panic would begin bubbling to the surface when I hit the open road. More than once, I have had to find a place to stop to steady my breathing as I attempted to navigate the lanes and honking cars. That is the thing with trauma: It never entirely goes away. It appears in the most annoying of moments. I could move through it, but it was still always there.

I stopped by the Chimacum gas station to pick up tarps and ropes to secure the art and was struck by how it probably looked like I was going to clean up a murder scene. Fear rushed in that someday Jeffrey may be purchasing these same supplies to dispose of my body. After the last batch of unwanted messages from him, law enforcement and I had no idea what he would do, and fear for my safety and the safety of others was mounting.

As I followed the dark valley road toward the Bainbridge Island ferry, buzzing with anxiety, there was still a hint of freedom. Even if just for a few hours, I was getting out of town and could feel the breeze of anonymity. I tucked into the ferry with my cup of coffee and watched the hustle and bustle of this commuter vessel. Women lined the restroom's mirrors with hairdryers and makeup bags, people jogged the upper deck circle, and colleagues in commute shared cups of coffee and breakfast sandwiches. I felt freedom in my solitude.

●　　　●　　　●

*The mile markers on the highway ticked steadily down—10, 9, 8—but all that surrounded me was the deep towering evergreens in the fall of 2006. I couldn't fathom that the trees would give way to the city and the Puget Sound, and the highway would end at a ferry dock. My car climbed down the mountain, and before me lay "The Emerald City" in her overcast glory in the fall of 2006.*

*After several years on the rugged Maine coastline, I had taken up with Ben. Ben had the charisma, charm, tattoos, and attentive nature I was attracted to. He supported my art and voice, and I fell into deep love and comfort with him. His stories of traveling and sailing around the world held my rapt attention.*

*In the summer of 2006, as he skippered a boat in Newport, Rhode Island, I found myself driving down to visit on the weekends. Ben was a man who commanded adventure, and I was living for it. Fresh oysters on Cuttyhunk Island, docking on Nantucket, all of it intoxicating. Not surprisingly, he would talk me into leaving Maine to pursue life in Rhode Island and beyond.*

*I often say I have a "broken picker" for men. I gravitate toward ones who would harm and not hold me in tenderness. That "broken picker" of mine should have set flare guns the size of fireworks off over the mega-yachts in Newport Harbor, but instead, it stayed quiet.*

*A few months after I moved to Newport, Ben would claim that the IRS had seized his bank account due to a tax error, and we needed to move immediately to Washington state, where he had work lined up. None of this makes sense when I look back, but I bought it hook, line, and sinker in my youth and trauma-formed brain. He urged me not to tell anyone, not even my parents, of this choice that we were making. We drove across the country through Ohio (within a few hours of my parents' house), and I said nothing. Brainwashing is an incredibly evil tool.*

*We would settle in Port Townsend, Washington, and only last about six months. He chipped away at my brain, working his manipulations on me. By the time we broke up, he had cheated on me, convinced me it was my fault, and raped me when I was trying to move my things out of the house.*

*I am stronger than I never knew. I would rebuild again.*

●　　●　　●

The ferry sliced through the churning Puget Sound, Seattle growing closer and closer. I rolled the truck down the ramp and into the clatter of the city. I only needed to drive a few blocks to collect paintings from an artist at the iconic OK Hotel's doors. Previously a haughty staple of the grunge era, it now housed artist studios and apartments.

The artist and I hefted his large-scale pieces into the truck, and as we did, the homeless shelter next door opened its doors. Suddenly, my vehicle was surrounded by curious men. I was standing in the back of the truck, answering questions that the crowd of men asked, feeling uneasy by the elevated platform of my display but amused and delighted by their thoughtful responses, when my phone rang.

Juggling art, conversation, anxiety, and fatigue in one hand, I answered the phone with my other, noting the number was from the Jefferson County Courthouse. To my surprise, the voice on the other end was Dee Boughton, a prosecuting attorney. He introduced himself and explained he was filing charges—gross misdemeanor stalking—against Jeffrey for stalking me. The first court appearance would be that day, and Dee wanted me to be there.

The world swirled around me, and I stood in the back of a pickup truck in Pioneer Square, a stone statue. I'm an intelligent woman, at least in a few areas, but I had no idea how the criminal justice system worked. As I'd filed report after report with the police station, I hadn't realized that a prosecutor may eventually prosecute. I also didn't know that it wouldn't be Me v. Jeffrey but instead The State of Washington v. Jeffrey.

Questions and confusion came tumbling down my cheeks in the form of tears. *What would happen next? What was I going to have to do? Would it stop Jeffrey from stalking me or make him angrier? What would he do with the anger?*

Back on the ferry, I stayed in the truck to be with the abundance of art hidden under the tarps in the bed. Unfortunately, I couldn't take joy in my anonymity anymore. I sat in confusion and anger at what had unraveled in the last few months and what was possibly to come. Looking back, I didn't know what was being asked of me or what would be asked of me in the following years. If I had known, I might have just driven that truck right off the ferry into the cold Puget Sound Bay.

Guarded by the tender and fierce presence of my friend Megan, I walked up the looming courthouse stairs and into the unknown. Megan is one of the great loves of my life—a pillar. Her carefree Santa Cruz upbringing is matched with kindness and compassion I have rarely encountered in anyone I have ever known. That day was no exception. Megan was with me that first day, and she would be with me on the last day.

We talked with Dee Boughton about what would happen next, eager to learn not just what was happening to me but also how this process worked. We made quiet jokes about how this was nothing like what we saw on TV in legal shows, but maybe if we were lucky, it would all be wrapped up with a tidy bow in an hour as television portrays.

Meeting with Dee, I felt like I was at my first day of law school. Charges had been filed against Jeffrey. At the hearing, if he showed up, he would be charged, then bail would be set. If he didn't, there would be a warrant out for his arrest. Either way felt like a losing situation. I didn't want to see Jeffrey or be in the same room as him, but if he didn't appear, that put me in greater danger of harm, and my head swam with worst-case scenarios.

I had not filed for a protection order yet due to my fear of standing next to Jeffrey. I was marched over to the clerk's window to begin that process. My hands shakily filled out the forms as if I were fueled by a truckload of coffee. I wanted to scream into the hallway—*I DON'T WANT TO DO THIS, JUST MAKE HIM STOP, GET HIM THE HELP HE NEEDS*—but I followed instructions and then went into the bathroom, as my stomach had turned against me.

In the courtroom, there were several bailiffs. I could see them search my face with compassion and pity. I realized they had dealt with Jeffrey over the years for past crimes, and there was some comfort in this knowledge. I'd never sat in a courtroom, and I sensed my life being ripped out from under me. I felt my agency slipping away with each passing second as we waited for Judge Landes to come out from her chambers. I had the steadiness of Megan sitting next to me, but everything was shifting into the voice of the unknowns.

When Judge Landes entered the courtroom, we all rose and sat down as directed, my wobbly legs obeying the orders. Then, the hearing began.

Jeffrey didn't appear in the courtroom, but he was fully present in my mind. As the hearing went on, I couldn't focus on the legal terms, future court dates, or arrest warrants. *If Jeffrey isn't here, where is he? He could be in the hallway, down the road, at my gallery, in my home.* His lack of presence made him present everywhere to me.

With stalking, this is part of the crime—the fear that each victim faces. If they aren't here, where is the stalker, and when will they appear next? Jeffrey is the darkness; he is the shadows. He resides in the deepest crevices of my brain. I never know what he will do next or when he will do it.

Granted a temporary protection order and a list of future court dates, I was sent back out into the daylight, clutching the piece of paper. The sunlight felt unfair as I pulled my signature shades down. The darkness my white sunglasses provided felt unsafe. Megan had to return to work, and I needed to do my due diligence to ensure that not only I was safe but so was Rachel, who was minding the gallery that day, until Jeffrey's arrest. Afterwards, I headed back to Dave's to hide and wait until I heard Jeffrey had been arrested. What was to have been a productive day had become splintered and unrecognizable.

By now, I had basically moved into Dave's without his permission because I felt safe there. I know he enjoyed having me around—I helped care for his child, cooked food, hosted family gatherings—but I could also feel the disconnect. Chalking it up to the stress I was under with my business and Jeffrey, I busied myself doing anything I could to create a better home and earn Dave's love. I was neglecting the apparent signs that though he felt sorry for me, he just wasn't that into me. If I cooked enough, cared enough, loved enough, or fucked enough, he would be able to fully commit and look over the external chaos I brought to the table.

I busied myself with these tasks as I waited out the night to hear if Jeffrey had been found. We were bonded in the situation, and though Dave couldn't fix it, he wanted to see safety for me.

By morning, Jeffrey had been arrested, and I stepped into the new day with victory in my heart. *He will get the help he needs, and he will stop stalking. Everyone is going to be okay.* Foolish, foolish Anna.

––––––––

In the quietest months at the gallery, winter 2012, I began to sink. I started cutting checks a bit later, hustling harder, and closing the gallery at a moment's notice to climb up the hill to the courthouse. It was a cycle that was not sustainable. I didn't reveal to my customers the reason for the sudden closures, and to my artists, I promised there would be a check in the mail the next day. My integrity was called into question by artists and customers, but I refused to breathe a word about what was happening. I held an unshakeable sense of shame in the situation I found myself in with Jeffrey.

When I occasionally broke my silence, I was always met with questions and accusations when uttering my truth. "Did you date him?" "Why did he pick you?" "You must feel special that someone is watching you." "What did you do?" It didn't matter that I had nothing to do with Jeffrey's behavior—I would still be blamed and questioned. I had already learned from experience and the media that the victim always holds the blame.

I needed to say—I needed to scream—it is never your fault. What if I had dated Jeffrey? Would it be my fault then? NO. What if we had been married. Then, certainly, I'd be to blame? NO. How about if I were just friends with him? NO. There is no justification for a stalker's behavior. There is no blame on the victim. Rather than deal with this unwarranted backlash, I chose to stay silent to preserve my broken spirit from fully shattering.

––––––––

It was the court date for the protection order, and I had been dreading the hearing. The few moments of sleep I got were filled with nightmares, and I'd wake in a panic. I steeled myself for battle by listening to the only song I knew to play, "Eye of the Tiger." It has, and will forever remain, my battle song from that mistake of a wedding day back in 2009. I wish I could say I jogged up the courthouse stairs in Stallone style, but I did not. Megan and Ellen had to walk me up the stairs. I used my own feet, but it felt like they each took an arm and carried my weighted being.

Jeffrey was in jail. His family would no longer bail him out—much to my relief. Worriment filled every nerve ending, as I had not yet been informed whether he would appear via jail camera or in person. There was a good chance he would be standing next to me as Judge Landes looked down from above, weighing his word against mine, only the piece of paper with my typed-out statement to defend me. I couldn't stop vomiting and shitting with the unknown wreaking havoc on my body.

Only minutes before entering the courtroom, I learned Jeffrey would appear by video from jail, and my body flooded with relief. I entered the courtroom, frayed from the needless emotional output, and waited for my future to be decided once again.

In Judge Landes, I began to see fairness and potential safety. She was an intimidating woman in her robes, but I could see care and determination for the law behind the exterior. Years later, I would learn of her work in the early domestic violence movement in Alaska in the 1970s and her push to allow crime victims to be fully seen in the offender-based criminal justice system.

That day, I read my short statement about why I was in fear of Jeffrey and wanted a protection order. Jeffrey, with his orange jumpsuit, wire-framed glasses, and receding hairline, squeaked back a confusing and accusatory line of defense. Judge Landes ruled in my favor, granting a three-year, five-hundred-foot protection order. With clarity, she asked whether he understood this distance, stating it was approximately a football field and a half. He acknowledged his understanding and disappeared from the camera as quickly as he had appeared. The screen went to black. I turned to light. This small victory would ensure my freedom. I just knew it!

In the early weeks and years, I flip-flopped back and forth between my certainty of freedom and resignation that Jeffrey would be an uninvited plague in my life forever. To live with that tension in my nerves and brain is something I was attempting to resolve back then and now have entirely accepted as my reality. I have found that in acceptance, I can begin to heal.

With a trial date looming in March, I was eager to push through and put my life back on track. I wanted to understand the legal process. I wanted to be in the loop as each step, each setback, and each decision was made.

I had, and continue to hold, empathy for Jeffrey, the voices and noise that fill his head and push him to behave by stalking people. But at the same time, I didn't want to give up my future or freedom. My quest for resolution took the form of learning. I researched the criminal justice process, schizophrenia, stalking, and protection orders. I started asking questions.

Prosecuting Attorney Dee Boughton kept me up to date on every hearing, and I would attend, tucked into the back row where Jeffrey couldn't see me on camera or hidden in the bathroom if Jeffrey was physically there, only sneaking in at the last minute. Once, I was even hidden in the sheriff's office at the courthouse, the holding cell a visual reminder of all that separated him and me.

Jeffrey, determined to have his voice heard, wanted to represent himself. He has always fancied himself a legal-minded person and, to my knowledge, has done a great deal of research on the law. Because of his mental health diagnosis, he was appointed a defense lawyer by the court and needed to undergo a competency evaluation to determine whether he was: 1. Fit to stand trial. 2. Able to defend himself in court.

His anger over being appointed a defense lawyer became evident quickly. He would threaten and lash out against the lawyers or create false accusations both sexual and violent in nature. They would be dismissed, a new lawyer would be appointed, and the trial date would be pushed back again.

My brain couldn't accept that Jeffrey may be able to defend himself. I grappled with the concept that if he was stalking me, wouldn't it be a continuation of the crime to let him defend himself? Additionally, I was baffled by the legal process and was growing wary of the postponements.

Often, I threw the "be back soon" sign on my gallery door and went to court hearings, the gallery bank account growing smaller and smaller all the while. Prosecutor Dee informed me that Jeffrey wanted personal information about me—my home address among the facts he was seeking. I wanted my information to be kept private and worked to advocate for myself, still refusing to use our local advocacy center's services.

One day at court, Jeffrey was physically in appearance, and I hid in what now felt like my new "office," the bathroom at the courthouse. Just as the hearing was starting, the bailiff snuck me into the back row of the courtroom. Jeffrey began soapboxing his rhetoric and, at one point, requested a new judge to oversee the trial. He exclaimed that he felt Judge Landes was ill and would die before the case went to trial, and therefore, there should be a different judge. You could have heard a pin drop in the courtroom as myself, my support, and the bailiffs looked at one another in shock at his brazenness. Jeffrey's antics and ramblings grew crueler and more pointed with each passing hearing.

My admiration for Judge Landes continued to grow as I listened to her calmly explain that she was in good health and there was no cause for her to be removed from the case. Her composed manner and fairness were clear, but she had no time for bullshit. Not that day, not any day. I have watched her in many hearings, as they often would be scheduled in a batch. She is a bulwark for justice.

Jeffrey's courtroom outbursts and requests weren't his only disturbing actions. Dee Boughton informed me that Jeffrey viewed my appearance at the court hearings as a sign of my love for him and desire to be with him. My brain popped like a balloon.

*Is there more to MY story that I don't know? Am I going to throw up on the floor? Is this why everything is happening? Is there a more serious threat I'm not being told? Where's the nearest trash can? What else is Jeffrey doing? I want to go curl up under a stack of quilts and hide forever.*

I was only privy to the evidence I was turning in. There was a much bigger picture regarding Jeffrey and his obsession with me and, I would later discover, with his other victims.

The last bit of control I held was ripped from me that day, and everything continued to spiral into the void. I now could not go to court hearings that were deciding my future just as much as they were deciding Jeffrey's. The truth was unavoidable now—I needed an advocate. Gulping up my pride, I went to Dove House Advocacy Services.

How naïve and pretentious of me to have waited that long. They met my nerves and grief with warmth and care. A small older woman with her bright suits and sunny disposition became my appointed advocate. She swooped in and empowered me with empathy and understanding. My advocate listened to me go over every detail from start to finish, backward and forward, a million times. She was a phone call, a meeting, or an email away any time I needed her.

Advocates are saints. They take on our trauma and face it for us. For victims, the mental turmoil of the process is often too much to bear, and advocates are there to explain and care for our trauma-riddled brains continually. Over the years, I have felt that just working with me must feel like a full-time job to the advocate, and then I marvel that they are carrying this burden for dozens and dozens of victims at the same time. They are mere mortals, but they are warriors walking amongst us.

Not being able to participate in the court process and staring at a crumbling business, I turned my attention to saving the gallery. With spring came tourists and, more importantly, a weeklong art retreat with hundreds of women who would flood my gallery to purchase my quirky curated selection laid out with them in mind. Twenty-twelve was to be the last year of the famed ArtFest, as the founder was stepping down, and all eyes were on me to take up the torch. Everyone was counting on me to continue this legendary week of creation and connection and to boost to our town's economy after the quiet winter months.

I had shown the work and made big sales of some of the top artists who taught at the retreats. I made friends with many of the participants, networked my butt off, researched, and consulted with people. The retreats appeared to be the next logical step for me. It would secure my gallery's success and grow my empire. With Jeffrey in jail, I rationalized that he wouldn't bother me again when he was released. I had shown him not to mess with me, and now I was going to show my community just how strong and powerful I was.

Ellen has always called me a "jammy dodger." It's an Irish phrase used for someone who pulls out a win/a bit of luck/the answer when all the chips are down, and it looks like failure is imminent. Taking on art retreats would be one of my greatest "jammy dodger" moments. That spring week, I made enough sales to catch up on my overdue bills and solidify my decision to take on this legacy event.

Back on top and in charge of my life, I came into a bit more normalcy. Due to the financial strain I had been under, I convinced Dave to let me move in fully but kept an extra room at my friend's house in case things didn't work out. I dove headfirst into being a stepmom, helping with homework, cooking meals, and assisting with the occasional school drop-off. Dave's large extended family would regularly gather for dinners and holidays, and I loved hosting and cooking. I found safety and joy in immersing myself in family life. Along with that, there were meals, sleepovers, and cocktail hours with Ellen and Megan at the brewery; in turn, our deep friendships, shenanigans, and laughter came back.

In these moments of simple joy, there was the interruption of the phone ringing or emails with news from court hearings and my unknown future. Lunch with Ellen would be disrupted by a call from

Dee about a hearing. Promptly, our laughter would end. While enjoying a drink at the brewery with Megan, I'd receive an email about a new trial date, and I'd stare into my drink quietly. I'd get a call while grocery shopping and forget to buy clementines. My phone would ring while trying to make a sale, and my shoulders would slump.

Even though I was clawing for normalcy and finding those moments of happiness, I faked it to make it with a smile painted on my face in whatever hue of lipstick I'd picked that day paired with my white sunglasses. The few who knew about Jeffrey grew wary of me continually bringing up the process. Even though they were my support system, they could not fully understand how it plagued my thoughts because it wasn't happening to them. There would be the comments of, "Get over it," "It's not that bad," and "He's going to leave you alone." I balanced these comments and fears with determination and hope as my days continued to be interrupted with court proceedings.

I knew of one of Jeffrey's other victims. It had been shared with me that a woman I knew from around town, Erica, had been stalked by Jeffrey for years. Needing to talk to someone who understood what I was going through, I reached out to her to see if she was comfortable meeting. We set up a date at a local restaurant to connect.

Tucked into the corner booth, cocktails in hand, lingering over tapas plates, we laid it all out on the line. Erica shared with me that she had gone to high school with Jeffrey. She had even once gone to a school dance with him but found him odd. Years later, in approximately 2008, he began stalking her, showing up at the house of her and her husband, following her, messaging her. I took her words in with great care and sadness. In a full restaurant, we were the only two in the room, linked together by our fear and this crime committed against us.

I left that evening feeling fully seen for the first time and also shaking my head in horror. *Thank god he hasn't been watching me since 2008,* I thought as I shivered.

I stared down at Prosecuting Attorney Dee Boughton's phone number lighting up my screen. Wearily, I answered. He needed me at court now. Jeffrey was going to plead guilty. I grabbed my purse, threw that pesky "I'll be back soon" sign on the door, and rushed up the hill to the courthouse.

My advocate was busy shielding another victim, so I texted Megan, Ellen, and Dave. No one could get there in time. *I'm fine. I can go alone. I don't know what I'm facing, but I'll face it head on.*

Once I arrived at the courthouse, Dee explained to me there was a high chance that Jeffrey was going to plead guilty that day, as charges had been amended. He was facing a misdemeanor stalking charge and would plead guilty to gross misdemeanor harassment. My face twisted as I tried to interpret the law, confused by the words Dee was saying. If there was ever a day I should have had an advocate with me, it was that day, May 30, 2012. The courtroom was packed with people for various hearings, and I snuck into the back row once again. I did not understand a damn thing happening around me.

What felt like seconds probably took an hour, maybe longer. My body was there, but I was gone; I was mentally floating out over the waters. There was nothing to tether me and keep me present.

My agency and voice were lost in the noise. I could not grasp what was happening. Dee and others asked me questions and provided information at a pace I could not compute. I did not know if I would pass out or vomit right there in the courtroom.

During a break in the hearing, Dee explained to me what was transpiring. Jeffrey would plead guilty to the lightest charge, misdemeanor harassment, if he could defend himself. The other charges, stemming from him getting into an altercation with another inmate, would be dismissed.

I drove my nails deep into the flesh on my arm, trying to bring myself back from the numbness that surrounded me. Minutes later, Judge Landes allowed Jeffrey to represent himself, and he pled guilty. She would now sentence him. Dee informed me the maximum sentence was for 364 days, but I should be prepared for Jeffrey to walk that day based on time served, as maximum sentencing is rarely given.

Judge Landes came back to the bench, and she asked if I wanted to speak and give a victim impact statement. Everyone awaiting other hearings turned and stared at me. I floated further away. I declined to give my voice because I didn't know what a victim impact statement was and didn't realize the importance of the victim's voice. Besides, at the moment, my voice was gone. The floating turned to falling, sinking, drowning, waves washing over me as I waited for Judge Landes to speak.

"I sentence you to 364 days," said Judge Landes, and the gavel fell.

The shitshow was over. I had never been as alone, surrounded by people, as I was that day. I began to cry, face buried in my hands, weeping out my confusion and injustice. People looked at me and stared in pity and curiosity. I gathered my purse and walked out into the sun, white sunglasses hiding my tears. Still overcome by the most intense loneliness I'd ever endured, I drove back to work.

From January until the end of May, there were approximately thirty hearings. *This is over; this is done. I am done*, I thought to myself.

# PART TWO

# FAWN

# CHAPTER EIGHT

# July 2012 – January 2013

"Many offenders do not stop their behavior after conviction but eventually resume their campaign against the same victim or against a new partner or other victim."[9]

Each passing month brought peace to the gallery and me. I craved the new—new freedom, new artists, new shows, new conversations. Art evokes emotion, brings visuals to words, hits on our nerves, and creates synapses. In my days spent at the gallery, I would marvel over a new show and conversation that surrounded it.

I wanted and needed the conversations in the gallery with my next show. I curated a show of large-scale abstracted nudes, focused on male and female genitalia, by a regional artist. After Jeffrey's sentencing, everything had returned to normal.

Those who knew about Jeffery stalking me took the approach of "get over it and move on." Some days, I did move on, but then I'd hear a sound, a phrase, a song, and I was transported back into the past. Trauma bubbled to the surface in the most inconvenient times, my brain being stalked by my history. As I sat with my secrets, the parts of me that no one knew, I looked at the paintings and saw the pieces of me that had no voice.

The show was a smashing success, not in sales but in reception. It was the talk of the town, and though we had a sign on the door acknowledging the adult content of the show, someone even went to the mayor's office trying to get the show shut down. Having felt censored my whole life, I couldn't have been prouder over the attempted censorship. Throughout the month, the gallery was filled with whispers and conversations of abuse, grief, and trauma.

In the far back corner of the gallery stood one piece, created by me. I had worked on it for two years and finally decided it was to the caliber and standard I would expect from any artist I showed. I had used my one-hundred-year-old typewriter to tell my story—not my story of being stalked but my story of everything else I held quiet. I had typed my story on white cotton fabric and then cut up every word, thrown it in a bag, and sewn it back together with hand-dyed black squares juxtaposing the pieces. Frayed fabric edges and threads created depth and begged to be investigated.

I told my story of harm and moving through life without letting anyone know how the words should be organized. Safely, I laid out my soul, but my secrets stayed locked away. I named the piece, "Sometimes when I lay down, words fall from my eyes like tears." It sold to an art collector in California, and I hope it gives them comfort to this day.

•   •   •

*High school gave way to college, and in 1998, I chose to attend the same university as my sister. Anderson University, a small Christian liberal arts school, had an incredible art department, and that was where I would put my focus. I had packed up my NFL aspirations in the years prior, feeling I couldn't trust men's behavior. I needed to channel my voice through art.*

*I've always made friends easily, and college was no different. I loved the dorm life with gaggles of gals chatting long into the evening. The art department created its bond of unique misfits and aspirations, and I was home there. Nonetheless, in the development of my artistic voice and college freedoms, I began to crumble. I had already accepted that I was not a Christian, the faith in which I was raised, and losing that platform of guidance left me teetering.*

*I hadn't processed and didn't understand how to unpack the injustices I carried, and my process became my actions. I shaved my head and grew my hair into dreadlocks. I behaved erratically and without thought for myself or others. I was a ball of chaos coming apart at the seams. Leaning into my agency, I decided to seek help and soon found myself at the tiny house on campus, meeting with a therapist.*

*I sat in a circle with other women who had been assaulted and abused, and I began to learn I was not alone. I found a salve in that circle, and I made lifelong friends in that room. I talked to my therapist for an hour a week. There was freedom in the confidentiality and in choosing to see a therapist without asking my parents' permission.*

*However, the freedom was short-lived after a session where I told the therapist that I had smoked pot and stayed over at the house of the guy I was dating—not having sex, just snuggling. Since it was a religious school, there were many rules: no sex, no drinking, no pot, no smoking, no fun! My admission to breaking the rules was met with a scolding, as she urged me to promise that I wouldn't commit these sins again because if I did, she would have to report me. Suddenly, I felt as though I couldn't be open with her. I continued to use the campus therapy services and see her, mainly because it was free, but my secrets stayed with me, and progress stalled.*

●   ●   ●

These art acts that were visually public and personally private helped me gain my footing again. I greeted my customers with a smile and a bit more brightness each day.

One summer morning, Connie, a middle-aged woman, stopped by. I didn't know much about Connie other than her warm smile and sparkling eyes from the few times I had met her at Al-Anon. I had attended when I was married to Carson to better understand sobriety, a path he had chosen and I wanted to support. By the nature of Al-Anon, I only knew Connie's first name and was happy to have her pop into the gallery for a look around.

We made small talk about the artwork, life, and all things Port Townsend. We started to say farewell as she headed to the door, but then she stopped and turned to me. She looked at me and asked, "What's going on with Jeffrey?"

Taken aback that Connie would know about Jeffrey, I searched my mind to connect them. Finding no connection, I stammered out, "Well, he's in jail now. Hopefully, his behavior will stop. My heart aches for his family and all that they have gone through."

She looked at me with her kind, now watery eyes and said, "Anna, don't you know I'm his mother?"

No, Connie, I did not.

Stunned, I sobbed, I reached out, and we met each other in a tight embrace. We wept, we hugged, and we talked. Connie shared with me more about Jeffrey, their family, and the shame they carried for his behavior. I took her stories in and held them with grief. I explained to her how sorry I was that her son's actions linked us, that I in no way blamed his family, and I knew they wanted him to stop these actions and live a healthy life. It's what I wanted too.

In our brief conversation, laden with our emotions, I began to connect the shame that society puts on the families of those who harm. I, as the victim, carried guilt and blame, even though there was nothing I could do to change the situation. Connie and the rest of her family shouldered a heavy burden as well, and even in that, she had the bravery and beauty to see if I was okay. Their son's behavior upturned their lives. They faced community judgment and backlash while they sat helpless in their grief. They had done everything in their power to advocate for their son's mental health, but as time wore on, they had to step away and allow Jeffrey to make his own choices. My heart broke for the family. In fact, it still does. Jeffrey's actions weren't just harming me; they were harming a community.

That was the only time I talked with Connie, and our conversation rests heavily on my soul to this day.

There would be other run-ins with the people and protectors I had met in my months dealing with the criminal justice system. That summer, Judge Landes and I would attend the same art gala fundraiser and chat with each other. Sometimes, she would attend a gallery walk. I'd see Officer Corrigan at the grocery store or around town, and he'd gently inquire about my well-being. Reflecting on the chance meetings, these moments in time, I realize now that these people knew what I had gone through, and they knew way more than me of what was to come.

Stalking is a psychological crime; it eats away at the victim's psyche and essence. Part of my silence was that I would often question whether I was overreacting. Should I just get over it? Move on? Why was I still carrying the burden of Jeffrey's existence and actions in my brain? Running into people like Corrigan or Judge Landes provided a sense of peace and validation. They removed me from the category of nameless victim and saw me as a person and, in doing so, mirrored back to me the severity of the crime being done to me.

As the temperatures fell, so did my spirits as I stared at the gallery books. I still wasn't where I needed to be. There had been town construction that compounded the financial problems, but the monumental loss of dealing with Jeffrey and the criminal justice process rippled through every month. I kept this problem hidden, not wanting anyone to know I was in trouble or why and set about launching a small series of art retreats the following year. I would host three retreats with twenty to sixty students, and the profits would allow me to keep the gallery going. I would rob Peter to pay Paul until things leveled back out. The chips were down, but I'd prove everyone wrong. My self-doubt fostered an attitude of controlled pride and determination.

Still dating Dave, I took control at the home I was forcing him to create with me. We had his son more often than his mother did, and I set about making sure his academics and behavior would excel. I took to painting the walls, bringing in new furniture, sprucing and cleaning up the home to ensure that I fit. I would dream and plan of redoing the kitchen and mudroom, taking every little bit of control and voice I could find, all while ignoring the undeniable signs that I wasn't the only woman in Dave's life.

There was the postcard from an old girlfriend, nothing to be alarmed about other than it didn't seem she was that far in the past and she didn't know of my existence. Another day, he left his Facebook Messenger up, and when I sat at the computer, there were messages between him and another woman staring back at me. He would talk his way out of it, and I would make another delicious meal, then settle into an evening of sipping whiskey with him on the couch. It wasn't good, it wasn't healthy, but the idea of starting over yet again with an uncertain future regarding my finances or Jeffrey's capabilities pushed me to stay.

My mom flew out after Thanksgiving to meet Dave and see our life together. She had taken very few trips without my father, and while I was busy with life and the gallery, I couldn't wait to have her visit and show off the world I had created. My mom lived a somewhat protected Midwest life and was often nervous and taken aback by my liberal leanings and lifestyle choices, such as living with a man outside of marriage and owning my own business.

That week, she leaned in with delight, and I smiled back, thinking of her watching the gallery while I ran errands, taking her to the pub to meet my friends, and having dinners with Dave and his family. Her eyes were wide with pride during the gallery walk that Saturday as she fully saw her daughter "in action," hosting, selling, chatting.

Within a few weeks, the world I had proudly shown off to my mom crumbled. During a fight one day, Dave told me that I would "never be a priority in his life," and I realized what a fool I had been. I had needed and forced this relationship; he had never wanted it. I was simply a collectible figurine of a woman for his mantle, a place to put his dick and someone to provide him food.

I would spend the next few weeks curled in grief at Megan and her boyfriend's house on the beach. That home, "Millside," had been my safety and refuge for years, or just a place to crash after a long night of dinner, drinks, and games. I welcomed its tender embrace and needed it as I tried to carry on.

I would learn of the other women in Dave's life, and before long, just like Carson, he would impregnate his newest conquest. I longed to have a child of my own, and each pregnancy by a former partner was a punch to the vagina.

Looking for a new apartment meant also looking for a place that would be secure. Jeffrey would be out of jail at the end of January, and though I hoped I would never hear from him, in an abundance of caution, I wanted my footprint in the community to be small. Luckily, a friend who managed apartments helped me secure a darling one across the street from the gallery. Remembering Judge Landes's protection order of five hundred feet, I could feel a bit more at ease with this location.

The entrance was a long wooden staircase along the back side of the block. The area below held other spindly stairs, an underground bar my friends had just opened, a music venue, a parking lot, and a nest of river otters. The locale, vintage in its façade and European in its setting, was eerie with its history of sailors and prostitutes from centuries before.

After signing the lease, I told my landlord about Jeffrey, asking her not to rent to him within my five-hundred-foot world. Since there were only four apartment units in the locked building, I felt safe and secure as I moved my meager collection of belongings into the updated apartment. I threw my mattress on the floor, put my clothes in the dresser, and looked around because that was all the furniture I had at the time. I had a decent holiday sale month, and though I shouldn't have, I splurged on a green velvet couch on a deep discount sale. I worked to put everything back in order just as quickly as it had crumbled.

In the final week of January, I looked at my phone. I knew it would ring the next day, and I begged it not to. After Jeffrey's sentencing, Officer Corrigan had told me to sign up for VINElink. This is a victim notification system that alerts victims or family members of victims of a change in status or custody of an offender in jail or prison. It's beneficial for keeping up to date on early releases and parole or learning if an offender made bail. It can and has saved lives.

I can remember calling to sign up for the service. The specialist at VINElink who answered the phone, whose job was to take my burdens off my shoulders and give me a glimmer of hope or voice, helped me as I stammered out my situation. I couldn't find words for requiring this service. I was angry, frustrated, and scared that I needed it. With gentle care, the voice informed me that when Jeffrey was released, I would receive a call from a Kentucky phone number letting me know he was out. I had signed up months earlier for the service, and that night, I sat in the uncomfortable silence that would be my future.

In the early hours of January 22, 2013, I received a Kentucky phone call. Jeffrey was out. I still hate when my phone shows a Kentucky phone number on its ID.

# CHAPTER NINE

# March 2013 – October 2013

**Victims of both stalking types (traditional stalking and stalking with technology) were also more fearful of someone close to them being harmed; losing their job, social network, peers, friends, or freedom; the behaviors never stopping; not knowing what would happen next; or losing their mind.[10]**

The 364 days of freedom quietly ended as I cautiously set foot into the world, knowing Jeffrey was free. I walked a tightrope of balancing my rational and emotional brains' responses against the fear that filled my cells. The emotional side begged me to stay free, believe in my safety, and go on with business as usual. The rational side, however, pointed out the obvious: With Jeffrey free, I was not. While I hoped that he would indeed leave me alone, that I had taught him a lesson, I didn't get to know, nor will I ever know, what was going on in his head and what actions he would take. It is one of the most frustrating parts of being stalked—being a victim of crime. I'll never know what he will do next. That part of my life has been taken from me and given to him.

One afternoon, while sitting in my car, parked in my beloved boatyard, I chatted with my dad while in between errands. My dad's quiet nature meant we didn't speak on the phone often; that was more of my mother's department to chat with me for hours and catch up. But this day, my dad and I spoke. I relished in time of any sort with my father, leaning into his quiet comfort and opinions on life. Our conversation rattled on as the waves lapped onto the beach. I relaxed into the beauty and bustle that surrounded me, feeling parental protection and pride radiate through the phone.

The sun danced on the water's edge, and paralyzed muscles took hold. My adrenal system dumped as Jeffrey appeared from thin air in front of my car, his smile leering at me. I yelled into the phone, "Dad, fuck, it's Jeffrey." My father didn't have a chance to respond as I hung up on him and threw my car into reverse. I peeled out of the boatyard, leaving Jeffrey standing where my car had been, smiling, as clouds of gravel dust filled the air.

After a few minutes of driving, I called my frantic father back, explaining that I was okay and safe, just scared. I could hear the fear in my father's voice as he suggested I not sit in my car alone anymore. In my mind, I was crossing off one more place I could safely go. Another place I loved gone, and this one was a tough pill to swallow. The light continued to dim around me.

Moving forward with caution, I set about trying to create normalcy, to bring a little fun into my life, and I pursued this with safety and the willingness for my plans to be derailed at a moment's notice. To safely plan one's life takes dedication, creativity, and quietness.

My gaggle of Midwest miscreants and I decided to start a euchre club at a local bar, The Pourhouse, to combat the winter blues. We would have held the tournament at my friend's Uptown Pub, but I knew that Jeffrey lived above it, and therefore, I didn't go to that neighborhood. To get to our euchre club, I made sure that every week someone would pick me up and drop me off. They thought we were carpooling, but if you took note of my driver, it was almost always a bigger male friend of mine.

If you haven't played euchre or played cards with Midwesterners, you need to know a few things. We may seem like sweet, passive people by day, but put cards into our hands, and we turn into shit-talking savages. The Pourhouse hosted us on Tuesday nights because it was their quietest night, and our volume would get so loud that we would drive customers out. One of my friends and I were so ruthless, we took on the personalities of Mona-Lisa and Jean-Ralphio Saperstein, the famously obnoxious duo from *Parks & Rec*... We were banned from being partners.

Those Tuesday nights of laughter, ribbing, and throwing down cards with abandon fed my soul. They reminded me of the silliness and joy from years prior.

"Excuse me," I heard from the table next to me. I glanced away from my game and saw a couple sitting and sipping on beers. The woman asked, "Are you playing euchre?"

"Why yes. Do you play?" I asked.

"Wait. Are you playing euchre with Green Bay Packers cards? Mark, look!" she said to her partner.

I laughed, replying, "Yes, we are. You want in on the next game?"

She got up from her table, looked at her husband, and said, "Mark, I can live here now." Then, turning to me, she said, "Hi, my name is Lea."

A five-minute conversation with Jeffrey changed my life forever, and so did a five-minute conversation with Lea, but in a very different way. For all the harm in the world, those split seconds that cause irreparable damage, look for the moments that bring bright change. That is Lea.

As we chatted over cards, I found out that Lea and her husband had moved to Port Townsend for him to attend the Northwest School of Wooden Boatbuilding, and Lea worked in the violence prevention field, flying all over the country to train communities, campuses, and military installations on how to be an active bystander to prevent gender-based violence. Noting this, I shared about my gallery and my background but not a whisper of Jeffrey. Lea and I exchanged numbers that night, and I hopped into my safety "carpool" to go home, thinking to myself, *Now that's a woman I need to know.*

I rationalized that the sightings I had of Jeffrey were coincidences. Jeffrey would be at the bus stop when I drove to get groceries. Clutching the steering wheel, I'd breathe shallow and frantic, whispering, "No no no, don't let the light change red." I averted my glance as the light stayed yellow and drove past. He had every right to be at the bus stop, the boatyard, the grocery store. And my world grew smaller as I charted a new path in my daily life of what I had the right to do.

When my laptop died on me one evening at my small apartment, I fretted over what to do. I couldn't afford a new one, and that meant I couldn't work in the evenings unless I went to the gallery.

I shared this news with my mom during one of our talks. She expressed fear over me working late in the shop, knowing that Jeffrey could be anywhere. I tried to challenge her; I wanted to protect her from my fears. In the end, she sent me a few hundred dollars to buy a new laptop. Having family support is a privilege I am aware of despite the unwanted situation. I had immense gratitude for that and continue to do so, thinking of the millions who do not. I can look back and question, would we have gotten to the finish line without it? Would I be alive without my parents' support? One of the many questions I will never have answers to.

---

*Who the hell is calling me at 6.30 a.m.?* I thought as I rolled over and looked at my phone. The glowing screen displayed my area code but not a number I knew. I ignored the call and buried my head in my pillow, hoping the headache from drinking Manhattans at the bar downstairs would subside before I had to go to work.

The phone rang again a short time later. Aggravated, I saw it was the same number, and my annoyance turned to dread. Could it be Jeffrey? I let it go to voicemail once more. Cautiously, I sat up in bed and hit play on the messages.

A man's voice on the other line greeted me. "Hello, Anna, this is Officer Holmes with the Port Townsend Police Department, and we need to speak to you regarding Jeffrey and some letters he has sent us. Give us a call back as soon as you can."

I slunk down under my covers and buried myself. Could I make myself small enough to disappear? While it wasn't a direct hit to my battleship, it may as well have been. With that, I began to come into a keener understanding, though I would not be able to vocalize it for years, about how stalkers will use the criminal justice system to communicate with their victims. In essence, they are legally permitted to recommit the crime.

Every nerve in my body shaking, I called the PTPD as directed. When I spoke to Officer Holmes, he began to share the horrors with me. The PTPD had received a series of letters from Jeffrey, and the contents were as chaotic as they were vile and threatening.

Officer Holmes stopped there; my clouded brain grew into a thunderstorm. Questions poured out of my mouth, as I felt I needed to know more information, more facts, more details, anything. I could not process without knowledge. Since then, I have learned the opposite to be true; sometimes, ignorance is the only way to process. But at the time, I was desperate to learn more. So Officer Holmes and I agreed I should come to the station to talk.

When I arrived, the officers summarized the information in the letters. Basically, Jeffrey believed that he and I were married. He also believed he was married to Erica and that I was their celestial child. He believed he was married to over two hundred women, but Erica and I were at the top of his list, and he lamented that he couldn't care for us in the way he thought we should be cared for. He went on to declare me an "evil person" and talk about how evil people "should be put to death."

Sitting at a small round table at the station, I told the officers to show me the letters. They asked me if I was sure and cautioned me about how upsetting they might be. "YES," I replied. They handed a copy of one letter over. Through poems and chaos, I found my eyes fixing on the ways in which I should die—put in a fire and roasted like hot dogs, my skin flayed by the bark of trees, put in a barrel filled with water and shot at. *Deep breath, Anna, deep breath.* I dropped the letter, my stomach, my heart, and my shoulders through the floor and into the darkest pit.

The letter I saw that day was one of hundreds, if not thousands, Jeffrey has sent over the years to law enforcement, judges, friends, other victims, advocates, prosecutors, and more. I took a photocopy of the letter with me but have never read another one since that day. I learned that there are parts of my story that I do not need to know—that my mind cannot handle—and that it is best to have ignorance.

I bow in sadness and gratitude to those who have taken on this terrifying role of receiving these letters over all the years. In doing their jobs as public servants, whether elected or through working in the criminal justice system, these people who receive these letters have also opened themselves up to harm, insult, criticism, and threats from Jeffrey. They have children, spouses, loved ones, and a community as well. It is a burden I wouldn't wish upon anyone, and I am humbled by the grit and determination of those called to these fields.

Though the courts and systems have prevented him from sending me letters directly, in my car, I keep a plastic bag and gloves to collect the evidence if one day a letter from Jeffrey does land in my PO box. For not only does he send these vile and threatening letters, but he also will sometimes ejaculate into them.

The officers tried to champion me by talking about safety planning, indicating that I should go stay with friends for the weekend, as they feared Jeffrey would escalate. They felt as though he was unstable enough to bring one of his threats to fruition but also had to let me know they weren't bodyguards and couldn't provide extra security other than doing more patrol drives by my business. My safety was, is, and always will be placed on my back.

I questioned why they couldn't arrest him. If he was threatening me and others, couldn't that be considered breaking the restraining order? They gave me more insight into the workings of Jeffrey and the workings of the law. Because the language was "Anna SHOULD be killed," not "I am going to kill Anna," he hadn't made a direct threat, and the most they could probably do was a seventy-two-hour psychi-atric hold. This speaks to not only our criminal and legal system but also to the ways in which Jeffrey and many other stalkers know how to dance around their victims with frenzied horror.

As our conversation continued and I didn't think I could handle any more, the officers talked to me about the gallery. Because it was a very public space, and I was a public figure, they had growing concerns of a larger act of violence happening in those beautiful walls. They pointed out that at gallery walks, I had two hundred to three hundred people come through each time, and from the perspective of potential mass violence, this was a perfect storm. Their words washed over and reminded me, *it's not just my safety—it's the safety of my community.*

Through the ringing in my ears, I heard a question that shocked me from Officer Holmes. "Have you thought about what you are wearing?" I looked up, stunned and broken, anger snapping in my eyes. HOW DARE YOU I wanted to shout, but my mouth could barely form words. Officer Holmes, seeing the angered defeat in my expression, walked back his statement with, "No, no, no, I didn't mean that in a blaming way. I meant it in a safety way."

He went on to point out that I was wearing a cardigan that went to my ankles, and I could trip on that if I needed to run. My heeled shoes could be a hinderance in escape. The large necklace I had around my neck could be used to choke me. He asked how I wore my purse. I replied around my chest so it wouldn't be stolen, and he quietly pointed out that someone could pull me down from behind with it.

●　　●　　●

*My fingers slipped through the fabrics of clothing on the rack that summer of 1996. I remembered that the school rules said "skirts must fall below the knees" as I loaded up an armload and headed to the dressing room.*

*Working two part-time jobs the summer before I started my new school to afford new clothes and distract myself from my own mind, I prepared for the reinvention of Anna. Transferring from the public school to the Christian school for my junior and senior year in a small town meant only one thing: I had done something wrong. I was a "troubled" girl who could be set straight by a Christian education. Stuffing the secret of Mr. Samuelson and the others' actions deep, I silently accepted the "Scarlet A" that would be nonverbally placed upon me. It was an unspoken NDA of which there was no monetary compensation because if people knew what Mr. Samuelson had done, it would certainly be my fault.*

*Selecting the perfect outfit to wash away my secrets and pain, I walked into my new life at Delaware Christian School. The junior class of only twenty-seven students held a few familiar faces, and I sat with Tina as she introduced me to her friends Laura and Hope. The other girls in the class looked skeptically at me, a "new girl," competition breaking into their ranks. They weren't wrong, as the boys also longed for fresh meat and poured attention my way.*

*I learned that day how to answer a question without ever answering it. "Why did you transfer here?" washed over me everywhere I went. "I wanted to be challenged more academically," "I didn't agree with the secular teachings of the public school," "I wanted smaller class sizes." Each one of my stories was met with a sideways glance—Oh, we know the truth. She was sent here for doing something bad.*

● ● ●

And then, guarded only by this knowledge and advice, I walked out of the police station.

I didn't go to work that day. The gallery stayed shuttered because why would I set foot in that space with all the knowledge and threats I had just received? Instead, I found myself back at my apartment, talking on the phone to my sister, Carrie. I needed to let the family know but couldn't speak to my parents in that moment. I didn't want to cause them fear or anguish.

As I spoke to my sister, I unconsciously changed my clothes. I looked up from our conversation to find a new version of me staring back from the mirror. She wore black tights, tall black moto boots with a knife tucked into the top of one, small denim shorts, and a black sweater. I could run in this, I could fight in this, I could survive in this. I stretched and moved while Carrie and I talked. As we ended the conversation, I took a good, long stare. My dark hair and bangs topped off the look, giving me an air of an Eastern European spy. I decided my spy's name would be "Black Water Snake" and headed out the door to seek safety for the weekend.

Ellen's house was first on the list of the safety tour. A little way out of town, it had been a place of refuge and fun for years. Someone from my friend group had always lived there, and I had spent more holidays and evenings there than almost any place in town.

Ellen and her girlfriend, Amber—my new employee after Rachel left to care for her ailing mother—were working on a jigsaw puzzle. I had a photocopy of the letter from Jeffrey with me, and we pored over it, trying to make sense of the words that held no meaning and process the threats that were weighted in their horror. We took a deep dive into researching schizophrenia—the various forms, the way it appears in some lives, how it can affect others. If I was losing control, I'd try to find some understanding in research. While pursuing that endeavor, I came upon a condition I had never heard of. It's a word that still sends shivers down my spine and bile into my throat: erotomania.

"Erotomania is an uncommon form of paranoid delusion. The affected person strongly believes that another individual is in love with him or her. This delusion develops and persists despite clear evidence to the contrary. The condition is very rare. Erotomania can start suddenly, and the symptoms are often long lasting."[11]

We collectively sank into the weight of the words we read. There were attempts to joke, lighten the situation, reassure me that he wouldn't harm me...they were just words. With nothing to stop or fix the situation, my skin crawled off my body, and I don't think it has ever settled back onto my shell.

Ellen purchased a child-sized baseball bat to keep us safe, and at night on her porch swing, we made up quite the tale of what we'd do if Jeffrey came to her house. Suffice it to say, our plan involved rappelling from the roof, a baseball bat, tar, a carpet, and glitter. You can choose your own outcome from that list of tools.

I have deep gratitude for the people and places I could find refuge and hide in, but you always must go home. Life can't just stop, and I had a business on the line. To protect my gallery and community, I needed to have extra tools, I needed to find peace and understanding with others, and my safety plan grew. I reached out to Erica, and we decided to get together. I called up a mixed martial arts expert to train me, and I asked a friend with a concealed carry permit to be appointed at every gallery walk. I treaded quietly in my community, shielding them from the noise happening in my life.

Guarded with a bag of McDonald's, two high-powered pepper spray guns, and a taser, I walked up Erica's apartment steps and settled in for an evening of anger, fear, stories, and connection. Friends had been as wonderful as they could be with support, but I feel in any crime, or big moment of life, you don't understand until you have stood in it. You can't fully understand the loss of a parent until you lose yours, and it's the same with the impact of a major accident, a sexual assault, or stalking. Erica and I met eye to eye. At the time, she was the only person who understood what I was going through. We gorged on McDonald's, we laughed, we cried, and we held our pepper spray guns, getting a feel of them, all while the darkness settled in around us.

---

The first question the former Marine turned self-defense trainer asked me was, "Can you kill someone who is trying to kill you?" Bristling at the thought, I stammered, "Yes." And we began.

I hate to exercise—I mean, really hate it. Often, I have felt not eating for a day is the same as exercising. With my trainer, that would not be the case. He would train me on strength, giving me tools I could use in my apartment to help build my confidence. He taught me how to do hand-to-hand combat, knife fight, understand situational awareness, work through adrenal dumps, and find weapons at hand. He would come to my apartment and locate safe places if I couldn't escape.

A friend paid for my concealed carry permit as a birthday gift, and I got a gun. Luckily, my trainer helped me figure out where to place it in my home. I learned with gratitude and fear, eventually having to end my sessions with him due to the cost and the crumbling mess that my gallery was becoming.

Hosting art retreats, hoping they would provide me the money I owed, was a dumb decision I will regret forever. I should have closed the business earlier, but I couldn't admit defeat. I couldn't let the stalking take me that far down. I thought if this could work, then I could have an extra revenue stream, spend more time away from the four walls where Jeffrey knew I existed, and hopefully land on top. As I hatched this plan and kept the reality of my world hidden from my community, I tried to get on with life the best I could.

The list of places I would go alone continued to shrink. There was the grocery store where Jeffery would hide behind displays while I tried to shop. I knew he was there. He knew I knew he was there, and he tested me to see if I would call the police for him breaking the protection order. I didn't call. Instead, I found a manager and had them escort me to my car. I began to go to the grocery store out of town or at odd hours when the buses were done running for the day. The bus was his main mode of transportation at the time, and therefore, I could somewhat plan around it.

Other times, I'd be in the Pourhouse, and he would come in, then leave, following the protection order, but where would he go and what could he do?

These questions regarding what he was capable of dictated every-thing I did and sent me into a spiral if I passed him on the street as his face crumbled into an evil smile. He continued to walk the fine line and blatantly break it in half. Choosing not to call the police probably emboldened him, but I hoped it would help him back off.

Another consideration was that during the prior year of court hearings, it had been revealed that he took the fact that I'd involved law enforcement as a sign of my love for him. As a result, it was challenging to know how to proceed, how to make it all stop. I seemed to be incapable of making the correct choice because it was a situation where there wasn't one.

It begs the question, in a crime like stalking, is there ever a right choice? To block on social media or not to block. To call the cops or not. To file reports or ignore. Each choice the victim makes could have posi-tive results, but we weigh the decisions on the reality that they could also lead to negative and very dangerous results.

One day at the shop, a regular customer came in and, to the tune of "How do you solve a problem like Maria?" she sang out, "How do you solve a problem like Anna?" She laughed as she sang it and shared that she had stopped by to shop the day prior, but I had been MIA again. Clearly, I didn't want to run my business. She asked why I was so lazy these days and gone so often. The thin skin I had left dripped off my body into a puddle of secrets on the floor. I stammered out an excuse about how I had meetings and no one to cover the gallery. In response, she shook her head and told me to get it together.

What if I had told her the truth? That really, the day prior, my land-lord had called to tell me that Jeffrey had tried to rent a unit in my building (which only housed four units in total). That I had closed my business and gone and hid for the rest of the day. That I had shared this with friends at the bar downstairs that evening, only to have them say that they hadn't wanted to tell me, but they had seen Jeffery loitering around my apartment building several times. That as I had climbed my apartment stairs that night, paralyzed in fear, I'd pissed my pants trying to unlock the door to my building. What if I had answered her sing-song question of "How do you solve a problem like Anna?" with the truth? But I didn't. I hung my head and told her I'd try to do better.

Ever the silverling, I still sought to find joy. I grew my friendship with Lea. I drove her to the ferry for her various flights, tucked into her house to watch 9 to 5, curiously learned all about her work, and cheered on the Packers with her.

Her work in the bystander prevention field was music to my ears. I had gone through forms of gender-based violence my entire life and started to think maybe I could find a place in this field, could give back to the people who had supported me in more ways than sitting on a board or hosting a fundraiser. I found a new kindred spirit in our friendship and eventually discovered the opening to a new path, which I desperately needed.

As my birthday rolled around, and since I was eager for a little fun, Ellen asked the question that I hated. "What is the theme of your birthday going to be?" I hate a theme or costume party, even more so now. You will never find me in a space where there are people in masks or scary costumes because you never know who is behind the mask. But at the time, I wasn't as aware and fearful as I am now. I answered her question perfectly: "You want me to do a theme, you can all dress up like me."

And thirty of my friends did. When we gathered at the Pourhouse on a Saturday afternoon, every version of Anna was there, from beehive to Black Water Snake. There was a sea of white sunglasses with burly builders wearing flowing sweaters and leggings or fur coats and sipping white wine. It was the purest form of community love, from those who knew what was happening in the shadows to those who just wanted to share in the revelry.

I look far back on that day, and it warms my heart, but I also reflect, especially on those unknowingly dressed up in my safety clothes, and think if only I had fully shared. But looking back now, recollecting the saltwater smells, the laughter, the white sunglasses, I smile.

Outside the brief windows of safety and good times, life became a personal jail cell. I had stopped walking anywhere other than work alone because if I did, I thought I may pass him on the street. It was always horrifying to watch his face shift into that skin-crawling grin. I would quietly meet up with friends for dinner or drinks or a game night. I preferred it when I could go to their house and then crash on their couch, enjoying the comfort of safety surrounding me for an evening.

My closeness with Megan and Ellen waned during this time. They were the ones to consistently see me at my worst. Not only had they held me through several years of the stalking at this point, but they'd also supported me through failed relationships. Now, they were watching me make very poor choices with my business. As it all spiraled around me into failure, instead of standing up and owning what was happening both personally and professionally, I turned into an ostrich, my head fully tucked in the sand, hoping to ignore the problems away.

We tried to keep the closeness, but often, my franticness fell on their shoulders. In my falling apart, I chose shitty men to date and made bad decisions. I would sit at my friend's bar downstairs drinking and didn't show up when those beautiful women needed me. I became a broken record when I saw them. It was a list of places I'd seen Jeffrey, whether he had left or not, how terrified I was for my business. All that is a lot to handle.

Not even my therapist at the time fully understood the psychological toll of stalking. It is indeed a sexual assault with all the wounds on the inside. I don't fault them; I fault a system that paints stalking as something romantic or humorous instead of revealing the horror it is on the victim's mind and life. And I fault myself for not pushing back and asking for more understanding.

After months of being the ostrich, of dodging payments, of the gallery being closed more often than open, of remaining on such high alert that I would shake while trying to sell a $25 piece of jewelry, the time had come to face the music: My gallery, my baby, my dream had died. And how I buried it was up to me.

There are times when we fuck up so gloriously, when we experience such unabashed failure, that the details of why we failed stay with us until long after. We cling to them and wear them as a badge of shame, neglecting to understand how we got to that point and shielding the failure not only from others but from ourselves. This is that time.

# CHAPTER TEN

# October 2013 – January 2014

There is a real and frighteningly significant connection between stalking and intimate partner violence. Stalking often co-occurs with intimate partner violence and can be an indicator of other forms of violence. Stalking can be a way to exert power and control during and/or after an abusive relationship.[12]

There's a door in the middle of Port Townsend. If you stumble upon it, I'd suggest journeying up the stairs. Because there you will find a beloved pub and restaurant, Sirens, and you can hear the faint echoes of sailors long gone, bar brawls, and working women.

I climbed the stairs, breathed in the history, and went to meet my friend Sally and some of her family, including her brother, Tom, whom she wanted to introduce me to. I knew bits and pieces of Tom's fabled past and thought it a kind compliment that Sally wanted us to meet.

Dripping in tattoos, quiet and sullen, he glanced up, his eyes snapping with light as we met. I may have been losing everything around me and sinking into the deep hole of depression, but I was still a woman, and he was intriguing to say the least. He fiddled with his skull ring, barely making eye contact until the conversation turned to cats, at which point his eyes snapped with delight again. To say Tom loves cats is an understatement, and that fact in contrast to his punk exterior made my heart skip just a little.

Once again, five minutes can change your life for the good or the bad, and little did I know through that short conversation I would make a friend, confidant, and teacher for life.

If you are going to lose everything, you might as well go all in on your failure. And that is just what I did with my business, reputation, integrity, personal and business friends, finances, and housing.

I had recently gotten to know Sally, and she had offered me the single wide on her property as new housing for very cheap. I needed very cheap. Without very cheap, I would be moving to Ohio to live with my parents or couch crashing. With Sally's kindness, I was able to overlook the death stain of a former tenant on the floor and set to work moving myself in. It wasn't glamorous, but I was lucky—lucky to have a spot to fall apart, to hit the bottom of the pit I was in and do so privately.

As our short time at Sirens ended, I asked Sally if she had a key to the house, as I needed to be able to lock the doors. She replied, "Oh, that's right. You have a stalker." Tom glanced up again with a different light in his eyes, that of protection and a hint of danger. I bid my adieu and bounded down the stairs into the unknown of closing my business.

With the encouragement of others, I hung a peppy sign on the gallery window— "boldly moving on to my next adventure, closing the gallery," or some bullshit like that. What I wanted to write in all red on the windows would have been "Fuck you, Jeffrey, and fuck ME for never telling my community." But I didn't. I set about carving a smile onto my face, nodding my head, and giving brief responses when people lamented my closing. Meanwhile, I dodged phone calls from artists I owed and turned my jewel box, MY GALLERY, my life into a yard sale.

Old and new friends came in to offer the support they could. The days leading up to the closing were a brutal dream. Every ex-boyfriend I had stopped by to flaunt my failure, to try to take advantage of me... and I mean that in the way it sounds. One ex came in, told me how bad he had fucked up, and tried to lock the door to the gallery and sexually assault me. I kicked him out and screamed at him on the street, still shaking as I went to meet a friend for lunch. It was a revolving door of all my pain and failure.

I began to email with Tom, talking to him about public loss, something he had experienced, and how to turn one's life on its axis in the most unpopular of ways. I wrote about preparing for my final gallery walk, making sure I had extra security in the form of friends with concealed carry permits, the depression that was taking over every cell, and the failure I felt. There was solace in writing the words and hitting send, not caring what the outcome was. *Just hit send*, I thought. *There is nothing to lose or gain.*

I almost didn't go to the final gallery walk. I threw up off and on all day but finally donned my bravest outfit, pasted on a red-lipped smile, and headed to face the music—and I do mean music, as I had been encouraged to make this a dance party. People swirled around me. I, in the middle of the tilt-o-whirl, was paralyzed as smiles and laughter wound around me.

And that was it. A few days later, the gallery was empty. I sat with Lea and a few others in the window of the shop, holding a wake for the space that no longer was. I gathered the courage to lock the door, slip the key through the mail slot, and walk away.

To this day, when I am back in Port Townsend, I can barely look at that space, and if I gather the courage to walk up to its doors, crocodile tears will fall. I now call that space my "Cake Baby." (If you know, you know. If you don't, then go watch the masterpiece that is *Bridesmaids*.) I grieve the loss of the gallery as I do the loss of loved ones.

———

I had stupidly agreed to attend an art gala for an organization in my community shortly after the gallery closed. Every customer and who's-who in the community would be there. I went with several other friends. I shouldn't have gone; it was a cake of failure being smashed in my face with every snide comment or question about my failed business.

Even the bolstering of those close to me couldn't stop me from falling, and fall I did. Succumbing to my grief, glasses of wine, sky-high heels (because I didn't give a shit about my safety anymore), and a very slippery wooden step into my trailer, I tripped and landed on my hands and face. At least now I could visibly see the bruises and scrapes I felt inside. When the wounds are all internal, psychological, emotional, there is something quite satisfying about seeing them on display.

The several days of healing forced me to look at the mess around me, including art I needed to get back to artists so I wouldn't get sued. I took stock of anything I could sell to pay off my debts: my wedding ring, my beloved couch. Any damn thing I could hock, I did. It still didn't add up to the amount owed, and I sat trying to become accountable and create plans to pay off the debts.

When I was in my community, it was an ongoing barrage of questions. In the grocery store, on the sidewalk, at the pub, on a walk, it was a relentless scratching at my brain as to why I had closed the business.

I caution anyone in my life who is closing a business to be aware that people are going to say the dumbest shit to you, and though they say it out of care, it will tear your heart out. They will tell you how much they loved your business even though they never bought anything there. They'll lament about your failures when you are on a blind date. They will mirror your failure back to you. If you can run away and take a week or space, do it!

And that's what I did. Friends of mine were getting married in town, and the next day, they had rented a huge house on Orcas Island for many of us. I hatched an escape plan, an escape from everything—from the constant gnawing of what Jeffery would do next, the community rejection, the barrage of questions—and escape from myself.

●　　●　　●

*My friend and I loaded my car to the brim in early January 2003 and headed out into the unknown as snow barreled down. Miles passing along over the rolling hills finally gave way to the rocky coastline of Maine, my new home. To the ends of the earth, where the sun first rises and the nights are longer than the days, that's where I wanted to be. Having finished college just a few weeks prior, I said farewell to friends and the region I had grown up in. It was time to carve my own path, and I wanted to be surrounded by rugged beauty and water.*

*After driving over the terrifying bridge with its pitched arch and movement in the wind, I got to the other side and made it to my new home, Deer Isle, Maine. Arriving at the winter rental, noting the piles of snow everywhere, we dug a space on the side of the road for the car and snowshoed in what we would need for the night, begging the fireplace to warm us and catch up with the chill in the old home.*

*While college had been the departure of living with parents, it had still been a protected environment as a religious school. In Maine, I felt myself crack wide open into adulthood and would make as many mistakes as I did strides. I'd take a job at local bar in Blue Hill, sleep around, and find myself in bad relationships.*

*On the flip side, I'd begin to make some of the dearest friends of my life. I'd launch an interior design business with a friend and begin to stretch my skills. Without exception, Sundays were spent with a group of people surrounding our ailing friend, Joe, and offering support through meals and laughter.*

*I'd spend four years in Maine, learning what it was to be an adult and what it wasn't.*

●　　●　　●

Years prior, I had met a friend named Heather and her now husband. They shared my love of sailing, eating, joy, and laughter. She and her husband ran a summer camp on Orcas, and since it was now November, all of its houses and cabins were empty. They invited me to stay on after the wedding weekend, provided me with my own house, and put me to work with Heather's landscaping company. We raked, leaf blew, and handpicked leaves off millionaire estates, and on rainy days, we made pies for Thanksgiving orders. We took the dinghy to get groceries or lunch at Friday Harbor, cooked meals, laughed, and cried, and I had a moment to breathe. I look back on that month on Orcas Island as saving my life, saving me from succumbing to myself, and often reflect *what if I had just stayed there?*

I sat on the water's edge, I patched the boat that is me, I dusted off the sails, and eventually, I returned to Port Townsend to begin righting my ship. Just as I will always grieve the loss, I will always feel the failure and work to right the wrongs.

Back then, returning was hard. My normal Thanksgiving with Megan, Ellen, and the crew wouldn't be; there were more repairs to be made there, and in my loss, I had on blinders to what was happening in their lives. I spent the holiday sunken in my failure and grateful for the invite from other friends.

Where was Jeffrey during all of this? I DON'T KNOW! Yes, there were the run-ins, but he had gone fairly quiet. But having a man who thinks you are married to him and who wants to murder you doesn't mean that quietness is good. It doesn't mean he's moved on. You just hold your breath for as long as you can until he tries to steal it again.

---

Despite the public embarrassment, my fear of death at Jeffrey's hands, and the mess I had made both professionally and privately, Port Townsend was my home. I had built a life there. It certainly hadn't played out as I'd wanted, but I did not want to leave. I did not want to be driven from my home, and I needed to face my mess, but to do so, I needed a damn job.

Other than doing landscaping on Orcas, I had been doing small jobs—a little marketing, hanging art for people's homes, helping write business plans—but I needed something steady. I figured I'd bought an art gallery with virtually nothing; I could create a job from nothing.

After listing my skills onto a piece of paper, I created a list of local companies that could perhaps use them. At the top of my list was Edensaw Woods, a large, high-end boatbuilding and architectural lumber company. That's right—a lumber company.

I approached Kiwi, the owner, Friday at the Port Townsend Brewery. He and his employees had been going there every Friday since the doors had opened, and despite my pain and the strained distance from Megan and Ellen, I continued my Friday brewery tradition as well. It was one of the few spaces I felt safe. Maybe it was the room of boatbuilders and carpenters that I felt protected by, or perhaps the sense of community. Either way, I was there.

Walking up to Kiwi and the crew, I felt nervous as they gave me hugs and kisses on the cheek. After the small talk, I turned to him and said, "I think you should hire me to do your marketing." He asked why and I replied, "You have one of the largest companies in town and very little outreach. I think I could grow your business even more."

We chatted for a bit longer, and he asked me what made me think I would be good at this. Without thinking, I said, "Kiwi, every Christmas Eve, you would come into the gallery and shop for your wife. I had your favorite beer for you and a tray of jewelry picked from things I had seen her fawn over. So when you came in, how much did you think you were going to spend?"

Kiwi, with an amused look on his face, said, "Around $100."

I looked him square in the eyes and asked, "And how much did you end up spending?"

He and I both knew the amount was much higher. He laughed and said, "Write me up a job description."

And that is how I became Anna Nasset, MD...marketing director for Edensaw Woods.

# CHAPTER ELEVEN

# 2014

**Given the increased risk of harm and lethality in stalking cases, it is vital to identify stalking separate from and in addition to concurring victimizations. Whatever way victims or offenders label their experiences, it is vital for workplaces to identify stalking behaviors when they occur because stalking requires a unique policy response.**[13]

Going after my job at Edensaw was also a calculated maneuver in my safely planned life. If I was going to stay in Port Townsend, I wanted to do so with some semblance of security, and what better place to work than a company that comprises 90 percent male employees? Yes, I have been a feminist since watching Anita Hill testify in 1992. Yes, I have been trained in self-defense. Yes, I believe in the undeniable strength of women. Though all of the harm that I have experienced has been at the hands of men, I found comfort in this group of guys that I had known for years, either through sailing, shopping at my gallery, or Friday pub nights. My choices were about safety, not about healing.

Did I tell Kiwi or the others about Jeffrey? HELL NO! There is a two-fold reason behind the secret I still keep when securing employment or housing, dating, etc. First, once I disclose about Jeffrey, there are usually questions, blame, and opinions. I've experienced and heard it all, and I didn't want to have to answer for the actions of a man I didn't even know. Secondly, would you hire someone who said there is a man who stalks them, thinks they are married, and wants to kill them? Most likely not.

What about the woman coming out of an abusive relationship whose ex-partner is stalking and threatening her... Would you hire her? Or the person who discloses they are moving because their neighbor stalks them. Would you rent to them? I beg you to consider the hiring and housing of victims and survivors; we need not be further harmed or punished for what has happened to us. We walk with the daily fears of personal injury and death. We don't need for you to put additional shame on us by considering us dangerous.

I walked into the large office at Edensaw for my first day. The sales team of six to eight men, depending upon the day, greeted me with laughter and cheers. They eagerly asked me where I wanted my desk to be, ready to move the empty workstation wherever I chose, assuming I'd want to be right in the mix. I took stock of the large room, the points of entry and exit, the road that dead-ended into woods, and pointed at the back corner.

"Why would you want to sit all the way back there?" they asked.

I quipped back, "Well, if I sit up front, everyone will think I'm the secretary, and that's not my job title, so I'll sit back there."

I set about setting up my desk, eyes scanning the road and doors. *Nobody needs to know my secret*, I thought as I settled in.

This job did not solve everything, but it was a step in the right direction. The mountain of debt from the gallery still loomed large. I felt safe, but Jeffrey could be anywhere, and I was still struggling with my relationships and friendships. My correspondence with Tom grew, as did his mystery, with him sending me pictures from faraway lands filled with sandy landscapes where he worked. I worried about the safety of this man I only knew through email and our brief meeting. As many bridges as I worked to repair, I also broke others, and my distance with Tom's sister, Sally, grew.

Many people who have experienced a lifetime of trauma create drama. We create turmoil, make mistakes, and self-sabotage to perpetuate the narrative of failure that we have so long felt. I look back on this period of losing the business and the months to follow as a time steeped in self-sabotage and also as a reminder of the patterns and behaviors I have broken. Grieve the past, learn the lessons, apologize, and do your damnedest to not repeat.

Several months into my new job, when Sally needed to build her father a small home where the trailer was, it was time for me to go, but I wasn't sure where. Port Townsend has long had an affordable housing issue, and only having secured steady income just a short time prior, I was at a loss.

I packed the scraps of my life into a friend's horse trailer and set about couch crashing and housesitting for a few weeks. My new friend Kyle, a steady rock of a man, newly retired and living in a condo on the water, offered up his place while he was away. Emily, the monochromatic mortgage broker, set up a guest room where I would spend several weeks. While my friendship with Megan and Ellen was growing new skin and taking on a beautiful new form, Megan and her partner were having problems, and Ellen had just moved into a studio apartment with her girlfriend.

Meanwhile, I did what I do best—I worked my ass off and found an incredible, AFFORDABLE apartment with a view in the beloved Uptown area of Port Townsend. As it was a small town, I had been informed by a friend that Jeffrey had moved from the Uptown area to the next town over, and I felt safe in my new housing.

Leaning on the learnings from my self-defense teacher, I made sure the apartment had multiple points of entry/escape, was in a second-floor location (nobody could break in through a window), and had a carport behind the apartment (where I could hide my car). I also kept my PO box to not have a physical address. There were even curtains already on the windows—a victim and survivor's first priority! I figured if I played my cards right, I could hide out in plain sight.

Then, I took to making my home, a small apartment with an entrance in the living room, which I lined with every piece of art and oddity I had collected in my lifetime. My friend Kyle gave me a small loveseat, along with a beautiful antique red trunk, in trade for design services. I found a vintage Formica table in the basement as well as a small bed. With the furniture in place, I went about curating a spot that one friend would say looked like "an adult version of a dollhouse." The apartment wasn't much, but she was mine and my safe refuge. I leaned into the concept that if you are only safe at home, then make it beautiful and make it yours. Every inch had a visual element, and every inch was my haven.

I adhered to my safety list. Though Jeffrey had been quiet, what we do know about stalkers is they can find you and will appear when you least expect it. To my knowledge, he never placed a tracker on my vehicle, but with all the technology we now have, monitoring someone's whereabouts is easier than ever. Therefore, victims stay vigilant, even in the quiet times.

I didn't walk alone or go to the movies. I grocery shopped at night when the buses were done running. No farmers' market for me. I only walked for exercise if a friend was with me. My car was always parked in the carport, and I entered through the back of the apartment building. This was my normal. It was second nature to me at this point, and I didn't ever stop to think how strange and unfair it was.

Even with the guidelines I lived by for my safety, I occasionally broke the rules, and I would pay the price. One evening, the deck of Sirens, and my friends, called to me through the early evening air. Feeling confident in my new apartment and job, I bolstered myself and walked alone, down the trail and into town, just a couple of blocks all by myself!

*What a brave woman you are*, I silently encouraged my feet as they stepped with caution. *Screw Jeffrey! You've bested him!* The thoughts filling my mind grew stronger. As my boots carried me to the stairway of Sirens, of course, there was Jeffrey, standing on the sidewalk in the doorway that led up to the bar. Never break your rules.

There were other people on the street, thankfully, and as my body flooded with adrenaline, my mind snapped into action. I had three choices: scream, walk away, or go upstairs and find my friends. I chose the third, ensuring each step of the way he wasn't behind me.

With heavy breaths and frenzied words, I stated the situation to my friends once I found them on the deck. "It's him. He's here. He was outside. Jeffrey. He didn't follow me. What do I do?" My words only made sense to those at the table who knew my situation. I calmed my breath, then explained my horror movie to those who did not already know. I steadied myself, surveyed the inside, and grabbed a much-needed drink.

After some time on the deck, my focus and bravery crushed, I went inside to use the bathroom. Turning the corner, I froze. With the Salish Sea air swirling around me, I turned to sand. There was Jeffrey, tucked behind a pillar in the corner. He had been watching the whole time.

Flight, fight, freeze, fawn? I thawed and fought. I grabbed the towering bouncer, screaming, "Get him out of here. Get him the fuck out of here." In that moment, I didn't give a shit who saw me, didn't care that my secret was out, that I was making a scene. *Just get him OUT!*

The bouncer escorted him out of Sirens, and I was left with the attention my performance had garnered. Several community members left their tables and gathered around me to help me calm down as I once again had to stammer out my story amidst living it.

My body slumped, as it was left with the effects of the system shock it had experienced. A feeling of sedation, even after such fear, took hold. A friend who lived in my neighborhood gave me a ride home. I dragged my body up my apartment steps, weary and broken but on high alert for Jeffrey's location. My adrenal system had been hit hard by the experience and was still working on overdrive, which led to me urinating on myself as the lock turned and I secured myself inside. My body was unable to regulate even normal functions.

My communication with Tom had moved into the chat feature of a game of Words With Friends, and I messaged him in whatever faraway land he was working in. I shared the situation and confessed that I had just pissed myself. Knowing Tom's heroic military service, I knew he was the one person that understood what it was to look into the eyes of death.

The next day, frail and fried, I called in late to work and headed to the Dove House to see my advocate. The blissful two years of not needing their services was over. Armed with her presence, I went to the Port Townsend Police Department. The officers greeted me with the sympathetic smile you give to the grieving at a funeral. Prior to Erica and me, Jeffery had stalked people for short periods of time, so there had been a collective hope that he would move on. We were nearly three years after that first night at the gallery, and in the police station, there was a mutual acceptance that this would never end.

While we talked through what happened, they asked why I hadn't called them the night before. The police report reads, "I hesitated to call the police because I was in shock, there was a bouncer and friends, and I did not want to relive what I did two years ago as it cost me my business and feeling of freedom."

After some encouragement, I begrudgingly filed my next police report. However, it was then discovered my three-year protection order, good until January 2015, had been misfiled for only two years. In other words, Jeffrey was fine to be at Sirens that night.

Frustration filled my body. Not anger—frustration. When mistakes are made, it's all about what happens next, about taking ownership and apologizing. I have certainly learned that with all of my failings. People who have dedicated their lives to the criminal justice field are no different. When a number is written down wrong or a name is misspelled, the ramifications can be grave, but I do understand that mistakes are made.

I held that in my mind as I climbed the courthouse steps and, with a heavy heart, filled out the paperwork for a new protection order. This time, there would be no luxury of Jeffery appearing by jail camera; if he appeared, he would be in the courtroom with me, and there was no way I was going alone.

I can only assume I didn't go back to work that day. Another day lost. At least this time, I could take a vacation day. A "vacation to hell" day would be more appropriate.

---

Though it was just a piece of paper, without my protection order, I felt lost, peering out my window through the curtains late at night, talking to my mom to calm me down. My sweet mom, on the phone with me despite the three hours' time difference, desperately wanting me to move home, sat in support and in her own fear. There is nothing wrong with Ohio or where my parents live, but for me, I just couldn't give up. Jeffrey couldn't win, and I couldn't bear losing my mountains and ocean.

The day of the court hearing arrived. I took a half day from work and accomplished nothing that morning as I stared out the window, fearing what the afternoon would hold. I arrived with my arsenal of friends at the courthouse where my advocate was waiting. Jeffrey paced the hallway; I threw up in the bathroom while friends guarded the door. His presence caused my body to reject anything I tried to put in it. Even now, as I write about him, I often find myself dry heaving with each word I type.

The assortment of onlookers in the audience gave Judge Landes pause. She asked, "What are you all doing here?" and each one replied, "I'm here to support Anna." This included a lawyer who had previously been assigned to represent Jeffrey. Nobody was messing around.

My legs wobbled as I approached the bench. I could feel the staples I had used to fix the hem on my dress pants scratch my ankles, and I began to read the statement I had prepared as I stood next to Jeffrey, only my advocate in between us.

Jeffrey began to plead his case, but I don't remember what he said. I have developed an ability to not hear him when he is talking, a skill I greatly appreciate. As he finished, Judge Landes spoke. "First off, Anna, I am so sorry we misfiled your protection order. That was our fault, and I do apologize. Jeffrey, I do not think you will stop stalking and harassing Anna. Anna, to make this right, here's a lifetime protection order. I don't want to have to do this again."

I smiled widely and thanked her. It was a huge victory. Although just a piece of paper, it was a beautiful permanent piece of paper to be folded and tucked into a special pouch in my purse, and it was all mine. You'd have thought I'd won the lottery, and in many ways, I had, as it is highly uncommon in most states to receive a lifetime protection order.

The officers had my friends and me stay back until Jeffrey had left, and then, they expressed surprise as well as we watched Jeffrey get into a car and drive away. Up until this point, none of us had known he had a vehicle. The officers and I took note of the car, and whatever joy I had slipped back into fear because he had wheels.

Frail and grieving, I sat in the afternoon sun at the Port Townsend Brewery with friends, sipping wine and smoking cigarettes. They congratulated me and discussed what an evil and terrifying monster they felt he was. There was solace in their reflections. I felt seen through the chaos.

---

I found safety sailing, crewing on the wooden sailboat *Annie Too* with Captain Ted at the helm. My body relaxed as we cut through the bay, tacking back and forth. Captain Ted, known for giving the best hugs in Port Townsend, along with other Edensaw employees and community members, gathered weekly to battle it out on the water. For me, it was the place where I could let go. From the water, I could see my whole town, and I could be in it safely. As I challenged my body and brain, I felt a calmness fill my being, one that I only experienced on the water. Returning to shore after each sail, my body tensed again with the unknown fear of where he could be.

After a great day sailing, I climbed the back stairs to my apartment and glanced over to the roof of the carport. Thrown on top of the roof were what appeared to be the guts of a salmon, and ice filled my veins. It had to be a sign from Jeffrey. He had referred to me as a Chinook salmon before and had described how I should be put in a barrel and shot at. Could this be him threatening me?

I gathered my weary strength and headed to the police station to file a report. The next day, I ran into my neighbor, who informed me that he had thrown the fish guts up there after fishing, a treat for the seagulls. I was a frayed wire of anxiety, unraveling faster than I realized.

The psychological crime that is stalking puts victims into the mindset that there is danger everywhere. We live in that constant fear of the unknown. While a salmon may just be a salmon, what if it is a sign that our death is near? From eyes open to eyes shut, our waking moments are filled with the distracting nagging of the unknown. It is an annoyingly terrifying headspace to exist in.

Every sign deserved attention and needed to be taken seriously. One day, when returning to work after lunch, I spotted Jeffrey's car parked at the top of the road that led to Edensaw. I had been working there for months, had gone to court twice, and spent time regularly with coworkers, and still no one knew about Jeffrey and his stalking. Now, just like with the gallery, I had the duty to keep others safe. So I set up a meeting with Kiwi for the next day. My biggest fear was that he would either be angry I did not disclose this information earlier or that he would be dismissive and make fun of me. I fought my mind over how to explain it all.

● ● ●

*One weekend in college found us just up the road from campus, packed with sleeping bags and a tent big enough for six people. The gaggle of misfits and thinkers I surrounded myself with did everything together—meals, walks, karaoke, trips, parties. There was a constant stream of events and play to involve myself in.*

*We headed out on an adventure to Mounds State Park, featuring ten ceremonial mounds built by the Adena culture Indigenous peoples of eastern North America. One of the guys with us, Todd, decided to drink more than the rest of us. When we tucked in for the night, crawling into our cloth home, he stumbled in, crashing down between me and Hilary. I shut my eyes, annoyed with his drunkenness but content in this safe cocoon of friendship.*

*My eyes snapped back open as I felt hands groping at me, fumbling to work their way into my body. I brushed Todd's hands away and stayed quiet. He moved on me again, grabbing my tits and advancing down toward my crotch. I brushed him off and woke up my friend next to me, whispering what was happening. He told me to ignore Todd, which I tried to do, but he came at me again, drunken fingers fondling my broken body. I sat up and said, "no," just as Hilary sat up as well. He had been trying to assault both of us at the same time. We both loudly protested and tried to explain. As confusion ensued, Todd sat up and threw up all over the tent.*

*We packed up our vomit-soaked sleeping bags, our soberness palpable, and headed home. There was a stop by the all-night truck stop for coffee, eggs, and a debrief. Leaving Todd passed out in the car, we sat in a huddled silence, and I felt my heart break in two. With the other injustices and harm that had happened to my young body, at least I hadn't known the perpetrators well. But I knew Todd. I had known him for years. I'd had a massive crush on him my freshman year, and now he dated one of my dearest friends, Jenny. I could feel myself breaking at this moment because if someone I trusted would do this to me, how could I trust anyone?*

●     ●     ●

Kiwi, in his Hawaiian shirt and brightly colored reading glasses, sat across the table from me, curious as to what we were meeting about. Tears filled my eyes and began to spill onto my cheeks before I even started talking, and his demeanor shifted from jovial to serious. Everything tumbled out of my mouth—the first meeting, the threats, the protection orders, safety concerns, court appearances, loss of business, and finally Jeffrey's car. With it all on the table, I got quiet and waited.

This was one of my first tellings of the story in its entirety to anyone who hadn't walked it with me, and I will admit Kiwi is not a man who I thought would start by believing and offering support. However, he reached over and took my hand. Looking me in the eyes, he said, "I am so sorry this has happened to you. I had no idea. You are safe here; you are part of our family, and we will protect you."

Many years later, Kiwi would connect me and another stalking victim who needed help, and he has offered support in the kindest of ways. The secret and shame I had carried quietly for so long saw a glint of light and support. I wouldn't be shouting my story from the rooftops anytime soon, but in that moment, I learned it's okay to share. You may just be surprised by the outcome.

Together, Kiwi and I hatched a plan. Edensaw had around sixty employees and covered a large area of land. He needed to protect his employees and stated such, but he also took into account what I wanted and needed. I didn't want questions from coworkers, so I asked that we keep this quiet. Kiwi agreed, but he wanted to circulate a picture of Jeffery through email to everyone, simply stating, "If you ever see this man, call the cops." I sat at my desk as he sent the email and melted into the ground, red-faced with shame, as everyone around me whispered their thoughts about who this stranger was.

Finding safety on boats, at friends' homes, and in any space I could eke out was key, and admittedly, it was a luxury that I could do so. Having no children or partner gave me the freedom to move in these ways. Evenings at Lea's, Megan's, or Ellen's were where I could find that space.

Now that Tom was back from overseas, he invited me to his place for a weekend of food, oysters, movies, and bonfires. Though we'd only met in person once, because of our months of emails and my heavy vetting of him, I felt comfort and security as I journeyed down the Hood Canal, winding my way to his place.

Arriving at his simple A-frame tucked in the woods, I was greeted by my pen pal. Tom's house erupted in a chaotically curated display of military medals, guitars, awards, memorabilia, figurines, and more books than my community library. Though nervous, I sank into a deep sense of safety and friendship. If you can be friends with a retired Special Ops and hide out at their house, by all means, do so.

When I would leave to visit Tom or drop off Lea at the Bainbridge ferry, even if I was just staying a few miles out of town at Megan's or Ellen's, I found myself filled with sadness and dread as I returned to town. The Olympic and Cascade Mountains stretched their way across the water, the brilliant blue sky splintering across the ocean, the charming Victorian houses winking happily with their bright flowers. It is a sickeningly beautiful place, but to me, I just felt sick.

The winds of change were also present. Lea and her husband decided to move to Montana, and I felt a pit of grief as I said goodbye to my dear friend. She had been a breath of courage and friendship when I needed it most. But life moves on.

Once a month or so, as part of my safety plan, I would look at Jeffery's social media. I have never followed his accounts, but that didn't mean I couldn't look at them, and from my work computer, I'd peer into his mind.

One day, while completing this safety task, my stomach dropped as I looked at a series of pictures Jeffrey had posted. The first series was around the perimeter of my friend Kyle's condo, a place I visited frequently and one of the few spots where my car was parked publicly. Kyle's condo sat along the water's edge in the heart of Port Townsend, and if I was there, my car was always visible. This was the condo I'd housesat before I moved into my apartment. It was where we had movie nights, sat on the deck, and chatted, and I realized I had made a dangerous mistake being there so often. Furthermore, I would now have to tell Kyle about the pictures.

I continued to scroll down, vomit filling my mouth. The next series of pictures were of my house, taken from downtown, looking up to the bluff where the house sat. He had captured my home and thus captured me. Once again, he walked the finest of lines, for directly below my house was the town football field, and he had taken the pictures from the field's edge looking up.

These pictures were also his way of referencing Judge Landes several years prior when I received my first protection order. She had stated that Jefferey was to stay five-hundred feet, one and a half football fields, away from me, my house, and my business. His calculated carnage in the picture series stunned me in its boldness, and I found myself in the ladies' bathroom throwing up. He was getting closer and closer, and I was slipping away.

# CHAPTER TWELVE

# January 2015 – April 2015

**Forty-six percent of stalking victims fear not knowing what will happen next.**

**Twenty-nine percent of stalking victims fear it will never stop.**[14]

The Uptown Pub was full on that Sunday in January 2015. Everyone was cheering on their teams vying for a spot in the playoffs. My friend and the pub's owner, Christel, poured drinks for us. Though the Uptown Pub was only a few blocks away from my apartment, my car sat parked outside, following the rules I lived my life by.

As I cheered on the Packers, I also sat texting my mom. She had taken my father to the ER due to severe back pain, assuming it was from an accident he had been in a short time ago. I was concerned, of course, but thought it would be a quick fix and he'd be home in time for the night game.

One eye on the game and one eye on my phone, I chatted away with friends. As the Packers threw another W onto their season, my mom texted, saying she needed to talk to me and asking me to call when I got home. Ignoring her request, I quietly slipped out the back door to the parking lot and placed the call.

"It's cancer. It's lung cancer, but it's spread all over, including into his spine, which has several fractures," she explained as I blinked into the salt air, attempting to take in her words. Time froze as her words sunk in and she continued to share what the doctors had told her. Dad would not be making it home that night, as they'd admitted him to begin creating a plan. The only thing I could comprehend was that my father, that sweet quiet man, would not be on this earth much longer, and as we hung up the phone, I burst into tears.

Walking back into the pub, everyone's joy stopped as they saw me sobbing. I blurted out, "It's my dad. He has cancer. It's bad."

I fumbled for my wallet as my heart began to shatter. Christel pushed my money away and helped me grab a friend to drive my car and me home. During the two-block drive, I texted Megan and Ellen. They were at my apartment forty-five minutes later. That's the thing about best friends—through ups and downs, mistakes and missteps, they will always be there.

As luck would have it, I already had a ticket to go see my family purchased. I was to fly to Ohio in a few weeks for my first visit in a few years. The other thing about best friends is that during an emergency, they become world leaders, and within the blink of an eye, my flight was changed to the next week and had been extended to be a three-week trip.

At Edensaw on Monday, I dragged my body through the doors. Several people already knew of my dad's diagnosis, as they had been at the pub. Being met with the kindness and care of not having to divulge was a moment I clung to after years of holding my stalking secret tightly.

I sat in Kiwi's office, a shell of human, a frail little girl, just wanting to go home. Kiwi is passionate about cancer. In fact, he started his own foundation that pays bills for people in Port Townsend with cancer. He said to me, "Go home. Be with your family. Let's get you a laptop and work when you can."

The rest of the week was a blur of getting work projects dialed in, chatting with Mom, texting Dad, seeing friends, talking with Ellen and Megan, and packing to go home. I fell asleep on the plane as it left Seattle and woke in the morning in Columbus, Ohio.

•      •      •

*I had been back at college for a week, but my heart was with my parents in Ohio that winter of 2000. Shattered bits of glass lay strewn across the kitchen floor in a perfect crash pattern. Looking at the destruction, I immediately regretted my impulse to throw the mason jar against my kitchen cabinet and quickly set about cleaning the mess I had made as tears fell down my cheeks.*

*I had just gotten off the phone with Mom, and my outburst was a reaction to anger and relief. Dad had been in and out of the hospital, trying to find a diagnosis to his nerve tingling, blindness in his left eye, and sudden weight loss. We had been searching for answers for what felt like years but was probably a month or so. Mom had called to deliver the answer: multiple sclerosis. I had known others with MS and thought it to be a death sentence. How would he move forward with his life, still only in his late forties, the breadwinner of the family? What did the future look like for him—for all of us?*

*I grieved and feared the unknown as I swept the shards into the dustpan before my roommate got home.*

●　　●　　●

Mom greeted me in the hallway of the hospital. Clinging to one another, we cried and then painted our best smiles on before entering Dad's room. Walking into the hospital room, I was shocked at the sight of my father. He had aged quickly in the last week. Now, as I look back at the pictures from before his diagnosis, I can see his decline, but how were we to know? I think of all the sad, pasted-on smiles I've received over the years when people were trying to be positive in a lose/lose situation, and each time, I saw straight through them. I'm sure my dad felt our grief-stricken pity that day and every day moving forward.

With Dad released and back home, I took to serving the best way I could by cooking. Even before getting to Delaware, Ohio, I had been scouring cancer cooking websites and came prepared with recipes.

We all knew he was dying, but if I cooked for his life, maybe I could save him. With my mom's credit card in hand, I headed to Kroger and shopped with wild abandon. It didn't dawn on me that it was the first time in years I grocery shopped without fear, but it was.

Armed with a full kitchen, I set about cooking, each night making a different meal and presenting it to my parents as though I were hosting a cooking show. During the day, I made batches of healthy muffins, soups, and quinoa burritos, piling it all into the freezer, cooking the pain and reality away.

At an appointment with the oncologist, I stayed behind in the exam room after my parents left to ask the terrifying truths. The doctor shared that it was indeed stage IV, and the outcome was bleak. He suggested if I went back to Washington to keep my bag packed and be prepared to hop on a plane at a moment's notice. When I left the exam room, my parents asked me nothing, but the truth was painted on my face.

On the drive home, Dad stated that he wanted a recliner for the family room, and as we passed a furniture store in a strip mall, we stopped. Dad, using his cane for support, an aging version of Goldilocks, sat in several chairs. Finally settling into the one that was "just right," he fell asleep promptly.

I found a sales associate and stated we wanted to buy that chair and I'd be back the following day with a truck. They explained that was the floor model, and it would take two months to get the chair to us. I pointed at my dad and said, "See that man asleep right there? He doesn't have two months; he's dying of cancer, and I'm getting that chair tomorrow." They disappeared to talk to the manager, and with the help of my parents' neighbor, I got that damn chair the next day.

Other than cooking, the days were filled with appointments, radiation treatments, countless errands, and a lot of TV. Carrie and her husband, Paul, lived forty-five minutes away and came over often. Dad's sister, Martha, came down from Toledo, and I busied myself caring for visitors and well-wishers who stopped by the house. I savored the thirty-minute drive that Dad and I would take to radiation, our quiet talks to and from, his questions about my life, his worries for my safety, him slowly processing his body failing him.

One day, as we drove home along the Scioto River, the song "I Lived" by OneRepublic came on, and Dad turned the volume up so the lyrics washed over us:

*Hope when you take that jump, you don't fear the fall*
*Hope when the water rises, you built a wall*

*(OneRepublic, I LIVED)*

I turned my face toward the river as I drove along, tears filling my eyes. Dad reached over and gently held my hand, both of us taking in how poignant the lyrics were in light of what was happening. He sat quietly looking out the window. The song continued on, talking of living life to its fullest until the last breath you take. Silently, we both thought of the moment to come when he would say goodbye. We drove on.

As the song ended, my dear dad whispered, "I don't want that song to end." *Me neither, Dad. Me neither.*

The next few weeks were precious and tender. My parents' best friends came to visit from Missouri, and I fulfilled my dad's requested meal of crab cakes by having a friend ship a dozen Dungeness crabs from Port Townsend to Delaware, Ohio. Members of the church came and prayed over my father, each remarking on his quiet leadership and how much they looked up to him. There would also be the occasional remark that the reason my dad was sick was so that I would get right with Jesus. I did not appreciate that take but simply muttered "thank you" and excused or busied myself.

I taught my dad to play cribbage, and we spent hours shuffling cards over the side table between the couch and his new recliner. When the snow fell, we spent the day watching *The Music Man* and *Fiddler on the Roof*. After he went to bed, Mom and I would sit and talk. I was doing my best to support her as she worked to keep Dad alive. Her notebook of medications, appointments, and schedules kept her grief at bay just as my cooking did.

---

In the beauty and grief, there was also anger—anger that this incredible father was slipping away. Just a few months prior, he had retired from being an architect for Honda. His swan song project, The Honda of America Museum, stood as a testament to quiet accomplishment. Never one to brag but instead sit and accept what would be, he showed the same stoic nature in his illness. I, however, am more like my mother; we are a little bit louder in our process. My dad had often been the peacemaker when my mom and I would butt heads over the years, and in his illness, she and I became a unified team.

Through all the years and the heartache I had caused my parents, there has always been love. When I left the religion they raised me to follow, moved across the country, made poor choices in relationships, and chose career paths that felt risky, there was love. I will forever be in awe and in debt for the way they have loved me despite not agreeing with me. It is a privilege to have such support, one I do not take lightly. It is something I wish for every person. In the dark days as death approached, we all clung to the love and gave however we could. The differences no longer mattered; we were there to love and serve.

One day, tasked with going to the grocery store, angry over my father's diagnosis, I headed to Kroger and put my earbuds in, listening to Sleater-Kinney as I shopped the aisles and threw food into the cart. Leaving the store, I caught myself. I had just gone into a grocery store with earbuds in! I was shocked at my lack of safety planning, my reckless willingness to do something so untethered to my reality.

Driving the country road home, traveling through cornfields and dipping down to snake along the river, I began to take note of other actions this time in Ohio had allowed into my life. At night, in the darkness, I would walk the trails next to my parents' property that my mother had lovingly mowed for years; I was walking at night alone. Some evenings, I would dip into town to meet Brett, my friend from high school, for drinks or dinner. I'd park on the street and walk the block or so to Vito's, our favorite haunt, by myself. My grocery store run gave me the slap-in-the-face reality of how much of my life had disappeared in my beloved Port Townsend. And when I headed back after three weeks in Delaware, Ohio, I carried that knowledge with me.

I kept my suitcase at the ready as I settled back into my apartment, the doctor's words lingering in my ears. *Be ready to come back at a moment's notice.* My focus and heart were in Ohio, but I tried to keep it together at work. The guys on the sales floor with me began to treat me like their daughter, and I found comfort in their kindness. Ellen and Megan were at the ready to support with conversation, laughter, meals, and drinks, and our friendship began to blossom once again.

After being home for only a few days, I headed down the flights of stairs to the basement where the apartments had shared laundry. The steep staircases led into the bowels of a terrifying basement filled with decades of abandoned possessions. My basket full, I gingerly stepped down, using the wall to steady myself, an eerie feeling washing over me, as always. Preoccupied by thoughts of my parents, I slipped, just a little, and scratched my arm as I righted myself on the steps.

I thought nothing of the scratch until a few days later when what looked like a spider bite appeared on my arm. Over the day, the swollen red circle grew. I began to track the growth of the swelling with a marker. It grew rapidly, and by day's end, I was at urgent care. The doctor was concerned but didn't think it was a bite, and then I remembered the scratch I had gotten. A hefty dose of antibiotics was given to me, and I was told if it didn't subside to come back the next day. It only grew more, and the next day, I found myself in the ER, receiving an IV of antibiotics. As I was being released, I was told if it didn't go down by that evening to pack a bag because I was being admitted.

Sure enough, that night, I was admitted for a three-day and three-night all-inclusive stay at the hospital. Bags of IVs hung around me.

I felt fine, but they couldn't get the infection to go down, my left arm remaining a topographical map of lines tracking the infection's growth. On the second day, they began to talk surgery to remove the infection! On day three, the antibiotics began to work, and on the morning of the fourth day, my mom called. Dad was in the hospital; he had almost died the night before, and I needed to come home now. She knew I was in the hospital, but I had shielded her from the seriousness. With all she was carrying at home, she couldn't process what was happening regardless.

Armed with laptops, Ellen and I sat in my hospital room and took over the world that day. I still hadn't been cleared for release, but I got a plane ticket for that night, just ten hours later. Emily said she would drive me the two and a half hours to the airport. Megan was at the ready to help pack and headed to my house to do my laundry. It begs the question, why are women not in charge of the world?

That day, we moved mountains. After being released and running countless errands, I arrived back at my apartment where Megan and Ellen helped me pack, including selecting a black dress. I had bought a one-way ticket; I didn't know when I was coming home, only that I wasn't returning until my father was gone. We hugged and cried as we said goodbye. I was going home to watch my dad die.

My friend Brett picked me up from the airport and took me to my parents' house. As I walked in, it was empty—quiet. Everything had changed in the two weeks I'd been gone. Oxygen tanks, a hospital bed, pillows, blankets, and medication filled the family room. I had been prepared for the physical change my dad was experiencing but not for the changes to our family home.

Brett, too, was taken aback. He'd been over many times and grew to be a necessary support in the weeks to come. He carried my bag up to my childhood bedroom, cracking a joke about always wondering where THE Anna Nasset slept and being caught off guard that the murals I had painted when I was young still clung to the walls. I took a quick shower, put back on my arm sling, swallowed all of my prescribed pills, grabbed Dad's car, and headed to the hospital, breathing in the last moments before I would begin to truly face the unimaginable.

The march to death was brutal to watch. There were still tender moments, but often, it was sitting and watching. My Maw-Maw, my mother's mom, had been helping while I was back in Washington. The lineage running deep in our veins, we too would butt heads, both finding the kitchen to be our place to cook the pain away. Mom and I would get in spats and disagreements. Carrie and Paul with their three young kids felt left out because they couldn't be there as much.

And Dad, his body decomposing around him, barely ever wavered from his quiet faith and acceptance, expressing anger very few times. The Norwegian word "uff da" became his go-to swear after a lifetime of not cursing. I could hear my dad softly utter the phrase, a term used to express surprise, annoyance, disappointment, astonishment, exasperation, and dismay, as he readjusted in his recliner.

The tension and emotion in the house could be felt everywhere except the family room, where he spent most of his time. That room remained calm. After Maw-Maw returned home, Carrie came over for a sleepover one evening—no kids, just her, our family unit together and alone one final time. We watched old movies, talked, and laughed, and after Dad fell asleep, us ladies gathered in the living room to continue to share that precious time together. The next day, things would begin to change for Dad, and he would enter the hospital and never leave. I think he already knew death was near, and he just wanted one more night at home with his girls.

During his week in the hospital, Mom, Aunt Martha, and I took turns staying with him the first several nights, but then, he just wanted my mom there. The Do Not Resuscitate bracelet was placed on his wrist, and he would look down at it sadly. He wanted to come home to die, and we set about putting hospice in place. He was to come home on Sunday, and we sat together at the hospital on Saturday, just the two of us. We talked, reflecting our love for one another. It was the conversation I wish for everyone losing a parent. Without saying the words, we were saying goodbye.

I went home to wait for hospice and began making soups—so much soup. If there was soup, there was hope. Brett came over to keep me company and wait for the angels of death to deliver their supplies. We went to the basement and looked at my dad's tools in his small shop. I riffled through boxes of painting and carving tools, all of the ways he'd wanted to spend his retirement. There on a shelf sat a small, framed picture of Dad and me when I was homecoming queen. On the back, eighteen-year-old Anna had written, "forever your little girl, I love you daddy."

The next morning, Mom called to tell me Dad had changed his mind; he didn't want to come home. He wanted to go to the hospice house located near the hospital, or as I call it, the death hotel.

I was livid. "He can't die there," I begged. "He has to come home. Everything is ready, and I have soup."

From the moment my mom had called me outside the pub in January until just nine weeks later with her phone call about him not coming home, I'd known he was going to die quickly, and I thought I had accepted it. It now came crashing down that he was really going to die, and no amount of soup could change that.

My dad, Mark Allen Nasset, in his quiet wisdom, knew what was best, and he was right. The ambulance ride home would have killed him; the two-block ride to the death hotel nearly did. We spent the night in his death suite, Mom and Martha sleeping. I sat up all night. For as long as I can remember, Dad and I would always drink black coffee. I filled Styrofoam cup after cup and sat holding vigil.

I talked quietly as he listened with his eyes closed, morphine and death filling his veins. Some time during the night, holding his hand, I said to him, "The reason I am still single is because no one stacks up to you. You have been the kindest man I have ever known, and if you aren't going to be here to look out for me, I need you to send me someone that can." He squeezed my hand one last time.

Several hours later, on the morning of March 16, 2015, he left us. Dad had been blind in his left eye for years after his MS diagnosis. As he was in the final minutes of life, I noticed the frantic look in his eyes and realized my mom was on his left side, and he couldn't see her. I told her to switch sides with me. She did, and his body calmed down. She then asked if she could lay her head on his chest, and the moment she did, he took his final breath. It remains the most tragically beautiful moment I have ever witnessed. That is love.

While we were preparing for the funeral, my parents' pastor came over. Mom and I sat with him, and he said something to me that I will never forget. It's something I tell anyone experiencing a loss of a loved one, a marriage, or a business. He told us, "People are going to say a lot of naïve and dumb things in the next few weeks. Remember it's because they love you."

And they did, oh how they did, but they also rallied around us. Our house was full of family members from near and far. Mom and I wrote out the eulogies we would deliver and selected flowers, passages, music. My childhood best friend, Vivienne, even flew from North Carolina to attend, knowing that while offering support to many, I needed support that day.

Hundreds of people filled the church, and we celebrated the life of my father. As the pallbearers carried my father's coffin, covered in sunflowers, out of the church, my sister and I surprised my mom by playing their song. Stevie Wonder's "You Are the Sunshine of my Life" played over the loudspeakers, and we followed behind the casket weeping, arm in arm.

Later that day, I would look at social media and begin to see posts from all over Port Townsend of people wearing my white sunglasses. Years prior, when Ellen's dad had died suddenly, I had made life-size cutouts of Ellen's face and had folks take pictures everywhere. I would later find out she got into my apartment, took all of my sunglasses, set up photos, and then returned them. This was her way of telling me she loved me, my community loved me, and I needed to come home.

Several days later, we would bury Dad in Toledo, where my parents were originally from and where they had bought burial plots in their young twenties. After the burial, Mom and I returned to Delaware, Ohio, and sat staring at one another. *What do we do now?*

I needed to get back to Washington, and instead of flying, I would be driving, as my parents had gifted me my dad's Honda CRV to replace my haggard car. Going home to Port Townsend with my newfound sense of freedom discovered through tragedy, I knew in the pit of my stomach that it wouldn't be my home for much longer, but I kept that knowledge private. I needed to make that choice on my own.

With grief, I could barely function, let alone drive across the country alone. I knew one person who would be up for the mission, and a few weeks after my dad died, I picked up Megan at the Columbus, Ohio, airport. We had a road trip to take, and we had decided if we were going to embark on such a journey, we may as well take the long way home. There were hugs and tears, Brett took us ladies to one final night at Vito's, and we hit the road destined for Utah. (Like I said, we took the long way!)

As you may recall, I've never enjoyed driving. It fills me with dread, and my current state of grief and anxiety didn't do me any favors. Megan, however, is one of the world's greatest drivers. Being her road dog, I fed her snacks, answered texts, and played DJ. We purchased our first of what would be many hats at the Cum N' Go gas station in Iowa, laughed ourselves silly at the truck stop boasting the best toilets ever— I mean, they were honestly a thing to behold—and wove our way across the country, settling in for our first night all the way in Nebraska.

The next morning, I took the first shift behind the wheel while she snoozed. Listening to Patty Griffin, I found solace in the gentle hills that laid straight before me. My time behind the wheel didn't last long, as anxiety set in with the winds of Wyoming, and Megan would drive

90 percent of the rest of our trip. Some people say, "Jesus, take the wheel." I say, "Megan, take the wheel."

Each of us had a reason for this road trip. For me, it was grieving my father, accepting that I would leave Port Townsend, reflecting on the past. Megan's road to change was different. She had been unhappy with her current partner for some time but didn't know how to leave without causing great harm. Our drive gave way to the conversations of the change and choices we both needed to make.

We made it to Park City, Utah, as the snow melted into spring and stayed with a friend of Megan's for a few days. Fabulous food and concerts... Well, they attended the concert; the crowd catapulted me into a state of panic, and I waited in the quiet pub next door.

As much as I wanted to go home, the dread, the fear, and the unknown of Jeffrey started to creep back in. We hiked up to hot springs, we made new friends, and moments of joy appeared again after the months of sadness.

We would continue our journey and hat buying, heading further south to the Escalante Pass. I didn't know what I was in for—I was just along for the ride—but Megan had done her research, and before driving over the spine of the mountain, we stopped at a liquor store. She bought me a bottle of wine, put it into a to-go cup, and ordered me to start drinking. As Dr. Dre provided the music, we drove higher than I knew possible, stopping for pictures and views whenever we damn well pleased, gob-smacked by the desert beauty. We arrived at Bryce Canyon in time for the sunset and to watch the full moon rise.

After several days in Utah, mountain passes where at one point Megan put me in the back seat of the car until we got back down, hikes into Zion, and the most incredible conversations, baring our souls and pains, we traveled north. The entire trip, I never talked about watching my dad die—I couldn't give it words yet. I needed to cling to that tragic beauty.

Heading north, I drove for maybe thirty minutes, my anxiety mounting with each mile. Megan drove us from Utah to Port Townsend. We arrived at the Port Townsend Brewery just as everyone was getting off work, and they gathered to meet us with hugs and tears, condolences and kindness. Conflict filled my brain. How could I possibly consider leaving this family, this place, this home?

# PART THREE

# FLIGHT

# CHAPTER THIRTEEN

# May 2015 – September 2015

**One in seven stalking victims move as a result of their victimization.**[15]

Experiencing grief and loss in the past was one thing, but nothing prepared me for facing my father's passing. There is that sense of "just get back to normal, keep yourself busy, go to work, see your friends, and move on." I, however, shifted into silence and learning. I read books on grief and watched documentaries on death, attempting to assist my brain in making sense of what I had just bore witness to.

I returned to work where my coworkers welcomed me with warm embraces. The guys surrounded me with care. Jimmy, one of my colleagues, announced, "Well, I'm adopting you now. You are one of my kids."

Ellen and Megan, along with others, would check in on me, asking if I wanted to talk about the experience. There was care everywhere, but somehow, I found myself sobbing in front of acquaintances, unable to share the deepness of my grief with those closest.

I became forgetful. I forgot dinners I had been to a few nights prior, plans with friends, meetings in the community. I showed up to work late often. Sunday nights and Mondays were the worst. I went back into the final twenty-four hours of my father's life and relived the moments of watching him pass that Monday in March. At Edensaw,

I could be found staring out the window, lost in sadness, lost in fear, seeking out answers, seeking safety.

Upon returning to Port Townsend, I knew I needed to make a choice to stay or go. If I stayed, I would live in constant fear but have my beloved town, though barely at this point. If I left, I could have safety but would have to begin life all over again in a new place with a new job and new friends. I knew better than to decide based on grief; the helpful books had warned me of that, and it was certainly not a decision that would change my life forever. I set a date six months from my dad's death: September 16. This gave me time to see what life would look like in Port Townsend, get my feet under me, and see what Jeffrey's next move would be.

One evening, armed with another frozen pizza, sitting at my kitchen table, hiding from the stunning landscape around, I turned on Netflix. It suggested that I watch the entire series of *Gilmore Girls*. I had seen bits and pieces in the past and found it cheery enough. I thought to myself, *I never really leave here anyway—why not?*

Lorelai, Rory, and the rest of Stars Hollow became my new family and community. The quirky cast of characters, soft perky lighting, lightning-fast dialogue, friendship, and foibles held me in a warm embrace. There I would sit every night, hitting "next" as the episode ended. There I found comfort. And when the series ended, I immediately started again with episode one. I would repeat this process several times. *Gilmore Girls* saved me and brought me a little more back to the light.

There have been studies that people with anxiety often rewatch the same shows. It allows us to feel comfortable because there aren't any surprises. We know what will happen next and can therefore rest into the program.[16]

I have probably rewatched all of *Gilmore Girls* no fewer than thirty times since my father passed. To this day, the people close to me know that if I tell them I'm watching *Gilmore Girls*, I'm in a dark place, and if I tell them I'm watching *Parks & Rec*, I am on my way back up and ready to kick ass once again. In a world full of images, articles, and reels of what self-care is supposed to look like, I will always find my well of renewal under a stack of quilts, curled up with the *Gilmore Girls*.

●   ●   ●

*Piles of quilts filled the gallery in the coldest month of January 2011, months before Jeffrey would pounce. Fabric art, emerged from the artists' depths, hung on the walls and piled on the bed I'd installed in the gallery.*

*I had craved the comfort of the fibers as my marriage crumbled around me. I leaned into my love of quilts, the history they held, and launched the gallery show to tell their stories and bring myself comfort. Quilts were an acceptable art form for women long before they painted canvases. Quilts were permissible because they were functional. The creators' lives lay before them—each secret, longing, and doubt stitched into the fabric.*

*The month I did the quilt show, conversation around sexual abuse reverberated from the gallery walls. It seemed like a fluke at first, but it kept happening. Not just with people I knew—with strangers too. Women confessed their stories in the gallery, held in a safe container of the fabric-lined walls.*

*It may as well have been 1811. Women gathered around the stretched quilt, talking in quiet tones about the burdens they carried, each stitch of the fabric a piece of stitching themselves back together.*

*On the gallery wall, I printed and hung this quote that I had found during my college studies. It is the clearest example of the power of the art form:*

> *"It took me more than 20 years, nearly 25, I reckon, in the evenings after supper when the children were all put to bed. My whole life is in that quilt. It scares me sometimes when I look at it. All my joys and all my sorrows are stitched into those pieces.*

> *"When I was proud of the boys, and when I was downright provoked and angry with them. When the girls annoyed me, or when*

*they gave me a warm feeling around my heart. And John, too. He was stitched into that quilt and all the 30 years we were married. Sometimes I loved him and sometimes I sat there hating him as I pieced the patches together.*

*"So they are all in that quilt, my hopes and fears, my joys and sorrows, my loves and hates. I tremble sometimes when I remember what that quilt knows about me."*

—*Marguerite Ickis, quoting her great-grandmother*
*in* Anonymous Was a Woman

*Looking at the gallery walls, I trembled over the collective stories held stitch by stitch.*

●    ●    ●

The six-month countdown to my decision was on, and I kept a mental log of the good and the bad. I began to pull myself out of my apartment and lean into all that was good in Port Townsend. I hopped on Captain Ted's boat whenever possible to sail my blues away. I pushed myself to go out with friends and support those who had supported me. I'd go to the grocery store, head to the cookout outside of town, write to or visit Tom. If I forced normalcy, always with an eye on safety, maybe I could stay?

Jeffrey was quiet during this time. Yes, he would be at the grocery store, in the pub, on the street, but he wasn't making direct hits or contact.

In my quest to discover whether to stay or go, I accepted a brunch invite from a friend who was in town for the weekend. On a bustling Saturday in Uptown, with the farmers' market thriving, I cautiously walked the few blocks to the restaurant with my friend alongside me. We weaved through the throngs of veggie shoppers and were seated in the cheery window of Sweet Laurette's Bistro.

Over eggs and Dutch babies and cups of coffee, we caught up and chatted about life, the Packers, work, and loss. I felt a sense of ease seeing my old friend, doing something as normal as brunch, and enjoying the brightness of the stunning Pacific Northwest spring day. People passed by our window seat. We waved at those we knew, smiled at those we didn't, and *shit, fuck, balls—it's Jeffrey.*

Fork held in midair, paused mid-sentence, I was paralyzed. He slowed his walking pace and lingered, just long enough to capture my eyes, handcuffing them to his own. I couldn't look away if I tried. Jeffrey's face turned upward in an evil smile, his eyes flashing bright, glinting, teasing at harm and death. Finally, he released my gaze and walked on.

As my fork clanged to the table, my friend, unsure of what had just transpired, asked, "Is that him?" My ghostly complexion answered the question. My brunch was over. I needed to go home.

My friend escorted me back to my house, and I fell into anger. Begging, pleading, "why me?" anger. My intent for the day had been to make a rhubarb pound cake, and I became infuriated when I realized I needed orange zest and didn't have an orange. Not having the orange was my undoing. I was beating myself up for not checking the recipe, pissed off that I couldn't make the cake, and frenzied in fear of having to leave my apartment.

*Fuck it! This is MY town!* I thought as I grabbed my purse and my knife and headed out the door. Farmers' market days brought hundreds, if not thousands, of people to my Uptown area, and I thought, *I can walk to the store, damn it. I can do this. He cannot take this from me. I will make my pound cake!*

As I weaved through the crowds to get to the small grocery, my head began to swim. I stood in the middle of the merry-go-round, watching people whirl around me. I could barely get my bearings. I began to self-flagellate again.

*He was just in this area. What are you thinking, you idiot? You can't leave your house. This is dangerous. What are you trying to prove? What if he is watching you right now? What if he thinks you being in the area means you love him? Why did you leave the house?*

The questions and blame filled my brain as I bought my orange. Every nerve ending in my body burst as I rushed through the crowds back to my apartment, locked the door, peered out the windows, and made the damn cake.

---

My friendship with Tom continued through it all, emails, messages through Words With Friends, and visits during the brief windows he was home. When his uncle and father died within a few weeks of one another, I took a day or so off and headed down to visit. Two friends linked through written word, Bananagrams, and loss.

We took his classic car out for our favorite drive; along the bottom of the Hood Canal, around the bay called Anna's Bay, we weaved our way up into the Olympic Mountains. Our first stop was always The Geoduck, the semi-famous dive bar, perched on the coast off Route 101. Feasting on oysters and big burger dips, we lingered over our Bananagrams and talked about our losses. I confided in Tom that I may move from the area, but I wasn't sure where yet, and we discussed possible locations.

Our journey back down the Hood Canal toward his home held the necessary pit stop at Hama Hama Oyster Saloon to feast on more oysters and sip cold rosé (for me) and Cabernet (for him). White sunglasses perched on my face, I looked out over the oyster beds. My happiness was no longer in Port Townsend; it was only truly found when I was gone.

As summer wore on in a splendor of sailboats, emerald-hued waters, and town festivals, I sat above it all in my apartment. I listened as Megan's band performed at Concerts on the Dock but from my balcony perch, high above, in my tower of safety. Town activities and crowds were off my list after my last risky errand to purchase the orange, but I still had to work, and part of my job was planning the Edensaw Community Cancer Foundation fundraiser. I turned my grief into soliciting donations, hanging posters, and hosting.

The day of the event, we all gathered to set up the giant tent, tables, and donations, my eyes scanning the parking lot of the Port Townsend Brewery for signs of Jeffrey. I had begun to share about Jeffrey with a few of my coworkers, and I felt safety in the lumberjacks, builders, and sailors who worked alongside me.

People streamed in for the event as music and the auction began. I scurried about multitasking, shielded behind my white sunglasses, my ever-present security blanket and hiding place. Meanwhile, I kept a watchful eye on everything, reminding myself to make sure I faced all points of entry and to be around strong men in case Jeffrey walked in.

It was our biggest fundraiser to date. I wore a yellow sunflower in my hat at the event in honor of my dad. I felt him smile down and protect me that sunny day.

A few weeks later, an unknown number glowed up at me from my phone on my desk. To this day, the unknown number, the telemarketer, any number that is not saved in my phone makes my heart quicken. I listened to the voice message from my corner spot in the large office. It wasn't Jeffrey, but in many ways, it was.

The state police were calling me. They needed to serve me and didn't want to do so at my work. Jeffrey was serving me to appear in court, they explained. I thanked them for their kindness in not showing up at Edensaw, hung up the phone, and exclaimed to the room of men, "That motherfucker. I'll be right back. I have to go to the courthouse. Jeffrey is serving me, and I want to know why—right now!"

There was comfort in the honesty I now expressed, my secret no longer hidden. It was liberating to show my pain and fear in real time to my coworkers. I wonder what they said when I left the office that day and headed to the courthouse on the hill, treading up the familiar winding stairs and traveling to the state police office.

I was greeted by pitying smiles, and the two officers on duty handed me the paperwork. I had been served, and I'm not talking a nice cocktail. Jeffrey wanted to go to court to get the permanent protection order removed, stating something to the effect of, "I still love Anna, but I haven't made contact with her and want to join the military."

I nervously laughed at the absurdity of the statement and asked the officers how he was allowed to do this. Wasn't making me appear in court and stand next to him an example of Jeffrey using the legal system to do the very crime I had the protection order for? They gave me a look as if to say, "Them's the breaks, kid."

Brimming with confusion and anger, I descended the stairs. On the floor of the district and superior court, I paused, looking at the space where I would once again wait to see what would be decided of my life. While taking in the weight of the grandiose vestibule, I felt a tap on my shoulder. Body clenched, I spun around, only to be greeted by Ford, the man I'd called for advice all those years prior.

His slow drawl greeted me as he asked what I was doing there. With a look of defeat, I said, "I'll give you one guess."

His shoulders fell a little. "You've got to be kidding me," he replied. We talked for a few minutes, and I felt safety in our history and his knowledge. I didn't need to explain; I could just be present in my sadness.

I walked back into work and threw down the paperwork I'd been served. The menfolk gathered around and asked me for the details, and for once, I offered them. In their kindness and support, there were some blanket statements, such as, "If he ever attacks you, just call me, and I'll be right there." Jimmy, my now "adopted dad," declared that he would go with me to the hearing, and I gladly accepted the invitation from my older friend and father figure.

Before the court date, I quickly learned that I wasn't the only one who had been served that day. Erica had also been served, and the terrifying connection put us both at ease. My new advocate would meet us at the courthouse the day of the hearing and urged us to write in preparation. Erica and I both set about writing statements as to why the protection order should not be removed, our fears, our concerns, all typed out and ready.

Crumpled statements clutched in our hands, we ascended the steps of the courthouse once more, our support teams surrounding us. Outside the courtroom, Jeffrey paced just feet from us as bailiffs stood in between, at one point sending him to the stairwell to wait, stating he couldn't be that close to Erica and me. Those with us stared on in horrified protection, getting a glimpse into the hell we had lived.

Once we were settled into the courtroom, with the familiar presence of Judge Landes looking down from the bench, the hearing began. I stood in front of Judge Landes, my advocate being the only thing separating Jeffrey and me. Jeffrey wore a strange combination of corduroy on corduroy, and he peered out from behind his wire frames, beginning to squeak out his reasons for asking the courts to cancel the protection order. Judge Landes listened and then turned to me. I asked if I should read my statement—it was starting to smear with the sweat of my hands—and she said no.

Judge Landes then proceeded to inform Erica and me that our protection orders would remain in place. After that, she turned to Jeffrey and made it very clear that her courtroom was not a place to recommit the very crime we had the protection orders for.

The slight sense of victory coming down from the bench brought a feeling of peace in being seen, supported, and believed by Judge Landes. It was a win, but still, I would leave the courthouse with the deep pit of loss. Why did I need to win? Why was he doing this? The waves of knowledge that this was never going to end crashed over me.

---

A few years before I became aware of Jeffrey, he had stalked a Catholic priest in Port Townsend, and a friend of mine who attended the church shared this with me. Running into her one day, I mentioned the priest and asked if she thought he would speak to me.

Clearly grasping at straws and seeking connection, advice, a Hail Mary perhaps, I scheduled an appointment with the priest. He shared with me his experience several years prior of Jeffrey attending the church for a short while before beginning to stalk him. The priest had acquired a protection order, and that had been sufficient for Jeffrey to stop.

As I knew from previous conversations with law enforcement, this was the way Jeffrey used to navigate—short bursts of stalking and then on to the next victim. I also knew from conversations that he had shifted, obviously, and had never let go of his fixation on Erica or myself.

Frantic for a solution at this point, I asked the priest what I should do. Having left the Christian faith years ago, I find it odd that this is who I was seeking guidance from, but desperate times call for desperate measures. He looked at me and said what I already knew: "If I were you, I'd move."

My six-month decision date loomed ahead, but I knew in every fiber of my being that he was right. I talked to others as well, my closest friends and those around me. No one wanted me to leave, but I also think everyone knew it was time for me to go. There is a profound sadness as I look back at those conversations—sadness in the acceptance we all felt around my possible departure.

I began looking in earnest for places to relocate. My mom, of course, wanted me back in Ohio, but I couldn't grasp returning to the flatland and sought other locals, scoured jobs, made notes of communities. I considered Montana, as Lea and her husband had moved there. I figured that could be an awesome place. However, with my dad's passing, I had promised my mom I'd try to move within a twelve-hour drive of her, and Montana was way further than that. I had loved my early adult years living in Maine and thought about returning to the Downeast region but perhaps to a bigger town, as I needed to start completely over. I looked at Portsmouth, New Hampshire; Portland, Maine; Madison, Wisconsin. I knew I wanted cold and snow, but I also wanted my beloved water to sail on.

Sailing had continued to be my salvation that summer in Port Townsend. Crewing for Captain Ted brought light to my life. A huge hug from the kind man, stretching my body while I pulled lines as we tacked, encouragement and laughter from my floating safety vessel kept my soul going.

One day, while walking into work, I was greeted by a sea of the saddest of men. The day prior, our beloved Ted, captain and friend to all, had hauled his boat, *Annie Too*, out of the water for the week to work on her. While doing so, he had developed pancreatitis and been life-flighted to Seattle.

Over the next week, we went in groups to the hospital. Jimmy and I drove to Seattle for a visit with our dear Ted, who was surrounded by more machines than I could count. Having just witnessed death a few months prior, I knew I was saying goodbye to my friend, the one who had put me on boats since moving to Port Townsend all those years earlier. I gave him a kiss on the cheek and said my farewell.

Many gathered to work on his boat and get it back in the water, and shortly after he passed away, hundreds of people processed behind *Annie Too* as the heavy haul-out boat lift gently drove her through the boatyard and placed her back in the water. I hopped on board with other crew members, and as we took her out into the bay to sail, I knew that I would soon be sailing away as well.

With my decision deadline looming, I noticed change was in the air. There seemed to be a breaking everywhere around me. Megan and her boyfriend and Ellen and Amber broke up within several days of one another, and our merry band, the chosen family I had spent the majority of Port Townsend days with, splintered. I sat in support with my friends. Both relationships needed to end, but I privately felt the sting of another loss.

My parents' wedding anniversary—my mom's first without my father—the fifteenth of September, just one day before my decision day, found me at Megan's house with my gals. Combating the blues of ended relationships, we were fully ensconced in the silliness of using the instruments of Megan's band to create our own rock band.

Laughter spilled out of the basement as we crashed on drums and keys, singing off key—well, I was singing off key. Those two have stunning voices. I glanced at my phone to see a text from an unknown number, and my spine stiffened. I clicked on the text and began to read.

"Hello, Anna, this is Bob, Vivienne's older brother who lives in Vermont. I am visiting her and wanted to offer my condolences of your father's passing."

I breathed a sigh of relief and thought, *How strange... I haven't spoken to or seen Bob since Vivienne's wedding fifteen years ago.* I wondered if he was still as attractive as he had been back then...

# CHAPTER FOURTEEN

# September 2015 – October 2016

Stalking frequently accompanies other intimate partner violence, and under certain circumstances, the combination indicates a heightened risk of lethality. In one 2002 study, researchers noted:

Both intimate partner assault and stalking are strongly associated with lethal and near-lethal violence against women, especially when these two perpetrator behaviors occur together and the perpetrator is a former intimate. Not all stalking and threatening behaviors pose an equal threat. Following and spying on the woman, leaving threatening messages on the victim's car, and threatening to harm the children were associated with a two, four, and nine time, respectively, greater likelihood of attempted/actual femicide.

Even when cases do not result in serious physical assaults or homicide, there are often serious psychological impacts on the victims that can last a lifetime. The impact can be further exacerbated if law enforcement, prosecutors, or other allied criminal justice professionals ignore or minimize the crime. [17]

The childhood crush on my best friend's older brother come true, it had all the trappings of a Hallmark movie. As Bob and I texted our lives to one another and progressed to phone calls, it became clear there was interest on both sides. Having made the decision to move, I was curious to see if my dad had indeed, from the great beyond, sent me my man. Bob's parents and my mom were ecstatic to hear we were connecting and eagerly encouraged us to visit in person. With a flutter in my heart, I boarded the plane bound for Vermont. Maybe, just maybe, this gal was finally going to get her happy ending.

Greeting me at the Burlington airport, he looked just as handsome as he did when I was growing up. We hugged one another tightly, our eyes sparking with the excitement of unknown possibilities. Arriving at Bob's cabin in the woods after dark, I was curious to see what the world would look like in the morning light. The next day, we drove along the bucolic and windy roads of the Mad River Valley, and though it was beautiful, it paled against the grandeur of the Pacific Northwest.

I found myself thinking, *Sure, this will work*, as I hiked up Lincoln Peak at Sugarbush, smiling at my hunky companion. Driving through historic and quaint Warren Village, eating dinner at a locals' hangout called The Smokehouse, and wandering Bob's property, I began to get a better sense of the land and community. I saw safety in the gentle rolling mountains, villages, covered bridges, weathered barns, and dirt roads. Vermont didn't feel like home, but maybe someday it could.

●　　●　　●

*Boxes created mazes that Carrie and I would run through and hide in every year or so of our childhood. My father's job as an industrial architect sent our family to live in different locations while he oversaw projects at car manufacturing facilities. Ohio, Pennsylvania, Ohio, Maryland, Ohio, Missouri, then back to Ohio, all before I was nine years old. Mom and Dad hid the stress of these moves and goodbyes of friends from us girls and turned the new locations into adventures into the unknown. Arriving at each new home, I delighted in my new room, placing my cherished stuffed animals and toys in a new order and settling into the next chapter.*

*Summers were filled with family vacations to nearby destinations, swim lessons at the local pool, and me whining while the rest of the family followed their passion for birdwatching. My parents would pick a new church that provided instant playmates. While attending church Sunday mornings, Sunday evenings, and Wednesday nights, one doesn't need to look outside the steepled building to build friendships. The Evangelical upbringing that I was reared in dominated my belief system and my social life. I was indoctrinated with the naïve comfort and privilege of middle-class, Midwest Christian life.*

*When fall came knocking, our beautiful bubble would pop with the daunting prospect of being the "new girls" at a new school. I, a budding fashionista, would search through the stacks of hand-me-downs that Carrie outgrew, attempting to create a look that would propel me to the top of the elementary school social ladder. Carrie, the intelligent one, would labor over the academic popularity she wanted to achieve. In solidarity, we stood side by side, our tiny backpacks weighing us down, waiting for our new bus, our new future about to begin.*

•   •   •

We could continue our long-distance relationship, meeting in Ohio to spend Christmas with our families and Bob visiting me in Washington to see the world I would be leaving. As we opened up our lives for one another to investigate, he had questions about Jeffrey as well as reservations. I assured him Jeffrey would leave me alone and it was over, but in reality, I knew it would only be over if I moved.

With great caution and conversation, we came upon the decision for me to move to Vermont. In my younger years, I had followed a man to Washington and promised to never make that mistake again. This felt different in every sense. Our parents were delighted; Paul, my sister's husband, had family in Vermont that they visited regularly; and there was nearly twenty-five years of knowing one another (yes, he the older brother and I the youngest sister's pesky friend, but a history nonetheless). I was leaving Port Townsend regardless; I might as well gamble on love.

Everything around me in Port Townsend seemed to support this decision. Ellen had fallen in love, Megan had fallen in love, lives were moving forward in various directions, and it felt as though mine should too after being stagnant all those years. But how, oh how, could I say goodbye to my home?

In the lead-up to leaving, I settled as many old debts from the gallery as I could, selling any possession I didn't love, hosting a "yard sale" in my apartment, fearing to have it on the lawn and draw the attention of Jeffrey. My mom helped me pay for the cross-country relocation, desperate to have her daughter closer and safe. There were weeks of dinners and parties, tears and cheers. My heart splintered and healed in the same breath.

The final weekend of goodbyes arrived, and I took a trip down the Hood Canal to meet Tom at the Hama Hama Oyster Saloon for our farewell and a final meal at The Geoduck. I stopped at a waterfall, and tears filled my eyes at the beauty. At the Hama Hama, I climbed to the top of a mountain composed of oyster shells and gazed out on the water, I posed for a picture, head thrown back in laughter. Then Tom and I walked to his car for a private goodbye.

We held each other, and I thought, *Please say it, please say it, please tell me not to go.* Though our relationship over the years existed more in writing than time together, there was, on my part, love and a desire to see if we could be more than just pen pals who slept together when we saw each other. But he didn't tell me to stay or that he loved me, and I sat in the seat of my friend's car weeping as we drove away. In my heart, I thought I would never see my dear friend, and love, again.

Megan and Ellen drove me to the ferry on Bainbridge Island to catch my flight. We made our jokes and told our stories, and a palpable sadness hung over us. We ripped the bandage off quickly, clinging to one another, saying goodbye, but not lingering. If we lingered, we would fall apart, and I wouldn't get on the ferry. I boarded alone, sitting with my giant suitcase next to me. I scanned around me, making sure Jeffrey wasn't somehow on the ferry. I wasn't safe yet. With a guttural sigh, I stared into the Puget Sound.

For the ten years I lived in Port Townsend, I had only seen orcas on a whale watching tour. I dreamed of orcas often, and whenever I did, the next day, I would hear of someone seeing them in our bay or at the beach, just a mile from where I laid my head. Orcas, my favorite animals, kept their distance from me, and it always saddened me. However, as the ferry sliced through the waves and toward my future, I gasped. Orcas appeared, swimming and jumping next to the vessel, saying goodbye to me. I openly sobbed, hunched over, body shaking, weeping as tourists stared. It was time to go find a new home.

---

Have you ever made a life-changing decision and immediately known you've made the wrong choice? I think Bob and I both felt that the day I arrived in Vermont. I know I did. Not the wrong choice in moving, and not the wrong choice in Vermont, but the wrong choice in partner. We both felt it and set about doing the best we could with our bad decision. Conflict in personality, lifestyle, and pastimes slammed us in the face, and as the summer wore on, the fights grew bigger.

After moving to Vermont, I worked to secure the basic needs: employment and safety. For work, I landed a new job as business manager for a farm and retreat center located on one of the most stunning pieces of land towering over my town of Waitsfield. Quietly alone with my secrets and shame, I worked planning retreats and events, helping with the non-profit work. The farm is a place where there are no bad views and everything smacks you in the face with its pristine beauty, but from my office, I sat in my darkness.

With safety an ever-present concern, I stopped by the Montpelier Police Station while I was in town getting my driver's license. When I inquired about their protocol when dealing with stalking, we chatted for a while, and they even looked up Jeffrey. I remember the officer let out a low whistle when looking at Jeffrey's priors. We chatted for a bit, and they shared with me that Vermont had just passed stronger stalking laws that would better protect victims and survivors.

At home that evening, I looked up the new laws and noted that the state representative for my area, Maxine Grad, had sponsored one. Feeling empowered and needing connection, for reasons I'm not quite sure of, I wrote to Maxine Grad and thanked her for her work. I even mentioned that someday it could save my life. Much to my surprise, she emailed me back and invited me to have coffee with her. She would be the first person I ever shared my story with in Vermont.

Bob and I were trying to make it work, looking for commonality and understanding. But when Bob would leave for a business trip, I'd lean into the peace. Taking a book to The Smokehouse, I'd have a quiet meal and a cocktail, yearning for someone to talk to.

During my first time sitting at the bar there, the door burst open, and I turned, interrupted by the commotion and revelry. A gaggle of friends roared in, everyone laughing and cheering, clearly regular locals. I looked at them, a tear in my eye. I missed being a part of a group. I missed my people. I desperately missed home. I would talk to Megan and Ellen for hours each week, a practice we still work to keep, but it wasn't the same. I was a stranger in a foreign land. In my new-found safety, I needed to accept loneliness.

I did begin to meet other women. A community organizer and I would start to take walks, a foreign practice to me after my years of safety planning. We attended the governor's debate at the Vermont State House in Montpelier, and on the way home, I whispered my truth about Jeffrey. Leaning into the safety I now had, the horrors of the past came out.

A petite and measured yoga teacher would invite me to an early dinner and drinks, both of us having moved to the Mad River Valley at the same time. I also befriended the relaxed and sporty sophisticate who ran the best restaurant in the area, The Common Man, with her partner. There were other women as well who would reach out and offer an invite.

I was desperately grateful for each text or call. With my relationship with Bob failing aside, I was beginning to walk again with newborn baby deer legs shaking. I pushed myself and would walk the area trails alone. In failure, I was finding freedom.

By fall, Bob and I faced our reality. Despite the hundreds of hours of phone calls, FaceTime conversations, and visits, regardless of all that we had discussed and covered, nothing had prepared us for the reality of living together. In our hearts, both of us knew there was no path forward, so we called it quits. All my possessions went into his storage unit for safekeeping, and with only my clothes and necessities loaded in trash bags stuffed in my car, I accepted a long-term housesitting gig in a remote village twenty minutes south.

---

Recognizing my sadness at my relationship ending, Megan, Ellen, and adopted dad, Jimmy, bought me a ticket home, and just six months after I left Port Townsend, I was on a plane back for a visit. The ferry where I had fallen apart guided by orcas carried me back to the motherland, and I was once again part of my gaggle of humans, laughing and cheering as I burst into the Port Townsend Brewery. I didn't care where Jeffrey was or what he would do to me. He wasn't even a thought in my brain. My soul sang with the reunion of MY people.

Every meal was booked with a different friend, my homecoming tour was packed to the gills, and I took every ounce of love I received and gave it right back. Dinners and house parties, sleepovers and silliness, the band was back together even if only for a moment. I allowed myself to let my guard down, feeling the joy I hadn't felt since 2011. My months of freedom in Vermont, though difficult and depressing, had changed me in a beautiful way. Maybe I could move back. Certainly not after I had just moved away—there was no way I could afford that—but maybe...

On my tour about town, I stopped to see my friend Amber, my former employee and Ellen's ex-girlfriend, at her new apartment. We chatted and caught up while she got ready for us to go get coffee.

I was lounging on her bed, laughing at a memory we shared, when my phone chimed next to me, then again, and then again. It kept chiming as I picked it up to see a series of message requests in my Facebook Messenger from a name I didn't know. The screen name stated Robert McCleod. I clicked on the first one, thinking, *Who is trying to sell me what?*

"I tried to send you a note the other day but it got lost. I was thinking maybe you are my type and when I was thinking of that in my head a lot of things [most everything started to make sense—which it hasn't for a while]. So I think "evil," like other labels are arbitrary points on an infinite series of numbers; it's maybe more important how one treats the arbitrary or things considered so. So, I did say that I loved you in my motion in court—I didn't really know at the time whether it was true: I just thought God wanted me to say that and hoped it might help in court, but I do think it is true."

"No!" I screamed, startling Amber, who turned. "It's Jeffrey!" I shouted.

"For what it is worth though and not because of anything you did I am breaking up with you: until I have the resources to have a bunch of girlfriends or wives at the same time it doesn't make sense to me to act otherwise, plus you are on the other side of the country and I'm sure there are decent men in those parts who would appreciate your company and you theirs without wondering in the back of your mind whether there was something wrong with doing so. I still am interested in possibly working with you in the future on getting good art shown and you are free to contact those artist on your own and or contact me, just as you would have been free to go to the Uptown Pub had Landes cared a whit about you or Erica's well being. I think you would made a very appropriate gallerist to the conditions of Washington and I bet you would be just as great somewhere else more able to be supportive of the arts. I hope you think of me if you so choose to endeavor in that regard and hold nothing against me given that I was actually born in Washington and have spent most of my life here."

My mouth filled with vomit as Amber came and sat next to me.

"I'm sure you would be an effective Gallerist: oh, though maybe in a more sane setting, Betty Parson would be a person to look to compete with: I am sure you know Peggy Guggenhiem was more of a collector and follower of Parsons than she was creative in her own right: but that was very shrewd of you to suggest you were like her given the way Port Townsend people are. You do remind me a lot of a wolf, like in all the good ways and all the bad ways: like I think a lot of people like you as in Roman mythology Rome was nurtured by a she wolf. You also remind me of Mawgli's mother in the recent Disney version of 'The Jungle Book.' Since Rome and Roman Catholicism is so prevalent around the world I think you have a really good future ahead of you if you just kept up doing what you did before but adjusted for geography and cultural limitations a bit."

My eyes lingered on several words: "Evil." He'd been calling me evil for years and talking about how evil people should die. "Uptown Pub." Did he know I didn't go there when he lived in that neighborhood? "Peggy Guggenheim." I had dressed up as Peggy for Halloween years before knowing Jeffrey existed. I threw the phone on the bed and rushed to the bathroom, barely making it to my knees before I violently vomited.

Amber, who had often been of the "it's not that big of a deal—he's harmless" camp, came into the bathroom. Once I had emptied my stomach, she said, "Get in the car—we are going to the police."

# CHAPTER FIFTEEN

# November 2016 – February 2017

## HOW LAW ENFORCEMENT CAN HELP

1. Listen closely to victims—even if what they say sounds unbelievable—and document everything they report.

2. Substantiating the crime of stalking requires building a case that establishes a course of conduct. If you do not have enough evidence based on one incident report to charge the suspect with stalking, take the time to discuss with the victim how to document and report the offending behavior so that you may build a case.

3. Investigate other reported incidents such as vandalism, burglary, and violations of protection orders to see if these behaviors establish a pattern of conduct.

4. Consult with your local prosecutor and U.S. attorney to learn exactly what evidence you need to collect to build and charge the case.

5. If the victim is still engaging with the offender, understand this may be the best way for the victim to remain safe.[18]

The drive to the station was only a couple of miles, but my mind traveled a thousand miles per second. *How brazen of him to make a direct hit. Had he seen me in town? He referenced me moving. How did he know I moved?*

I had tried my best to keep everything hidden. In that moment, I worked to piece together the parts of my story, my life, and this crime that I will never, not then and not now, get answers to.

Weighted by my questions, angst, and shame, I walked into the station, sobbing uncontrollably when I saw Officer Corrigan. In all those years of reports and visits to the police station, I had stayed measured, cracking jokes, expressing gratitude. That day, I fell apart.

Snot and tears dripped down my face as I apologized to Corrigan and others in the office. "I'm sorry I came to visit. I shouldn't have. None of this would have happened if I weren't here. I should have just stuck to my plan..." I sputtered out between heaving sobs.

Officer Corrigan looked at me and gently said, "This is not your fault. This is your home. You should not have had to leave your home."

My body eased just a bit in hearing these words; the sense of support and kindness from law enforcement was much needed. We set about once again filing police reports, collecting the messages, taking screenshots, documenting and logging it all. The thin glimmer of hope was that we possibly had what we needed for felony charges, which could place Jeffrey in prison for a larger amount of time—maybe even a few years—if he was convicted.

•     •     •

*Everyone else is doing it. What's the harm? I thought as I swallowed ecstasy for the first time during winter break of 1999. The giant circus-themed party was a confetti-filled event of cotton candy, cocktails, bouncing bodies, and drugs. My pure Midwest upbringing had not prepared me for a party of this caliber. I relished the freedom as the drug took hold, and I danced into the evening.*

*I remember my "no" as he forced himself onto me. I remember trying to get him to stop as my panties slid off my unshaven legs. My "nos" continued, and he did too. I gave my body over to the inevitable when he entered me despite my pleas. I woke in the morning, alone, with blood on the sheets because I had been a virgin.*

*I didn't tell my therapist, fearing I would be in trouble. I had broken two of the rules of our school. I had taken the drug. I was to blame for putting that substance in my system. I rationalized with myself that this was my fault. I tucked the rape into my bag of secrets, carried them on my back. The secrets were heavy; the burden weighed me down, but I put one foot in front of the other.*

*Despite my somewhat outrageous behavior from time to time, I found a fantastic group of friends. We were like-minded, fearless, funny, irreverent, and bright-eyed, looking into the future of the world we would create. I'd left the Christian faith my freshman year, as many of my friends had. We went to a Christian school but found safety, and the unraveling of our belief systems, in one another.*

•    •    •

Officer Corrigan also shared with me about the other victims mentioned in the messages Jeffrey had sent me. They were newer victims, but he seemed to not be letting go of them. Both were female. One worked in the district courts; the other, in the county jail. My heart ached for them and our shared journey.

We talked further, and in order to collect evidence, the police asked me to do something but only if I was comfortable with it. They asked that I not block Jeffrey's message requests because we needed more. With the burden of collection on my shoulders, the weight of responsibility yoked to me, I agreed. Then, as so many times before, I was sent back out into the dangers that lay outside the police station doors, sunglasses hiding my fear.

I had lunch planned for that day with my pal Kyle. When I arrived at his condo, he was eager to see me until he saw my face, screwed up in anguish and defeat. He had walked much of this journey with me, as a courtroom supporter and confidant, and he knew what my expression meant. Jeffrey was back.

I slunk onto his couch and showed him the messages, and we talked as I stared at the sea lapping upon the rocks below his home. I wanted to jump over the ledge and let it swallow me, carry me away, never to appear again. Instead, I mustered what strength I had and curled into the passenger seat of his car as if I were a ninety-year-old woman going to an appointment, small, frail, and confused.

We headed to the Spruce Goose and had a lovely dinner at the Port Townsend airport. I picked at my sandwich while small planes ascended and descended over the Olympic Mountains. I would be on a flight soon, carried back to Vermont and back to the loneliness of safety.

Later in the evening, while out at a friend's house, everyone tried to distract me, working to tether me to support and joy but to no avail. Even as they tried to cheer me up, the messages from Jeffrey began to flood my phone. So much of this journey had been spent alone, but my dear ones were able to see the effect in real time, my physical response, the mid-sentence stop, my body changing shape.

> "William Corrigan did call me today: and I hope you can convince him there is no need to be concerned as 'I broke up [with you],' and you are safely way, way away. And needn't travel a long way for nothing."

*I NEVER DATED YOU, YOU MOTHERFUCKER. YOU CANNOT BREAK UP WITH SOMEONE YOU WERE NEVER WITH.* His message gave me no peace.

> "Please just take that into consideration for my sake and others as I am no longer just a boy and could hurt people. I think too that

you are going to have to better 'own,' your own nature if you you are going to be able to have more productive relationships with men. Even if you're a wolf in a spirit animal sense and personality sense, wolves deserve love to. I think you might have to find another 'wolf,' like person though, though I don't know. Maybe you're more like a husky: I did see a Husky last night right after I sent you a message and it looked really happy, just standing outside someone's house on the side of a road, smiling. I wish you the same satisfaction and contentment as well as peace in your own life. My friend is also from Ohio and he suggested that you must have been molested by your father but that what happened must have been helpful in your processing such things. I have no clue whether that was actually true, but I do hope in some way you benefited from meeting me. I did notice your wildness when I first walked in the gallery and I'm not particularly scared of wolves or huskies as I am more like a raccoon, and used to go to a lot of Huskies games with my grandfather, but I think it makes a lot more sense than the hypocrisy of the state where the state kills people and doesn't eat them, and wolves at least eat the things they kill. Raccoons kill dogs they don't like and other pets in groups but I also think they are more civilized than canines arguably, where having an apposable thumb helps in such matters. Civilization has it's faults and especially in Washington though I don't think it's all Washington's fault: I just think it was sort like washed up on the tide of Western and for that matter Eastern civilization but the tides didn't come back soon enough for it to really be normal like other places or have 'continuity.' I like being outside too but like Cows and house dogs I kind of like the indoors as well. Raccoon like people tend to suggest a different way of looking at evolution and I hope I've offered you a more satisfying vision thereof. For example not for political reasons but based on my love of science I think Marx is helpful to consider regarding validating one's notions."

Around me, everyone sat in horror as my phone chimed again and again and again. Each message was more confusing and viler than the last. I stepped outside and screamed into the wind, "HOW DARE YOU SPEAK OF MY LATE FATHER. HOW DARE YOU!"

"Of course you want me and I want to get in a fight with some cops at some point: but I think it's important for you to take a minute and consider why you never committed to Port Townsend and kept your toes on the East coast: like maybe there was some good reason for that you haven't been willing to consider. Like maybe you were cunning and saw it was a trap to begin with, the way Raccoons walk right into those things—I actually saw a video from a news agency online where a raccoon was trying to break into a jail. I did that back in 2009. Honestly, I was hoping I could stay in jail for thirty years or something, but it got way crazy: one of the guards literally tried to kill me four times with one of the doors and then they put me in with inmates they thought would fight me or I would attack, which I found inappropriate. There is a legalistic side of me that is just as strong as the wild side: and it takes offense at corruption very easily and I kind was a fan of Asperger's syndrome for a while and then I think I've developed it in some ways as method of getting things finished. The only reason I told the cops that they ought to kill you [where I had no such desire myself to do harm to you] was that that you had lied and it seemed malicious of you to act the way you had and I thought of Port Townsend sort of like a flock of sheep. But now I am willing to admit that wolves need to be wolves too, and it's not my job to tell the cops what to do."

It had been decided I would stay a few extra days in case the police department needed me, but I wouldn't stay in Port Townsend. And as luck would have it, Tom, whom my heart had said farewell to, was back for a surprise and very quick visit to his house in Washington. I would travel south to him in the morning and spend my remaining days in safety. Until the morning came, my friends turned my phone on silent, took it from me, and tucked me into bed. The messages continued throughout the night, each worse and more bizarre than the last.

While Amber and I rode to meet Tom halfway, we stopped several times for me to vomit on the side of the road. There wasn't the grief I felt when moving away six months prior. It had been replaced with a wretched agony that I could never come back. But then, there he was— Tom. My body and safety were released into his arms, and I fell deep back in. My friend, my protector, my confidant would keep me safe in the days to come. He, too, would witness my turmoil firsthand as the phone beeped out new messages.

"But love you too. You do sort of center my thinking even better than gravity: I just think the idea of being buddies with a husky would make my grampa happy; he went to school at the UW and so did my father and brother."

I sat hunched over Tom's table filled with its cluttered curation. He leaned over me, hands on my shoulders. I held the phone up for him to read while my head burrowed into my arms.

"Fuck, six years of this? And he keeps getting worse. I'm so sorry, Anna," he said as he gently squeezed my shoulders. "What can I do?" he asked.

There are a lot of things I would like a former Special Ops to do to Jeffrey, but instead, I replied, "Let's make a drink, eat snacks, and watch a movie." He made us Singapore Slings and cut up cheeses and meats. Then, we snuggled into the couch and watched *It's a Mad, Mad, Mad, Mad World*, because, indeed, it is. Having both fought in battles and wars, we fell asleep as Spencer, Ethel, Caesar, and the gang raced to find their treasure at all costs.

French press coffee and poached eggs were served by Tom. We sat across from each other at the narrow breakfast bar, discussing the adventure of the day. We both knew there was only one adventure on our agenda—to take the drive. And once more, we loaded into the car, let iTunes pave the way, and set off for The Geoduck.

As we drove around Anna's Bay on that dreary day, my phone rang. This time, it was a number I knew, and Tom pulled over immediately, not knowing where the cell reception would fail us.

Officer Corrigan greeted me from the other end of the line. Jeffrey had been arrested. I jotted down next steps, things I needed to do, and other comments from Corrigan while Tom patiently waited. After I hung up the phone, he squeezed my hand. Tom is a man of few words, and his hand squeeze spoke volumes.

We drove those winding roads once more. Lingering over my oysters and burger dip, looking out at the gloomy hues of the Hood Canal, I took my first full breath in days.

---

I have always wanted to live where there are certain days you can't tell whether you're looking at mountains or clouds. Standing on the back deck of my remote housesitting spot, I looked into the night sky, squinting to find where the mountains started and the sky ended. I was the loneliest of alone, up a dirt road, in a foreign area, miles from work and the few women I had met.

I roasted garlic and smeared it onto bread. I made gallons of soup—if I couldn't save my dad, maybe the soup could save me. Lorelai and Rory from *Gilmore Girls* became my best and constant companions. If I was home, they were my friends, my family, my saviors.

Work at the farm had been down to part time due to their programming and events taking place in the summer. On my first day back in the office after my vacation-turned-nightmare in Washington, I sat my bosses down and came clean about everything. I told them about Jeffrey, revealed my real reasons for wanting to relocate, and explained that there should be no fear on their part, as he remained in custody. They offered support and asked questions, and I did my best to get to work and push it all away.

Phone calls from law enforcement, advocates, and the courts would interrupt my work time, and my focus would be gone for the rest of the day. I stared out into the lonely beauty of fall in November after all the leaves had gone, trees waiting to be blanketed and hidden in snow.

The rawness and visibility in landscape matched that of the news cycles. Clinton and Trump were about to face off on election day, and I, like most women, sat in horror over the words and rhetoric coming from his mouth. Certainly, there was a kinship across the nation among all who had experienced sexual violence, but that did not soothe my soul, as the glass ceiling did not break that election night and instead weighted us down.

Needing additional employment, I reached out to the few women I knew and was surprised when my friend and restaurant owner immediately offered me a job serving tables at The Common Man. I hadn't waited tables in over a decade, and this restaurant was known for its incredible fine-dining service. It wasn't the career move I had intended when relocating, but it seemed like most people in the Mad River Valley worked in the service industry, especially during ski season, and this was a good way to keep my evenings full, keep my bank account in the black, and possibly make new friends.

My first day on the job was Thanksgiving. *Better than being alone*, I thought. Nervously donning my black server outfit, I met and greeted people all evening, then sank into my seat for staff meal after service, quiet and timid amongst the community of long-time friends.

My housesitting stint was winding to a close, and I had been desperately seeking permanent housing. Scouring ads and putting the word out to the few people I knew, I sat in the uncertainty of unsecured housing. I would answer an ad to find the apartment had just been rented.

Defeated, with clothes in large trash bags, I moved from one housesitting gig to another, keeping watch over beautiful homes with panoramic mountain views and curated spaces. I had become a bag lady, not just in how I transported my possessions but in the weight I carried. This combined with phone calls from the police department, advocates, and courts meant my days were a complex dance of piecing together every aspect of my life.

Finally, I received a message back from a landlord. She had an open unit, a small studio apartment located in an old farmhouse in the historic Warren Village. "I'll take it!" I blurted out, and she suggested I go see it first.

Warren Village, with its precious history, pristine New England homes, and babbling brooks, had captured my heart since my first visit to Vermont. I thought perhaps my luck may just be changing. I coordinated with the current tenant and climbed up the old staircase on the back side of the house. The door opened, and a sparkly siren of a woman appeared.

"Hi, I'm Mimi. Come on in."

There wasn't much to see in the studio apartment—deep red old wooden floors, a small kitchen, a loft. Shockingly, a jet tub filled the tiny bathroom. Most importantly, there were two points of entry/exit. I was home.

Mimi and I stood on the deck and smoked a cigarette as we got to know each other. She and her husband were moving to the larger unit, a converted barn, just down the stairs. Could I possibly have secured housing, a neighbor, and a friend in one hour?! Nailing down this basic need removed a bit of the weight I carried.

I signed the lease, luckily avoiding telling my landlord about Jeffrey, as he was incarcerated, and forked over all the money I had made at The Common Man. Then, I borrowed an air mattress, Bob helped me move my boxes from his storage unit, and I hauled my trash bags of clothes up the stairs.

My first night at the studio, which I came to call "The Nest," was New Year's Eve. I woke in the morning, vulnerable and alone on my underinflated mattress. I needed curtains, and I needed them up NOW!

Knowing I was moving into The Nest, I had gone to Big Lots the week prior and purchased the things I had just sold when relocating: a dish rack, a pot and pan, a French press, a kettle, towels, curtains—the basics one needs at the deeply discounted prices I could afford.

I found the curtains and rods and stared up at the large window. Since the window trim was hanging on by a thread, I could feel the winter draft and felt gratitude that heat was included in my rent.

Realizing I didn't have a screwdriver or drill, I looked down my deck to see Mimi outside sipping her coffee and having a smoke. I cautiously walked down and inquired whether she may have a drill or screwdriver. She said, "Certainly. Is there anything I can help you with?" I explained I needed to hang curtains, and she offered to help, which I gladly accepted, thinking, *Mimi, I need more help than you could ever know.*

She had already privately noted that I had unloaded a meager number of belongings and no furniture into the space, but she didn't question it. Additionally, here I was with my priority being to hang curtains. And in her kindness, she did not pry—she simply helped and began to establish trust with me, a rescue pup of a human, that would lead to my openness down the road. Often, all we need to do is hang the curtains for someone.

My sister, Carrie, her husband, Paul, and their kids visited a few days later. Paul helped me move some chairs in, and the kids jumped on my air mattress and delighted in the loft upstairs. I sat in shame and embarrassment over how little I had to offer or show for my life. From gallery owner to bag lady, there I was in all my failed splendor.

We adults talked in hushed tones, not wanting the children to hear about my break-up with Bob, the current case with Jeffrey, and how I would put my life back together. Their default was prayer and Christianity, and while I respect their choices, this was not for me. My default was resiliency and rebuilding.

Carrie and I clung to one another as we said our goodbyes. We were still the balloon and the string.

––––––––––––––

Another call from the Port Townsend Police Department came in; my case had been misfiled as a misdemeanor and not a felony. The case would be refiled, but my last shreds of hope fell from my eyes because with this misfiling, Jeffrey would be released.

Once again, I choked on my own vomit as I waited for the Kentucky number from VINElink to blink on my screen, the notification of his release. When it rang, I answered and punched in my code, hung up the phone, and stared. When would he strike next?

Frantic to reignite my safety plan, I notified my landlord, ran escape drills in my head, and figured out where the nearest police station was. Then, night after night, I sat on the phone with Megan and Ellen and wondered what would happen next.

January 11, 2017, at 3:03 a.m., I woke to the chime of the Facebook Messenger app on my phone. *He's back.*

"I meant everything I said to you. I apologize about saying those things to the cops but I said them in the knowledge that they would never do anything to hurt you. As I was saying to NAME REDACTED, I'm willing to plead guilty to the charges if she refiles the case in district court with Judge Landes. And I give my word I won't report and I gave my word I wouldn't report her or any of the other prosecutors to the Washington State Bar Association for prosecuting the case even though you lied and perjured yourself prima facie in the petition the order is based. My current attorney, NAME REDACTED, said that the case was not refiled and dropped in superior court because you live in Vermont but I was under the impression that the prosecution wouldn't go forward with it as I'd threatened to report them to the W.S.B.A. if they proceeded with the case. I also felt guilty for pleading to harassment when the original charge was "stalking," and Bert Boughton changed the charge after I said they'd only win if he changed charge to 'harassment,'—which was actually in the original message(s) I sent you. Beyond that I feel bad that I didn't serve any time for actually assaulting NAME REDACTED which the plea agreement was formed by."

With a heavy sigh, I rolled over and looked at my phone. Over the years, I have taught myself to scan for words that could be threats and tune out his political and religious ramblings, sexual comments, and the vast number of times he calls me a liar. As my eyes skimmed over the first message, I stopped on the word "Vermont." One could assume he had somehow figured out I lived in Vermont, but this was the first time he'd said anything, and the alarm bells in my brain began to clang once more.

Several more messages came in as the early hours wore on. I sat up straight in bed, shaking.

"I do love you and I was watching 'I AM LEGEND, starring Will Smith and at the end he dies to save a mother and her child and I thought of you as they went to some place in Vermont to defend against the zombie apocalypse—with an antidote to the disease he'd given them. I apologize for getting mad and being nasty when you claimed you were the next 'Peggy Guggenheim,' you probably were and maybe Modern Art and contemporary art would not be what it was and is without her and you—"

My body moved to the bathroom, and I curled over the toilet, retching. All the while, my phone continued to chime.

"I already...I apologize for being so zealous about 'making it,' when I met you, that I might have missed the very possibility that you might be interested in me in a relationship that was non professional. I thought you were a much more decent woman than the one I was seeing at the time and I think we are much better sexual partners than others."

"I NEVER HAD SEX WITH YOU," I screamed into my pillow. "I don't know you," I cried out.

"P.S. I am glad you are safe in Vermont. The other part of the Kim Yong Un thing is that while it may not seem like an issue now, when he gets the missiles he'll be under tremendous pressure and scrutiny to use them."

"P.P.P.P.S. There is the issue of NAME REDACTED. She thought I should be evaluated for competency because I used the word 'competency,' in a sentence. Then she was giving me the gooey eyes in court after I pointed out the lack of cause for my being evaluated and passed the evaluation plus being found neither a threat to 'myself or others.' The psychologist from Western State was quite sympathetic to my story as he had been an artist and cartoonist prior to having to find other work to support himself and family. Like the psychologists who evaluated me before and came to the same conclusions, they seemed personally concerned with regard to the success of my case. But then the premise of sanity as it is commonly 'understood,' doesn't make much sense outside of a coercive environment like a court or psychiatric hospital. Because a person is 'dangerous,' doesn't mean they should be locked up: everyone is dangerous—they, the law and church just don't want people to believe that as it hurts their bottom lines—which they aren't even supposed to have. When Ford Kessler told you I was 'dangerous,' or the like, it probably just got your attention like when I told the court and NAME REDACTED that my release was a matter of National Security: in a cult like environment—normal relationships between the sexes is not allowed, but normal sexual motivations between the sexes is not something that can be taken away."

*Is this other victim he is writing about okay? Why is he talking about Ford? Is he alright?* The chaos of protection and security filled my brain as the minutes ticked on and the phone kept chiming. Receiving the messages as he was writing them put a darkened hue to the situation, as if he did indeed own me.

"P.P.P.P.P.S. It makes sense in both your cases as I'm probably the only person who could get either of you 'off,' in a ... any sense of the world, word. 'Evil,' isn't a condition one can easily get out of as I've defined the cause of it and its not a very 'light,' issue either though, it somehow reminds me of that book 'The Unbearable Lightness of Being,' by Milan Kundera. It sort of reminds me of the book 'The Curious Incident of the Dog in the Night Time,' too."

Reading the word "evil" once again, I couldn't even muster a whisper to continue defending myself against this monster. Depleted and wobbly, I used the wall to support me as I once again collapsed onto the toilet.

"P.P.P.P.P.P.P.S. Am I the greatest legal mind of my generation? Probably. I was the devil's advocate once literally. I just know there are more troubled people than he."

"P.P.P.P.P.P.P.P.S. I also am sort of scared of myself when it comes to the law. But being a criminal in a corrupt society in a cult like state and under a law the bible calls 'the strength of sin,' seems safer than being a lawyer therein."

"P.P.P.P.P.P.P.S. I also still have a few years to resolve the Kim Yong Un issue, and I don't rush things. I do think you're the best lay I've had. Maybe not the 'greatest.' But the best. And I like that. And it seems like healthy sex. So give me a note or whatever if you ever want to hang out again."

Sitting on my bed's edge at nearly 5 a.m., I began to fall—fall into the weight, grief, fear, anger, chaos, and confusion. The phone continued to chime.

"Like that night you were talking about or when I was outside the Sirens and you were 'on the deck.'"

"I apologize too for holding the fact I found you 'sexy,' against you."
Silence filled the early morning hours. I peered out the windows, then drew the shades, put an extra quilt over my shivering body, and didn't leave my bed until my shift that night at The Common Man.

From my bed, I would call the Port Townsend Police Department and talk to Officer Corrigan, sending all the evidence to him but wondering if Jeffrey's words for once held some truth. Were they not going to file the felony charges due to my distance? Officer Corrigan didn't have the answers, but as he inquired around, signs pointed to this being the case. I clung to scraps of hope and pulled the quilts tighter around me.

I put my dirty waitress clothes on, warmed up the car, and went to serve the rich. Rosy-cheeked and oblivious, they came in from the cold, sharing tales of the days on the slopes and asking questions that pried into my life. As the night wore to an end, with customers gone, we staff sat with our shift drink, counting our earnings.

One of my fellow servers, Izzy, made small talk with me. Izzy, a short dreadlocked nugget, has the superpower ability to make friends with anyone and to sniff out those who may need a new one. She asked if I wanted to stop at a bar down the hill on our way home for a nightcap. And there at The Hostel, an old farmhouse turned bar/hostel, just a few miles from my apartment, I sat with a glass of wine and told her my story.

A few nights later, and in the beginning bustle of a long holiday week, Izzy and several other employees invited me back to The Hostel after work for a drink and to hear live music. It was a mixed crew of kitchen staff, the bartender, and servers, and despite my secrets, I was excited and yearning for community.

When I arrived at The Hostel, the place was packed to the gills, and I found myself parking far down the dirt lane that led up the parking lot. A large tour bus was parked along the road, and the number of people was staggering to me as I walked into the cozy pub.

Beer, sweat, and patchouli filled the air. I hadn't been in the Valley long, but long enough to know we were in the thick of tourist season. Being in the service industry, our group got our drinks before any of the tourists and stood in a small circle, shouting to one another over the noise. It was the first time I'd been out with a group of people since moving, and I felt a sense of community.

We joked about our worst customers, laughed about the evening, and toasted. However, a little while later, our small circle was interrupted by a drunken tourist. He appeared out of thin air. I still remember his high and tight short dark hair, digital camo ski jacket, and red military fun run T-shirt. He joined us without permission.

We all looked at one another as if to say, "Do you know him?" None of us did, and as he made a few off comments about the females in the group, we closed our circle off from him. He wandered off, and we chatted on.

The odd encounter with this man, the throngs of people, and my fatigue led me to leave after one drink. I bid my adieu and headed out the front door of The Hostel, keys in hand. Walking along the porch, I noticed the same man who had intruded on our group sitting alone, smoking a cigarette. I walked past him, thinking nothing of it, and continued through the snow-covered parking lot, waving at a local girl

I had just met as I passed the tour bus (which I had found out was a booze cruise bus for the rich young revelers inside).

I turned to look behind me and saw the man from the porch hustling toward me. *He must be getting on the bus*, I justified but quickened my pace. When I glanced back again, he was past the bus, and he had accelerated into a jog.

My years of self-defense training kicked in. Working through the adrenal dump, moving to escape, not fight, my body took over and propelled me. I broke into a full run, glancing back and forward in swift head turns. He was getting closer and was clearly faster than me.

I pushed my body forward, clicking my key fob to unlock my car doors. Then, in one motion, I threw my body into my car, hitting the locks and putting the key in the ignition. He grabbed at my door, yanking the locked handle, using his strength to try to open it. His eyes, filled with frenzied danger, met mine. I threw my car into reverse and sped off.

I do not know how long the moments were between leaving, making the five-minute drive home, and calling The Hostel. It felt like mere seconds. When I called the bar, the assailant was nowhere to be found. The booze bus was being loaded, and for all I knew, he was already on the bus. All women remaining at The Hostel were escorted to their cars when they left, and no one ever saw him again.

I have seen that look—the look of pure evil—a few times in my life. I know what that look means, and I know I saved my own body—if not my life—that night.

The next day at work, I told Izzy and the others who had been there the night before about the event. The guys from the kitchen, kind and protective, felt horrible. They had discussed how eerie our conversation interrupter had been and apologized for not offering to walk me to my car. I could feel their care and support, and I could also feel myself slipping further and further away.

Each moment of each day, I dreaded the chime of my phone and simultaneously wondered when the Facebook message request would happen again. Due to the crime, the stalking, an unknown fear and suspense filled every brain cell and hogtied my ability to function.

On January 17, 2017, the next attack arrived.

"Hey love, if you want me to move out to Waitsfield let me know. I spent some time in Connecticut, New Jersey and New York the year before last; I applied to the graduate art Program at Yale a few times. I was curious what it was like as I had never gone out of New York city or Washington D.C. except to catch a plane. I spent a fair amount of time in 'Wallingford,' watching five dollar movies in the afternoons and writing a bunch of poems. Socrates may have been disingenuous in his motivations for arguing various things and not really interested in 'the truth,' per se but I think he may have had some point about poetry corrupting a society: I guess the caveat though is that where a society is based on laws and laws generally lead to people confusing normality with morality, then poetry can be some kind of alternative to that..."

Fingernail scratches down a chalkboard filled my ears. *Who fucked up. Did I? I kept everything so private. How did he know about Waitsfield?* I propelled myself to the bathroom just in time for everything to evacuate my body through both ends. The trash can caught my vomit and my sanity.

"I've been putting off slapping a cop and dealing with the unknown attached to that the past few years because cops are basically blue collar or from that background and it doesn't seem fair to slap one and then put them in a position where they had to fight me where I'm scared I might end up killing one because of whom they work for and what those people are doing is killing me and everyone else and it's not fair to lay such a thing on the cops because they in biological reality don't really have a choice with regard to what they were doing, because of where they came from and the position and relatively low pay they get combined with the real and abiding dangers and risks that go with their occupation, the trauma that comes from that and the consequences for themselves and others: so at a certain point there seems to be an exception and or the cops no longer are even cops and no one really can be a cop or fulfill reasonable expectations within that position where money is such an influence on the end result, but also the present and the perception of the past..."

*He's going to kill cops?! Why do I have to be the one to carry this burden of knowledge? It's three in the morning in Washington. Go the fuck to sleep, Jeffrey.*

"I'd like to call you. I think we belong together like the wolf and the boy in the Cormac McCarthey book 'All the Pretty Horses.' I want to be 'Mr. New,' to you. I feel I love you. I won't bother you again. I love you. Goodbye. Write me back. I appreciate you. Fangs and all. I want to be with you. I don't care if we look at art in totally different ways: I like you as a person. You're so sexy. You're a beautiful woman. I love you even though it's 'inconvenient,' to. I like your style even though it's not mine. I love you even though it doesn't make sense to the peasants. You're a real princess ala Machiavelli. I think I can say I'm a Prince too."

And then, the Facebook Messenger phone app began to ring. Jeffrey was bold enough to try to call me. I stared at the screen, remembering to take a screenshot, then gingerly put the phone down on the quilt next to me. Lungs heavy and lightheaded, I walked away and looked out the window once again. If he knew where I was, he could be anywhere, including my home. I checked the lock on my weathered apartment door and looked out through the old windowpanes to the yard below.

---

While talking to Officer Corrigan, I could hear his voice dripping with sadness as I shared with him this new batch of messages. Both of us silently processed the harm that could befall each one of us, knowing the bullshit county prosecutor was doing nothing. I needed my own plan.

Because Jeffrey had mentioned Waitsfield, Corrigan wanted me to talk to law enforcement in Vermont in case he came here. He guided me to take all my files and evidence, along with Corrigan's business card, and go to the Vermont State Police (VSP) barracks as soon as possible.

Since it was a very rural area, we didn't have local law enforcement, and the VSP barracks were twenty minutes away. I had already driven there and timed it with one of my safety drills. At the moment, I had to get to work at the farm but promised I would go in the next few days.

Also, on my list of to-dos before heading to work was finding a therapist. I could not survive this—I knew it. I was a tattered rag doll being thrown into a well, and there was no one to throw a rope to me. I went online, found one who looked like we would be friends in real life, and booked a session.

Professional help was one thing; I also, once again, had to speak to those around me. I had to do my due diligence so that no one else would be harmed if Jeffrey came to Waitsfield. With that in mind, I gingerly told Mimi and her husband, Colby, over a cigarette on the landing. They took in the information with steadfast support and compassion. Were these two creative creatures able to hold this and maybe hold me?

Finally arriving at the farm, brain filled to the brim with all that had transpired in the last week—the night terrors of messages, the almost attack at The Hostel—I was completely checked out during our weekly meeting. I shared with the owners about the latest batch of messages, as I had been doing. They were concerned and offered support, but then they turned and sadly informed me that, to save money, they needed to cut my hours to five a week.

With that news, my rag doll body smashed to the bottom of the well and lay broken, bits of stuffing seeping out between stitches. In one week, I had narrowly avoided a physical attack, had Jeffrey tell me he knew where I was living, and lost most of my job. I went home, turned on *Gilmore Girls*, and crawled into bed.

I followed Corrigan's orders and gathered all the evidence, put it in a nice manilla folder, dressed as professionally as I could, and walked into the barracks on Friday of that week. I greeted the officer on duty with pleasantries and asked to speak to him privately. We headed into an office, and I began to clearly lay out my situation, stating I was being sent to talk to him by the Port Townsend Police Department and holding the folder in front of me as if to hand it to him.

He stared blankly at the folder, then at me. "What do you want me to do with this?" he asked in an accusatory tone. "There's nothing we can do for you here," he continued.

The folder dropped onto my lap; my shoulders slumped. I stammered, "Well, I know you can't do anything here, but, but, but the cops out there... Well, if something were to happen, they wanted you all to know who Jeffrey is, who I am, that this is a very serious and dangerous situation."

He looked at me as if I were the girl who cried wolf. I could feel his annoyance sucking the air out of the room. The officer stood up as if to say, "We are done here," and I followed suit.

Crestfallen, I got in my car and drove to Montpelier for my first therapy appointment. *This better work*, I thought, *because I cannot survive myself much longer.*

# CHAPTER SIXTEEN

# March 2017 – October 2017

**Seventeen percent of stalking victims describe losing a job or job opportunities.**[19]

With the week of breaking almost in the rearview mirror, I sat in my studio apartment, eager and nervous for the next day, January 21, 2017, the first Women's March. I desperately needed the camaraderie of marching with all women, and yet, with my body on high alert, I knew the crowds would put me on edge. *Nevertheless, she persisted.*

Cracking open the antique steamer trunk that had once belonged to my pal Kyle's mom, I dove in and pulled out bolts of fabric—a large red piece and an antique blue and white pattern with delicately bold floral and stripes. My beloved sewing machine, which had sat forlorn under the table I had procured, moved to her rightful position on top, and I set to work, snipping and sewing to make a large flag. The red served as the flag background, and I tacked on the blue and white fabric as the female symbol.

In the morning, dressed in all black, harkening back to my Black Water Snake days, I went to Montpelier early, not only to beat the crowds but also to survey the area and make sure that my car was parked for easy escape in case my anxiety overwhelmed me or there was a mass shooting.

Thousands upon thousands gathered in Montpelier that day, as they did all over the country. I located my friend and raised my flag high. Peering out through the throngs of bodies from behind my white sunglasses, I felt seen in a way I have never felt before or since. Just as I stood in support of every survivor there, they stood in support of me, and for once, I allowed myself—forced myself—to stop and take it in. I felt the overwhelming rush of connection and kinship with each step toward the capitol. The moments of dropping into emotion were few as I constantly scanned the crowd for signs of Jeffrey or other potential danger, but even those drips of connection wetted my parched lips and would keep me going long after.

After thirty-three years of gender-based violence, Jeffrey, the near attack—all of it—stacked upon me, that week weighed me down into a deep depression. More days than not, I didn't leave bed until my shifts at The Common Man or for my few hours at the farm. I lay in the depths of pain I hadn't felt since college when I attempted to take my own life, staring above me at the rafters, wondering if that was the only way out.

●　　●　　●

*After Todd tried to assault Hilary and I, that spring of 2001, he offered us an apology at our friends' urging, and I accepted it because it was the only time someone had taken ownership of their actions. I tried to put one foot in front of the other but found myself falling flat on my face; I missed classes, went deep into my loneliness, and was miserable in my existence. I realized that there was no way out; I was a vessel meant to be used and abused. The only way to stop this cycle, I determined, was suicide.*

*Those close to me knew I was in a dark place and did their best to hold me, but people can't be around 24/7, and in the dark moments, I found myself sitting and staring at a bottle of painkillers I had from a car accident that I had been in earlier that year. The bottle tempted me to take it down and wash away the pain with a bottle of vodka.*

*One evening, when I was sure everyone was busy and my roommate was gone for the night, that's what I did. I drank in my end and was sitting in my demise, waiting for the drugs to take hold, when a surprise knock on my door broke through the silence. Opening the door, I saw Jenny's face—Jenny, whose now ex-boyfriend Todd had tried to assault me just a short time before. Looking at her face, I turned and threw up on the floor.*

*Jenny, whose own heart had been broken by Todd's actions, cleaned me up and sat with me long into the night, talking, caring, and making sure I wasn't leaving the earth. Things didn't change overnight, and they would get worse before they got better, but the care Jenny showed me, mirroring that I am worthy and loved, kept my feet on the ground.*

*The feelings of wanting to die didn't run out the door that evening, and when I found them clawing through my brain with ferociousness, I knew I was in trouble. This time, I just asked for help. A dear friend took me to the ER, and within a few hours, I was institutionalized. Wearing an orange jumpsuit, I would begin one of the most terrifying and revealing weeks of my life. I stared into the abyss of how my life would continue to unravel as I looked at the faces around me, and I began to dive fully into my brain and trauma.*

*The elderly psychoanalyst who worked with me helped me peer into my "winter of discontent." I learned and began to accept that these things that had happened weren't my fault. I deserved respect and autonomy. I began to leave the "just get over it" mentality and accept that I was carrying a lot of trauma that I needed to unpack to find lightness.*

*My week in the mental health facility was filled with others' voices as they battled their minds and the inward work while I unraveled mine. I even made a friend, a fellow student at the university. He is gay, and that was against the school's rules. He, too, had tried to take his own life, and we found a deeply connected friendship in our lonely secrets.*

●　　　●　　　●

I leaned into the tools I had gathered over the years. I talked nightly to Megan or Ellen while I was on my way home from my server shift and they were arriving home from work, our time difference pairing nicely to offer support during those dark hours. I reached out to my old professor, Knapp, who had helped me all those years prior when I'd attempted to take my life, not to ask for help—just to let someone know I wasn't okay. In addition, I kept up with my therapy. It didn't take the pain, the depression, the grief, anxiety, PTSD, any of it away, but my tools kept me going.

On the darkest of days, when I couldn't see a way out, I would go to the post office in Waitsfield to check my mail and made sure I always complimented an older woman. Their smiles, that brief connection, mirrored to me my worth and need to stay on this planet.

Days, then a few weeks, passed with no messages from Jeffrey. There was no ease in this; in fact, I experienced the opposite. More fear and concern filled me with each passing day. Not knowing his location while he knew mine was terrifying to my core. If there was a man who looked like him dining at The Common Man, I would run down the back stairs while the bartender made my drinks. I'd make it to the toilet barely in time, scrub my hands, then dash back up to grab my tray of drinks and deliver them. No one knew the terror, other than my friend Izzy, who was truly beautiful in unknowingly making sure I didn't fall off the edge of the world with her invites to interact with others.

Painful acceptance shrouded me on February 9, 2017. I'd accepted my fate as the Facebook Messenger app chimed at me. The Port Townsend police couldn't help me, the Vermont State Police didn't care, and I was alone walking this journey, waiting for Jeffrey to catch me. At that time, I felt either he was going to murder me, or I was going to take my own life. I couldn't live with this the rest of my life.

"I don't think you should totally feel ashamed for being attracted to your father as to a certain degree that is normal, especially when he is charming, relatively wealthy and powerful. I don't think people should be ashamed of being attracted to you because you have similar qualities though perhaps in a more ontological sense. Sexiness may simply be the fact that a person doesn't follow the law or other hypocritical worldliness. It's not how you look that is so sexy to people per se but the things you advocate and don't simultaneously. People aren't attracted to 'you,' they are attracted to what you represent: you, your soul is inviolable. You can't be forced to do anything in that regard and you needn't worry about old lecherous men or relatively young lecherous men. It would seem problematic though for you to continue pushing to get me arrested; if I'm what you want you can't have me as allowed above and if you want what I represent you're not going to get it that way either..."

Numb, I sat in my bed, waiting for the next, and the next, and the next. I didn't need to vomit; a calmness had come over me.

"I know REDACTED NAME still wants to prosecute me but that's because she has basically the same psychological background problems as you and thinks its a way of flirting to send or try to send people to prison."

"It just seemed really tacky. He apparently was a cop before then and got in a lot of trouble in Texas for beating people up, so he became a prosecutor, and when that started looking bad became a priest or something equivalent: I never thought of beating him up but he sure flinched like he thought I was going to when I passed him on the street one day at lunch beside the movie theatre. I've been told that the prosecutor is 'ultimately responsible,' or something to that effect for corruption in the law and I ought to slap a prosecutor, and maybe a female one— yeah I think I'd consider that, but there is that movie 'Bridesmaids,' or whatever about that girl in Chicago and she meets a

cop and—the actor I think is actually Irish and not a cop per se
or could be if he wanted to be at the same time, and he says in
the film that 'Cops are like priests,' and I think they are actually 'ultimately responsible,' or something for the enforcement
and application of the law, and so it wouldn't make sense to not
slap one at some point: I just think that killing one like Corrigan appeals very much to me as well. I guess I can kill him with
kindness though! I've done that a few times before and maybe
that is what I'm doing to you now."

The messages flowed in at the rapid pace I was used to. I looked at
the door. *Is he here? Is he outside? Is this the end?*

"I sort of doubt it though, because I still find you attractive.
I've also never felt like harming you or had God as I understand him/her/it/them wish for me to do any such thing to
you. I mean I think it would be cool if you came and hung
out with me in Port Angeles. You are certainly rough around
the edges but you've got the best structure out there as far as
precedents go for consciousness and appeal. I also think it's
not necessarily racist to want to be with someone of the same
race as one. You remind me or Michelle Obama reminds me of
you and I think she's definitely his better half. If you're pissed
off at me, get a grip. I could say all sorts of mean and true
things about you but I'm not. I will though if it goes to trial
and the the petition is allowed into evidence. That is just the
way the 'ookie cookie,' crumbles. 'Oookie Cookie,' was a game
that boys used to play in Washington in the nineteen twenties: they would all jerk off onto a cookie and the last one to do
it would have to eat it...

"Anyhow, kindness is lethal, so beware. At this point I'm trying
to kill you with it, but also 'lying,' appropriately..."

Lying down on my bed, I felt my fight was gone. *I* was gone, sinking under the quilts and pain. The phone continued to chime next to me.

"So, maybe you've never been #1 in my mind; I am old fashioned and you seem to be as well: like you seem to love the 1950's in a way that I do as well..."

"You didn't seem very happy in your gallery when I first met you I must say: something like a wolf at the zoo all caged in, so... maybe you wanted what came to be. I always feel bad when I see wolves in zoos. I stole a dog that was outside Safeway this last year but I didn't take it far enough away so it's owner found it again: he was a douchebag, but I'm glad I did it; it makes me feel mad but I can understand animals I think as well as St. Francis of Assissi did: I once played chess with a raccoon and it very nearly beat me: those guys—yikes, maybe that is why the Russians never invaded, and never will. They jumped my boss and his wife when they went camping up by Bellingham, apparently if they don't like a dog they'll lure them out into the sea and then drown it.

"I do love you and I do feel a bit inappropriate saying that to you as I am terribly selfish in many respects with my time and it disturbs me to think of putting anyone out. It also is humbling to me that I love you, perhaps like its humbling to love a bitch, a dog I mean: though in that vein..."

Minutes, hours, a whole day of silence went by. I got up to put a meager bit of food into my body. Coffee, wine, bathroom, and back to bed.

On February 28, 2016, Spain's Aleix Segura Vendrell achieved the world record for breath-holding with a time of twenty-four minutes. I believe I beat his record that day, holding my breath for nearly twenty-four hours before the phone chimed again.

"I suppose there are other women like you so if you don't find my appeals, entreaties, come ons and requests to your standards I'm not going to die because of it. I can't accuse you of being unloving yourself as jail, the forensic unit and as I've heard on a number of occasions—prison is better than many if not most of Washington, but PA might be even better.

"Unless you have more to prove in PT, maybe you'd like it here too.

"I did see a brunette at the library this evening who I fancied like you. She had some anxious and nervous significant other as it sounded you did when you actually failed to return that quite excellent painting I gave you in the same manner REDACTED NAMES accepted you as their friend. You are quite appealing as materialistic people go, I guess a bit like my mother. I guess it's because you don't let it get to you."

Then, silence.

---

The weeks that followed were chaos. Nobody knew where Jeffrey was, and everyone was concerned. Though the county prosecutor in Port Townsend had declined to take the case, I found my resolve to fight for my life and freedom, for the safety of other victims, for the protection of communities, and I filed every damn message he sent me with the PTPD.

Officer Corrigan, not the most tech savvy of people, decided to have Facebook do an IP address search to find out Jeffrey's location, and he and I embarked on the bumbling process of figuring out the information I would need to provide. I began to give voice to my situation with a few more of my coworkers at The Common Man, and one server helped me locate a computer guy in town who could help me with the process. Facebook is a slow machine, and I wonder about the lives lost due to its delays. With paperwork filed, we all waited for the results and feared what he may do.

Erica, his other long-time victim, and I kept in contact during this time, my heart aching for the safety of her and her growing family. To our joy, we discovered he had been arrested again on different charges. That night, as my shift at The Common Man ended, I poured a small glass of champagne and toasted to whatever amount of freedom I had, dreaming that maybe he would stay in jail this time.

I made a hair appointment and had my hair styled back to how it had been during my gallery days, cutting off the foot of locks I had grown, chopping my fears off. Afterward, the stylist asked if I wanted to go grab a drink. Needing friends and community to fill my soul, I said yes, and we headed to The Mad Taco.

The small barroom was the same size as the Port Townsend Brewery, and it was Friday, after all. While I was thousands of miles away from old friends, it felt comforting. The packed room, crammed with locals I had seen around, coats strewn on the backs of chairs, mud and slush on the floor tracked in from the snowy day, felt familiar. My stylist introduced me to various ladies, and I shyly began to take a step forward into this new community I lived in. The unknown timeline of freedom pushed me to dive in and make the most of the moments.

Jeffrey's incarceration didn't last long, as he was able to make bail, and I began to hold my breath again, waiting for the next message to arrive, but all remained quiet.

Eventually, the search warrant of Jeffrey's location, the IP address, would come back from Facebook, and Corrigan would deliver the blow to me. Jeffrey had been in Port Angeles, Washington, located in Clallam County (the next county over from Jefferson County where Port Townsend is located) for the bulk of the messages he sent me. This meant that not only could the PTPD do nothing, as it wasn't their jurisdiction, but they would also send the case to Clallam County where no one knew of Jeffrey, no one knew my years of terror, and no one would help me.

I crumbled into defeat and depression yet again. Letting go of my rope ladder, I bounced to the bottom of my well. The only hope I clung to was that he would be prosecuted for stalking another victim, giving us all a brief window of freedom.

The Common Man season was ending during the summer, which led to my newest job hunt. And as so many survivors before and after me, I did the logical thing and began to look for jobs in the advocacy and victim services field, searching for healing in the world that had helped me for so long. Thankfully, the advocacy center I applied to didn't hire me. I would have been a shit show, but it planted a seed, and I started to research and learn about the careers in that field. I paused the seeking of employment but not the education. I found a program offered through the state of Vermont, the Vermont Victim Assistance Academy (VVAA), and applied for a scholarship. Then, I waited.

Spring and summer were budding around me. My hours at the farm increased back to twenty per week with their summer programming, and I picked up odd jobs doing design here and there. I was in a holding pattern, but I was making it work, and holding felt best in case I needed to flee or disappear.

This season gave way to visitors as well. Emily, the mortgage maven of Port Townsend, paid a visit, and I basked in the familiarity of friendship as I toured her around Vermont. Carrie and her family also stopped for lunch on their way to visit her husband's family in Maine.

Then, "why can't I quit you" Tom arrived. He had been studying for his master's degree through an online program at Norwich University, something I didn't know until moving to Vermont, and Norwich happened to be located just over the mountain pass from me, a mere twenty minutes away.

When his weeklong residency and graduation came along, he opted to stay with me, snuggled into my studio apartment. Despite how complex our relationship was, his presence provided the salve and safety I yearned for. I could let my guard down when Tom was around. He had protected and served our country in the most heroic of ways; he could protect me for a few days as well.

Meals at The Pitcher Inn down the street, drinks at The Smoke-house, and drives reminiscent of our Geoduck adventures ensued. That tattooed war hero even went to the Vermont Quilt Festival with me and listened as I shared my knowledge and love for the art form. The connections to home kept me tethered.

Shortly after Tom left, I had a scare. My period was late—so late, in fact, that there was no way I could have been pregnant due to the timeline, but I took a test. I was delighted by the negative sign but also sat with the shock. I hadn't had my period in four months, AND I hadn't noticed. But what I *had* noticed lately was hot flashes. I chalked it up to my anxiety and fear, but I started to piece it all together. I had stopped having my period right around the time Jeffrey sent the last messages to me.

*Surely trauma couldn't have put me into early menopause. That's not a real thing*, I bargained with myself.

I did research into the connections between trauma and perimeno-pause. It's a very real thing. I had my period twice more over the next year, both times when I was happier and at ease, and then never again. At the age of thirty-seven, I went through full menopause.

If you had seen me in my youth babysitting and caring for all the kids, you would have assumed I would become a mom, and I would have too. As a young woman, I couldn't wait to have children. Some of my friends would save their baby clothes that I had complimented for when I had my child.

However, as the years wore on and Jeffrey's presence grew, I knew I couldn't bring a child into the world. How would I shield them or save them from Jeffrey's madness? The choice had already been made for me in my mind, and now, my body followed suit. I celebrate the births of my friends' babies. But in private, after each announcement, baby shower, Mother's Day, first whiff of the newborn's head, I struggle and mourn deeply.

I had heard tales and experienced a small glimpse of the Warren Fourth of July, but nothing prepared me for its reality. Warren, a village of a few hundred residents, would welcome fifteen thousand people for a morning parade and all-out party.

The village vibrated in preparation the night before. Mimi, Colby, and I busied ourselves setting up for the next day. The event of the year would end in my yard for many locals and friends. I had become a Valley girl, and I burst with excitement. Mimi, ever the stylist, and I decided to go with vintage Fourth of July, each selecting our 1950s picnic attire.

She and Colby told stories of parades past, but none of it landed until the morning of the Fourth when, at 7 a.m., there were already people partying in our yard. *If you can't beat them, join them*, I thought as I threw on my blue and white plaid dress and headed out the door.

By 9 a.m., every inch of the street was covered with people streaming down the mountain roads, hugging, shouting, laughing. There was red, white, and blue as far as the eye could see, and with it, dread. I marched down the street with throngs of people to watch the parade, but as they celebrated freedom and independence, I saw mine slipping away. The fact remained that no one knew where Jeffrey was during this time, and while I had tried to push that out of my mind over the last few months, he could indeed be anywhere.

From behind my white sunglasses, my eyes scanned the crowds. People were shouting and losing their Vermont minds as Senator Bernie Sanders marched along the parade route, their voices amplifying my fear. As the gigantic articulated floats crafted by communities garnered cheers and awe, I wanted to crawl inside the sculptures and disappear. Frivolity surrounded me as people danced in the street in front of the "almost" famous General Store, and I marched back to our house, trying to disappear in Mimi's footsteps that led the way.

While hundreds partied in the yard, riding down the hill on dirt bikes and lawnmowers, waving flags while bands played in the background, I ascended the steps to my apartment, and my breathing began to shake. Quick inhales took over as I sat in the plastic seat on the small deck, hyperventilating, gasping for air and quietude.

Somehow through the noise and chaos, Colby heard me, and he flew up the stairs, grabbed a paper bag from my kitchen, and handed it to me. I breathed into the brown craft paper bag as he rubbed my back. As much as I feigned being okay, I very much was not, and the revelers below felt far away.

The next day was a big day. One of my favorite people in the world would be in Vermont, and I jumped in my car, drove over the mountain pass, and parked at the Middlebury Inn. Upon entering, I was greeted with squeals and hugs by my dear Lea. She was working with the college, and we had one night to reconnect and rehash the last few years.

Lea, "you poetic noble land mermaid," the Ann to my Leslie Knope á la *Parks & Rec*, sat, and I told her everything, every damn thing that had happened in the last few years, in the last few months, in the last few days. I spilled it all out, and she held it in a beautiful container, filled with the sarcasm and strength that only she was capable of conveying.

I also took a quick trip out to Blue Hill, Maine, where I had resided in my early twenties, to visit my dearest friends, Missy, Emily, and others. Even before I made the six-hour pilgrimage, I told my friends, "Do not post anything of my visit." Still on high alert, I never posted about adventures or whereabouts until after I returned.

I welcomed the warmth, laughter, salt air, and bottles of rosé as us ladies caught up on the years that had passed, and I began to open just a little to all that had transpired. Our friendship had gotten lost in the shuffle of different coasts and schedules, along with my ability to be present. Visiting Missy and Emily was another reminder that maybe Vermont was the right choice, even if it was hard to feel it.

---

The farm had informed me they would no longer need my services after the summer season, and up shit creek I paddled again, looking for various jobs in the community and throughout the state.

I received word from Andrea, the coordinator of the course I had applied for the scholarship to, that I was accepted, and my heart jumped with delight. I didn't know what I was doing or where it would lead me; I just knew it was time to start whatever this next chapter of my life was. I enthusiastically accepted the scholarship and began a barrage of emails to Andrea, my nerves and lack of knowledge apparent.

In late August, with all quiet on the Jeffrey front, my phone blinked that familiar unknown number across the screen. I tried to telepathically read who was on the other line, just knowing the unknown hadn't been working in my favor. The ringing stopped, along with my breath, and I waited for the voice message to come through. Was it Jeffrey? Was he here? Had he found me hidden in the hills of Vermont? The voice message landed, I gingerly hit play, and a male voice spoke.

"Anna, this is Detective Trevor Dropp with the Port Angeles Police Department. PTPD sent over your case a while ago, and I have been assigned to investigate. Can you give me a call back?"

I jumped, I screamed, I danced, I tossed my Hama Hama trucker cap high into the air with glee. Someone 3,091 miles away cared. They believed even if they didn't know me. The distance mattered not—they wanted to investigate.

I rushed past my panic attack lawn chair and down the stairs, bursting at the seams. Through frantic words and gestures, I blurted out to Mimi and Colby a synopsis of the call I had received. They never knew Washington Anna, her gallery, the horrors she faced from Jeffrey. They knew only the small bits I had shared, had only seen the cracks of the effects in me.

Despite their little knowledge, they jumped up and celebrated with me. Then, they asked what Detective Dropp had said when I called him back. "Oh, shit, I should probably do that," I exclaimed, running back up to place the call.

My call to Detective Dropp found me gushing with gratitude while he managed my expectations. He was only assigned to investigate. He didn't know if anyone would prosecute, but he would do his job.

Unfortunately, his job was complex because still no one knew where Jeffrey was. Dropp asked if I knew Jeffrey's location. That would have been great if I did, but wasn't that part of the problem? I never knew where he was! I did tell him I'd check with Erica, the other victim, to see if she knew. She and I hadn't chatted in a while, but I thought maybe she would have information. Once again, victims being their own detectives!

Feeling slightly less optimistic, I still did what I always did and sent a thank you email to Detective Dropp. I ended the email with this: "Also, once again, I wanted to thank you for calling me and pursuing this. I had given up hope that anything was going to happen after it got moved around so much. Even if nothing does happen, it was great to receive a call and feel heard by you and the community. There are many reasons I'm pursuing a certification in victims' rights, but one of the biggest is how lonely and 'unheard' you feel, so thank you so much for hearing me and taking the time!"

Within a day, Erica messaged me back. She had done a little nosing around and found Jeffrey had been in King County (where Seattle is located) jail since April on charges regarding another victim's stalking case, and no one had told us! APRIL?! How had the cops not known this?!

We were both livid. The panic attacks, the sleepless nights, the chaos that filled my brain, the trauma that rewired my body... I could have had a break since APRIL? I don't get angry often, but I was pissed. Yes, I could have been putting his name into VINElink daily to check, but that wasn't my job. Had I dropped the ball, or had the system? Either way, he was incarcerated, and I gave that information to Detective Dropp.

With Detective Dropp on the case and Jeffrey behind bars, I had one thing I wanted to do with my minutes of freedom: adopt a dog. Often, victims will get a dog as protection, but I always felt the opposite, for having a dog meant taking them for walks and being more visible, which was counterintuitive to my safely planned life. But maybe now with the case in King County, my potential case, and yet another case with another victim being built in Port Townsend, I could stretch my legs and enjoy a walk with a pooch by my side.

I looked at various adoption agencies, remembering we had a local agency that brought dogs up from the south, and I found myself scrolling through the available dogs at For the Love of Dogs Vermont's page. Too big, too medium, male dog, male dog, too big, too big... STOP THE PRESSES. Who is that nugget peering back from the screen? Her pointed ears dwarfed her bug-eyed, snaggle-toothed dark face. They stood at attention, and I swear she could fly with them.

I clicked on her profile, wondering why anyone would give her the name she currently had, Trinity. I quickly discovered this six-pound chihuahua mix was aptly named. She was indeed the holy Trinity with only three legs, and she would be mine.

While talking to Ellen that night, after sharing pictures, she said to me, "There is only one person I know who would get the tiniest, three-legged dog with abuse history and then most likely carry her around in a bag...and it's you." My best friend knows me so well, and her statement was very true. I had already been looking at bags and baskets I could put her in. We both decided to keep with tradition. Ellen had a chihuahua named Willie Nelson, and despite the miles, they would be brother and sister. Therefore, Trinity became Dolly Parton.

In the weeks waiting for Dolly to arrive from Tennessee with the other rescued pups, I accepted a new job. I took on the position of server, along with doing marketing and events, at Tucker Hill Inn. I had been to the new restaurant at the inn and met the new owners, Patti and Kevin, several times. They had bought the inn to spend more time with their kids and moved from a big city to run it. The dream was not matching the reality, and they needed help and growth to carve that time out with the little ones.

Patti's curly bob matched her perky personality, and Kevin, having retired from corporate life but being unable to let go of some of the teachings, gave me confidence in this opportunity, having pursued me for the position. My farm job would be firmly phased out by fall, and I eagerly went to work at Tucker Hill.

Dolly arrived in my life when I needed her most; we both rescued each other. I openly cried when they handed me the tiniest bundle at the rescue pick-up day. She shivered in fear in my arms and hooked her only front leg around my neck as if to hug me. My heart burst with love that day and has every day since. I had bought toys and treats, and I was ready to begin our adventures together. I took her home and realized there had been a little false advertising regarding her ability to use steps. I scooped her up and showed her the apartment.

Everything scared her, and rightfully so. She sat quietly on an old quilt, taking in her new world and cautiously inching closer to me. She snarled and snapped as I tried to get her outside again. Eventually, she calmed, and I was able to carry her down the steps. She settled in, and I began to learn many things about her that her years of abuse had instilled in her.

Dolly hates kitchens (any kitchen anywhere), children, toys, square-shaped food bowls, other dogs, most men, most women, when you scratch her butt, any loud noise, large rooms (she prefers to walk along the edges of rooms) the list grows daily, even now. For everything that Dolly hates, she provides me with all the love, and I see her fear and anxiety—I know it. She is me in dog form, and as her voice grew from quietness to barking at every damn thing, my voice began to grow as well.

---

Detective Dropp was unable to interview Jeffrey right away. He was planning to do so, but Jeffrey was transferred to Western State Hospital, a psychiatric hospital he had gone to on multiple occasions.

Even with all that had transpired, everything Jeffrey had done to me, all the loss and fear I had experienced, the only thing I wanted was for him to get the services he needed. I wanted him to be able to experience life without causing harm. I know our system is broken in handling people with mental health diagnoses, and our prisons are packed with people needing other services. With Jeffrey, we had seen long ago that he wants to feel the way he feels, and that is in many ways his right, just as it is my right to go to the police and pursue safety. I have no answers for this—just sadness that the years have led to this.

I told Detective Dropp, "Hopefully this will get him the help he needs. I doubt it, but please keep me informed as time goes on when he gets out and what your steps will be."

Over the next few months, that is what Detective Dropp did. He sent an email every now and then letting me know that Jeffrey was still in Western and that he hadn't forgotten about me. He was going to investigate this case.

Just as Jeffrey appeared in my life out of thin air, information about my case would appear with the same cadence. The end of October 2017 brought just such news during a routine check-in with Detective Dropp. Jeffrey was still in Western, but Detective Dropp had been able to investigate through the Facebook search warrants and by obtaining Jeffrey's phone and had met with a prosecutor, James Kennedy, who was willing to move forward with charges. My eyes lingered over the words in the email, a faint glimmer of hope filled me, and I cautiously set up a call with James.

James, a retired Army officer who served several tours in Afghanistan and later became a lawyer, met with me on my level. Perhaps it was his military leadership skills, his passion for victims, or how he was raised, but he met me where I was at. When we talked for the first time, I felt fully seen. I had always felt somewhat used by the legal system and hated my role in it, but for the first time, I sat at the table (even though I was thousands of miles away on the video call) with those supporting me and prosecuting Jeffrey. James educated me on the difficulties of prosecuting stalking, discussed with me the lengthy process, managed my expectations, and got to know me as an actual person, not simply the victim. I walked away from that conversation with empowerment, knowledge, and support.

With my secrets tucked back inside, I walked into the state complex in Waterbury, an old asylum turned offices—fitting considering my situation and as an active victim of crime—and took my seat for my first class at the Vermont Victim Assistance Academy. Notebook and pen poised, I listened as the forty other classmates introduced themselves and their jobs. Every single person in the room, except me, already worked in the field. They were employees from restorative justice centers, members of the Vermont National Guard, detectives from the attorney general's office, parole officers, and advocates, and I shrunk with intimidation. I didn't understand what any of these people did or why their work sent them there. Everything was overwhelming.

When it was my turn, I quietly said, "My name is Anna Nasset. I'm a community member, and I don't know why I'm here other than to learn."

We broke into assigned groups and began working on charts on the walls. We were looking at victim journeys through the criminal justice system and examining how the victim may or may not be feeling. I saw myself everywhere in the chart; it was my roadmap. I stood in my blazer, the only one I owned, with the seasoned victim service professionals, not sure how to participate, certain I would sound like an idiot. We moved through the chart, and I listened with care.

The end of the chart was the point where sentencing has happened. The man next to me, Detective Ben Carver, in his pressed suit and lavender shirt, towered over me, intimidatingly tall, and he asked me, "What do you think a victim would be feeling in this moment?"

I looked at him blankly. He wanted to know my opinion. Did my voice even matter? I craned my head up to face him and said, "Well, I imagine if the sentencing was in the victim's favor, a sense of relief and celebration, but I don't think that would last long because they still have to face what happened to them despite a positive ruling. And wouldn't they also have a gnawing feeling of what happens when the offender serves their sentence and is released?"

He nodded his head and said, "Interesting. I hadn't thought of all the pain and fear—just the happiness of a strong conviction. Thanks for that!"

The rest of the two days flew by quicker than my pen could keep up. I sat in awe of the rock stars in the field who came to present. They were like celebrities to me, dark angels fighting to protect victims of unspeakable crimes across the state.

The second day, I switched tables and sat with Detective Carver and his partner at the attorney general's office, along with a few other women. I had mostly switched because there was a guy in the class who resembled Jeffrey, and I wanted my back to him, but also because Detective Carver was the first person whom I'd felt seen by, so damn it, we were going to be friends.

As the second day ended, I thanked Andrea, the coordinator of the class, for accepting me into the course and asked if we could meet for coffee and to talk career options. She agreed.

At the train depot coffee shop in Waterbury, I sat and nervously waited for Andrea. She arrived, seeping with kindness and straightforwardness, and we started talking. She asked me a few questions about my skill sets, and I explained graphic design, development, events, and marketing. I told her I wanted to do something that kept me in the shadows. I wanted to be the wing woman to an agency—someone they could lean on.

We continued our conversation, and she asked the questions that changed everything. "Why do you want to work in this field? Your background is so different. Why change now?" I stammered out a response, and she read right between the lines. "Why did you move to Vermont?" she asked, looking at me squarely.

I gulped, and the story spilled out over the next few minutes. When I stopped, she applauded my bravery and then reflected on how unique my situation was. She shared with me that most stalking victims aren't believed, that most know the person stalking them, that it isn't a crime that's taken seriously. Yes, I had experienced the negative response with the Vermont State Police, and this had taken years, but everything else was mostly positive. I took this new knowledge in, taking in my own privilege at the same moment. We continued to talk, and I learned.

Then, as we were winding down and finishing our cups of coffee, she said, "I think you should start a business offering the skill sets you have. That way, agencies that can't hire someone full time but desperately need your help can get it. Also, have you ever thought about public speaking?"

The first part I agreed with. The second, the public speaking, I laughed about and thought hell would need to freeze over seventeen times before I spoke publicly.

# PART FOUR

# FIGHT

# CHAPTER SEVENTEEN

# November 2017 – May 2018

**WHAT TO SAY**

"I believe you."

"I'm sorry this happened."

"I am here for you."

"You can tell me as much or as little as you want."

"It's not your fault."

"I'm glad you told me. I'm so proud of you."

"What can I do to support you?"

"I can stay with you tonight. Would that help?"

"Do you want me to go with you to the hospital or police station?"

Even with the best of intentions, "why" questions can sound accusatory and make survivors blame themselves.[20]

In the early morning, driving the winding roads of Route 100, I headed to Killington for a small day conference for victim service providers. Once again, the only friend I had in the room of hundreds was myself. Andrea had told me of this conference put on by the state of Vermont, and I was going to take on every educational opportunity I could. Plus, there was a session on stalking from the National Stalking Center.

Eager to learn about my own life and the things I had experienced, I settled into the training.

Noticing the guns and suits around me, I felt at ease by the presence of law enforcement. I know this is not necessarily normal and that I have privilege in being able to say this, but I felt protected. In that environment, I could let go of my constant concern about safety and be in the presence of learning.

After the presentation, I nervously walked up and went full "fangirl" on the trainer from the National Stalking Center. I will always remember her kindness toward my naïvety. She invited me to sit with her at lunch, and we began to talk. When she asked about my story in a measured and thoughtful way, I shared pieces, unsure of what to say, questioning whether it mattered, constantly apologizing for what Jeffrey had done to my life.

As lunch ended, she handed me her card and said I should think about speaking. *What is it with these people thinking I could be a speaker?* I thought as I tucked the golden ticket into my purse. I headed home in the dark, on high alert for the possible moose or deer, high on the knowledge I had gained, and elated over my one connection made.

Working in the service industry in Vermont has its odd advantages, the biggest perk being mud and stick season. These two seasons—when the snow melts and the state turns to mud and when the leaves fall, giving way to a barren landscape waiting for snow—are considered the off seasons. With these seasons comes an unwritten agreement amongst restaurants and inns to give their staff a break, and everything shutters for a few weeks in mid-April and mid-November. The other months of the year, you work so hard, there is no time to spend the money you make, and you tuck away a few dollars to get you through the closures.

November 2017, I found myself eager for stick season and excited to spend time with my mom in Ohio. Dolly and I packed up my dad's old car and headed down the road to home. As I drove along, I ruminated over the thought that you can have many homes without owning property. I existed in Ohio and Washington and was beginning to find home in Vermont as well. The roots in Vermont hadn't taken hold yet, but an idea had.

Once more settling into my childhood room, I grabbed my small journal, looked over the notes from the course I was taking, and began to jot down ideas for a business plan. I lingered over business names, writing list after list of words, pairing them together to see if my matchmaking skills worked.

I spent hours at the coffee shop, the same place where I had sat and worked when my father was still alive. The grief of his absence hit me as I lingered in the spaces of home once again. While planning my next step, I also stepped back in time, peering at my own timeline that had brought me to this moment and acknowledging the gnawing sadness and reality that if Dad hadn't died, I wouldn't have seen safety, I wouldn't have moved, and I wouldn't be sitting here now planning my next phase. His presence hung over me, and I leaned into its embrace instead of staying in the futile world of "what ifs."

● ● ●

*That fall day in 1991, while home from school, I chose to forgo* **The Price Is Right** *viewing and settled onto the couch of our family room with blankets and Lipton soup. Who was this bold woman on the TV? She was a commanding presence in her teal suit, sitting with her family lined up behind her and a tower of white men leering over her, asking her questions about pubic hair on Coke cans. I was transfixed.*

*Anita Hill didn't look like me, her bravery and poise in contrast to my eleven-year-old white self with feathered bangs and glasses. CSPAN held my rapt attention. More importantly, Anita held my breath. Never having seen a woman stand up and recount the problematic behavior of men in power, or anywhere for that matter, I knew I could trust her. Of course, the men questioning her would believe her and Clarence Thomas wouldn't be appointed!*

*After prayers with my mom as she tucked me into bed, I cried that night that Justice Thomas was appointed to the Supreme Court. At the age of eleven, I didn't know what the Supreme Court even did. I did know that they didn't believe Anita. She had stood up and spoken her truth.*

**Why didn't they believe her? Why did they put her through all of that just to not listen? Why should women stand up against men who hurt us if we aren't going to be heard? Will we be punished for telling the truth? Will I be brave enough to speak if something bad happens to me?** *I thought as I drifted into sleep.*

*Anita Hill was, is, and always will be my first and brightest hero.*

●     ●     ●

Finally, the list of words came together, and I felt satisfied with the pairing, Stand Up Resources, because I was finally standing up, and I wanted to provide resources to victim service providers and agencies. I wrote my mission statement, bought the domain name, and began to design a small site. Whatever journey my father's passing had sent me on, this piece felt the truest to my being. I had long said I would never own another business. I love when I prove myself wrong.

There was the continuous conversation with my mom, her urging me to move back to Ohio while I resisted. I could never fully put into words that while I loved my mom and the visits to my hometown, I needed to keep marching to my own drum, carving out life in small communities, taking the mountain climb instead of the straight, flat path. Our impasse grew into acceptance and promised trips of cross-country skiing and summer adventures. I packed up and headed home, full of ideas and excitement.

I worked at Tucker Hill on New Year's Eve, not telling anyone about my new business. I drove home well before midnight, toasted with Ellen and her girlfriend over the phone, and climbed into bed with Dolly. The next day, I launched my website and quietly opened my business.

At the next session of the Vermont Victim Assistance Academy, as I sat with Detective Carver and others, we started the session once again by going around the room and saying our name and who we worked for. This time, I said with confidence, "I'm Anna Nasset. I own Stand Up Resources, which provides marketing, design, and development for victim service agencies." It wasn't the same voice that I lost in 2011. It was different, tinged with fear and grief but strengthened in resiliency and knowledge. The sound of it was foreign to me. I chose to lean in.

The months rolled on, feet of snow grew on the ground, and Vermont became a winter playground. At Tucker Hill, I had taken on the job of bartender, and I stood at the ready for the mobs of people to fill the cozy barnwood-covered room. By day, I worked on business plans, reaching out to agencies in the state, trying to land my first client, and by night, I served drinks.

I studied my notes from the VVAA course and prepared to push myself over the ledge of comfort. Through conversation with Andrea, I had agreed to sit on a victim/survivor panel for our next VVAA session. Terrified, I drove to Montpelier and walked into the Vermont Network Against Domestic and Sexual Violence to meet the other panelists. I thought I would be looked down on and hear familiar phrases like, "It's just stalking—it's not that bad," but instead, I was embraced by my peers.

Afterward, I met Detective Carver for a drink, and I excitedly shared about the meeting. He encouraged me to submit to speak at a national conference for advocates and law enforcement. I laughed at him.

"I can do a ten-minute talk on a panel, but what would people learn from me presenting my story?" I asked.

He went on to explain how people in his field need to hear stories of success from survivors. It helps them learn best practices that they can implement into working with victims. He rattled off names of organizations that hosted such conferences, National Organization for Victim Assistance (NOVA), End Violence Against Women International (EVAWI), and many more. I jotted them down, went home, and noted that NOVA was currently accepting proposals for their conference. I threw together a proposal, as the deadline was the next day, and hit submit.

Shutting down my computer, I laughed. *This is ridiculous. There is no way they are going to accept me. My story isn't that important.* My normal mode of self-deprecation taking over, I headed to work at Tucker Hill.

I wrote and rewrote the ten-minute speech I would give to my classmates. I worked with the Vermont Network Against Domestic and Sexual Violence to help craft my story with educational points. I even met with a fellow panelist who had schizophrenia to ensure that when speaking about Jeffrey's mental health, I did so with care.

I poured everything into my speech, and looking at my own words, I began to make sense of my story. I peered back into the life loss, the crippling fear. Still, I couldn't make heads or tails of why I had agreed to speak. I talked it all through with my trusty companion, Dolly, and though she is a great listener, I had to find the answer myself.

At Tucker Hill, Kevin and Patti knew I was taking this course and would often ask "Why?" to which I would mumble some response. The day of my talk, I had already asked for the evening off, giving a fake plan because I didn't want to tell the truth of why I had moved to Vermont: fleeing Jeffrey. Though I was beginning to be vocal, I was still selective and wanted to keep the work I was pursuing private from the life I was living.

When I did choose to share my reasons for moving to Vermont, I was often asked if I knew or had heard of Sue Russell. Her name would frequently appear in the new circles I was working in with advocates and law enforcement. I did not know Sue but would quickly learn of her story, which had happened in the Mad River Valley nearly twenty-five years prior.

Sue had been out in town with friends, having drinks at The Smokehouse. When she'd left to go home, her car had gotten a flat tire. A man stopped to assist and offered to drive her home to where her husband waited. But the man did not drive her home. He instead drove her deep into the woods, sexually assaulted her, brutally beat her, and left her for dead. Sue survived and would turn our area and the country on its head as an advocate and speaker.

She and her husband relocated to New Zealand after the offender in her case served his twenty-one-year sentence. Though the Mad River Valley had shown up in monumental ways to protect her, she couldn't live there in peace and safety. Sue moved from the Mad River Valley shortly before I arrived. Within a few months of me hearing her name, we would become pen pals and sisters in survivorship, an unwritten bond tying us together.

———

Preparing this talk was also preparing me for what was to come with my own continued journey with the criminal justice system. After months of waiting, Detective Dropp was able to interview Jeffrey once he was moved to Jefferson County Jail. Jeffrey had been moved there to serve a one-year sentence for stalking another victim, and after Detective Dropp met with him, James informed me he wanted to take this case as far he could. He wanted to fight for me and the other victims, and he saw in me the strength to go the distance. Whatever James saw in me, something I had never seen when I looked in the mirror, I was willing to rise to the challenge.

He talked to me about the tedious process, the unknown and unlikely outcome, the months and months of work that lay ahead. He also informed me that he wouldn't file charges in this case until Jeffrey had served the sentence in Jefferson County Jail because, as soon as you file charges, the clock starts on time served. James wanted to give me and the others the longest amount of freedom possible. I was in.

Nervously sitting next to Detective Carver at our third session of the VVAA, I fiddled with the edges of my ten-minute talk; today was the day I would deliver it. Once again, we went around the room introducing ourselves, and when it came to me, I said, "My name is Anna Nasset. I'm the owner of Stand Up Resources, which provides design and development to victim service agencies, and I'm a survivor." Detective

Carver gave me the "smile and nod" look, not the pitying smile I had received from countless victim service providers over the years—a real, "you got this, and I'm proud of you" smile.

As we settled into the day of learning, the idea washed over me that people would learn from me that day. As I took my seat with the other panelists, I stared out at my classmates, many of whom were surprised when I sat down, and every edge of me hummed with nerves. I opened my mouth, and I shared my story for the first time. Just as five minutes changed my life forever, ten minutes of talking altered the course of my life again.

---

Vermont being one of the smallest states in population led to me meeting many people in the victim service field at a rapid pace. I said yes to any learning opportunity, began to learn about legislation that involved this field, and leaned into the time off that mud season provided to engage and get involved.

With mud season also came a swift, hit-you-over-the-head love. The kind you know won't last. At first, I resisted, knowing he was getting divorced. He was so kind, handsome with stocky stature and twinkling eyes, genuine in his questions and interest, and I thought, *To hell with it—why not try?*

But I also gave him my business card and said, "Go through my entire website. If you are still interested in me, let me know." I had just added an "about" section to my website and shared a few sentences of my story and how I came to Vermont. I figured that would run him off, but instead, he came over to my apartment a short time later, eyes filled with tears, and gave me a hug I melted into.

Our relationship included day trips around the state, evenings lingering over favorite meals, and coffee and chats long into the morning. It was the whirlwind I needed. I felt seen for the first time in years, and also, it was fun.

When not intertwined with my new beau, I kept up with my learning and worked to secure my first design or development client. I eagerly attended my first National Crime Victims' Rights Week ceremony, and this time when I walked into the room, I knew people—not well, but I was able to sit with my imposter syndrome amongst the staff of the Vermont Network.

I shook hands with the governor at the awards ceremony. I went to the capitol to hear testimony on gun laws and accepted the invite when Governor Scott signed the new gun legislation into law on the capitol steps while the NRA screamed and scared me. I purchased books, read articles, and checked my email to see if anyone wanted to hire me. My work email received one or two emails a day, mostly spam, but I knew one day I would see a work request.

I assumed the email in my inbox that late spring day was a newsletter from NOVA when I clicked on it. I had been glued to the TV that afternoon with the Cosby guilty verdict having just been given. My eyes were half on the TV and half on the email when I read, "You've been accepted to present at the annual NOVA conference in Florida." I dropped to my knees in tears, my body filled with shock, delight, fear, and adrenaline. Ten minutes at a table with peers was one thing; a ninety-minute session amongst strangers was very different.

On occasion, when I had the gallery, I would have to speak at a fundraiser or event, only for a few minutes, and that was a good thing because I was terrible. I'd talk too fast, mispronounce words, and jump around. "There is no way I can do this," I told myself.

I walked circles in my studio apartment for hours and texted the man I was dating. He burst into my apartment a short time later, gathered me in his arms, and congratulated me. "Grab your coat," he told me. "We are going to The Smokehouse to celebrate." To every person we ran into that evening, he proudly exclaimed, "She just got asked to speak at a national conference!" And I began to let his pride in me wash over me and find confidence in myself that yes, I could do this.

Spring rolled into summer, and I found myself writing my story and living it at the same time. Though charges wouldn't be filed for some time, there was still a lot of work to be done. I wrote my own affidavit while writing my speech. I drove thirty-five minutes to find fax machines in Montpelier to fax paperwork. I went to the Vermont State Police to have them witness the affidavit and was met again with the same disdain and disrespect I'd received the year prior. I walked out shaking my head, thinking, *There's some people who could use some training.*

Many trips with legal documents were made to Montpelier, and if Detective Carver was in the area, we'd meet for a coffee or cocktail. The support not only professionally but also emotionally when I was having to handle the legal aspects meant the world to me.

On a sunny May day, I attended the last session of the VVAA. This time, when asked to introduce myself, I said, "My name is Anna Nasset. I'm the owner of Stand Up Resources, which provides design and development to victim service agencies. I'm a survivor and apparently a speaker!"

Several classmates looked at me with a smile and a nod, and I beamed back. With my graduation certificate in hand, I walked out into the warm afternoon sun, pulled my most fabulous white sunglasses over my bright eyes, and forged into the unknown.

# CHAPTER EIGHTEEN

# June 2018 – January 2019

**Stalking cases can last a long time, and your loved one's reactions, wants, needs, and feelings might change over time.**

**Continue to check in and be a source of support. Ask questions like, "How can I help you feel safer?"**

**Ask the victim how they feel the safest being contacted and use that medium to contact them.**

**Some stalkers monitor victims' social media accounts, phones, and/or other forms of digital communication.**[21]

Have you ever known the moment a relationship was over? There is a sudden change in the way they look at you. The sparkle fades in an instant. I saw that happen. There were no fights, just his divorce and life catching him, and with that, he released me to see what else was out there in his new single world. I clung on tightly for the next few weeks as the relationship crashed down, a fading firework in the night sky.

I turned my tears into words and wrote my speech. Hundreds of Post-it notes on my all-in-one dining, office, and sewing table were put into order. Post-its of years past. I looked through the evidence piles

I had in the form of screenshots and messages, selecting to share the ones that didn't give the horrific vileness, choosing to not allow my story to be taken over by voyeurism. I became the superhero of my own summer, focusing on victims' rights by day and adult babysitting—aka bartending—by night.

One evening, as the last customers shuffled up to their room at Tucker Hill Inn with bellies full of delicious food and Lawson's beer, one of the waiters sat down for his shift drink. An older character, as hilarious as he was friendly, he plunked down onto the bar stool and said, "How's it going, Lady Luck?"

I laughed and said, "You have no idea how unlucky I am." After some prompting, I told him why I had moved to Vermont, explaining about Jeffrey. Other pieces of my past came up, and his compassionate shock held me.

Driving home, I thought, *How odd. When I do reveal my experiences, it's often to people I don't know that well and not the ones I'm close to, such as the owners of Tucker Hill, Kevin and Patti.* I fiddled in the discomfort of my seat, knowing I would soon have to share my truth. I needed to get the days off for the conference, but that could wait.

Having only had bad experiences with public speaking in the past and lacking the skills to feel confident about the future, I invited friends to a series of practice speeches. The first one was hosted by a friend at her yoga studio. While I don't do yoga, I was grateful to use her space. Mimi and others sat on pillows and yoga mats as I stood and told my story for the first time. With my laptop on the floor to share my slides, I nervously clicked and spoke.

Afterward, we sat in the weight of my words, sipping wine and reflecting, no one knowing what to do with my story. They knew what I had shared with them in the past but had never seen the enormity of it. That was all left in Washington and in the walls of my apartment. In my releasing my words, they began to see me to my fullest.

Looking into my glass of wine after a long shift, I sat in a booth with Kevin and Patti, chatting about service, gossiping about town, engaging in normal end-of-the-night banter. I gathered my wits and asked for a week in August off. "Just during the week, not the weekend," I explained.

Kevin and Patti looked at one another and then said, "Sure. Where you are heading?" When I explained I was going to Florida, Kevin commented, "Why the hell would you go to Florida in the summer?"

Before I knew it, the words spilled out, the truths, Jeffrey, moving—all of it tumbled out onto the wooden table. As I stopped to regain my breath, Kevin looked me in the eye, slammed his hands on the table, and exclaimed, "I knew it! I knew your story never added up. Patti, haven't I said that since we met her? It just didn't add up!"

I burst into laughter—we all did. It really was the reaction I needed in that moment. "Busted!" I said through my giggles. And I added two more supporters that night. My team was growing.

I would conduct a series of practice speeches at friends' houses. Small groups gathered to offer support and critiques. As my release continued, my being and sense of self became unveiled and clearer. In this opening to friends, I was unconsciously also preparing the team of support I would need in the year to follow and trial that would come. As my friend Sue Russell says, "The more who know, the safer you are." I would add to that—the more who know the safer AND more supported you are.

---

On my yearly pilgrimage to Maine, I didn't listen to my music or podcasts. Instead, I listened to myself. I had voice recorded myself speaking, and I listened over and over during the six-hour drive, pulling over on backroads to make notes.

I arrived at Missy's with bottles of rosé and a copy of my speech. Lingering in her garden, I began to share it with her but found myself stopping. Sharing with the newer people in my life was one thing; sharing with people I'd known for years became too painful, so I left her a copy to read on her own.

Emily, Missy, and I gathered once again for a weekend of salt water, wine, lobsters, and laughter. While we were sitting at an outdoor bar in Blue Hill, Emily's husband joined us ladies, and as we chatted about my upcoming conference, he looked at me with a perplexed gaze. He naïvely asked, "Wait, you are going to teach people how to stock shelves? I didn't know such a thing existed."

All three of us fell off our barstools laughing as his confused look grew. "No, not that kind of stocking," I replied before explaining the conference to him. It was a poignant moment of humor and how quiet I had been for years. Another team member of support was added that day, and I would need every one of them.

Throughout the summer, Jillian, my victim witness coordinator, would check in once a month or so to let me know I wasn't forgotten and they were still building the case. Occasionally, she'd even ask for help. I had reached out to Jillian and James about the NOVA conference, and I was fine to speak if I didn't share anything from the 2016 – 2017 messages that they were building the case on. I sent my whole speech to James, and he responded with this email:

"I just read your entire speech. I found it incredibly powerful. I have worked with victims of crime for many years now, but I have never actually been placed in a position where I was in their shoes and saw the world how they see it. But that is what your speech did to me.

"Do I have your permission to share it with my office? I think my coworkers would benefit from reading this.

"As to your question though—No. I don't see anything here that needs modification. Hell, I was thinking 'how do I get her to repeat this entire thing while on the witness stand?'

"I am sorry that life has thrown you this curveball, but what you are doing with it is inspiring, truly. I am now trying to think of venues in WA where you could come and share your story, though I fully understand that you might not want to come back here—yet."

I wept when I read it. Could this man whom I'd never met take this case the distance? It reinstalled my faith to keep with the case despite the lengthy delays.

•　　•　　•

*I was met with stares, awkwardness, and unintentionally invasive questions after my stint in the hospital following my suicide attempt. I walked in the fog of medication and embarrassment, well enough to be out but not well enough to fully grasp how dark I had gone.*

*I also sat in the acceptance that I had missed a lot of school and would require an extra semester to graduate. Meeting with my faculty advisor in the fine arts department, Professor Knapp, I sat a small shell, uncertain of what to do next.*

*Knapp, as we all referred to him, an equally brilliant and comical man, sat across from me. His eyes twinkled with concern, and he asked me, "Anna, what would you like to focus on? How can I support you in graduating?"*

*I looked at him and said, "I want to study women's art history and quilts and textiles—anything created by women."*

*He nodded his head and helped me create my own curriculum of women's art history. I began to make dresses, every one with the same silhouette, dress after dress. I took out my grandparents' typewriter and ran white cotton fabric through the old machine. Steadily, my story began to fall onto the fibers. I used the typed textile to line the dresses I created, and then I lovingly stitched them back together. Unless you knew of the lining inside, all you saw was a dress.*

*A semester later than my peers, I hung the dresses in the university gallery on a clothesline. Knapp and I stood back and smiled. I had found my way back to life.*

•　　•　　•

Though I retreated into the work of building the training, I found the world around me opening up with invites to relax on the river, meetups at The Mad Taco, birthday parties, and BBQs. Sure, I still had the annual panic attack requiring a paper bag and my neighbor Colby during the Fourth of July parade, but I had come to terms with that part of the day. I cautiously said "yes" to the invites, and one evening found me next door celebrating my neighbor's birthday. The theme being prom, I threw on an old gallery gala dress that had collected a bit of dust and headed over.

Walking into the kitchen, I noticed a mullet-clad man in a tutu gesticulating broadly to those he spoke with. I paused. I didn't know him, but I knew him. After reaching into my brain, it came to me. He had been the ringleader of the gaggle of friends bursting into The Smokehouse two years prior, right after I moved to Vermont. The ones who'd caused my eyes to mist up with homesickness as I watched them.

Soon enough we were introduced. "Hi, my name is Brian, but everyone calls me Mullet." *Well, that's on brand,* I thought, looking at his 1980's hairstyle. Once we started talking, we never stopped. There may as well have just been the two of us there that night.

Mullet used to live in the Mad River Valley but relocated to Boston, where he was getting a Master of Liberal Arts from Harvard and a law degree from Suffolk University at the same time. He was a former schoolteacher and had indeed had a mullet since he was ten years old.

I shared with him about my work, and he excitedly bobbed his head, locks of hair bouncing along, as I talked. He had to head home to Boston the next day, but we agreed to stay in touch and grab a drink next time he was in town. I walked home thinking to myself, *Is this my first friend who truly understands my work?* My team grew one person at a time, but in meeting Mullet that evening, my team grew exponentially.

NOVA loomed just a week away, and listening to my recorded voice, I hit the road for a night or two away with Tom. A month prior, he had let me know he would be in New Hampshire for a training session in the White Mountains and asked if I wanted to come stay with him. Obviously, I wasn't going to say no, despite Megan and Ellen rolling their eyes so hard I could hear it through the phone.

I settled into the old Thayer Inn in quaint Littleton, New Hampshire, and waited for his arrival, our reunion as sweet as ever. Over the next few days, as he attended training in the mountains with colleagues, I wrote. I sat at cafés and worked and reworked my speech and slides. During the evenings, over dinner with Tom and a colleague of his, I shared my day's adventure, and they shared theirs. Tom was the friend and support I needed before I embarked on my trip.

I returned to Waitsfield to give my last practice talk in the community room in the local church/community center. The local paper did a story about me, featuring a picture of Dolly and me smiling into the sun, and with that, my story went out to a wider audience than I could have imagined just four months previously.

The evening of the public practice session, I arrived early and began to set up chairs. *Twenty will be more than enough,* I thought. Tom was still in New Hampshire, so he couldn't get away to attend but would join me the next night after my shift at Tucker Hill.

Detective Carver came early, and I felt a deep air of protection settle over me when he entered. I saw him scan the room as others filed in—customers from Tucker Hill, friends, strangers, Patti, Kevin, and the entire staff filled the room. Detective Carter and I began to unfold more chairs. Others arrived, community members I didn't know, State Representative Maxine Grad, my therapist, more friends; the crowd grew to around forty-five. I stood at the podium, shaking, and began to talk. Looking out into the sea of faces and support, I soared.

Before I left for the airport a few days later, Tom presented me with a gift he had made me. Years ago, he had told me that when you said my name all at once, Annanasset, it sounded like a town on Long Island. He had made for me my very own model Long Island Rail Road train station, complete with the LIRR and blue and white station sign, identifying the stop as Annanasset. I squealed with glee and hugged him deeply for this thoughtful craftiness. We delighted in our farewell meal at The Pitcher Inn, and in the early hours, I put my suitcase in my car, headed to the airport, and flew into the unknown.

---

I always wanted to be an expert in something. I thought it would be American quilt history, but as I sat on the plane and a woman next to me asked where I was traveling to and why, I had a moment. I explained where I was going, and her eyes widened with excitement for me, as if I were an expert in the field of stalking, and I thought to myself, *Well it's not quilt history, but I guess it's where I'm needed!*

I still had no real idea why I was going to NOVA, if anyone would attend my session, or what would happen afterward. I had fundraised and gotten sponsorship just to make the trip. I wasn't being paid, and this was a costly endeavor, but the conversation with the woman on the plane gave me courage as I made my way to the hotel in downtown Jacksonville.

I settled into the hotel bar, eager to meet attendees and possible friends, and looked around me. The room was full of potential colleagues, and I felt terrified and alone. The memory from years ago, the loneliness I felt when first moving to Vermont, came to mind, and I pushed myself to make the most of the moment. My inner dialogue of self-doubt turned into a pep talk, so when the gentleman next to me introduced himself, I was up for a chat.

Daniel was there with the Army. Stationed in Germany, he worked as the head of the SHARP program over there. None of these things made sense to me, and I timidly asked, "What is SHARP?"

He kindly explained it's the Sexual Harassment/Assault Response Program, and there is an office on every base and an advocate in every unit. The look on my face must have said I had never heard of this, and he shared with me that NOVA is where SHARP advocates come for their educational credits. In an instant, I second-guessed my decision to come here. *Why would anybody in the military want to hear me speak? I have nothing to offer them.*

As our conversation continued and I shared that I was there to share my story, Daniel said, "Great! I'll bring you to Germany next year to speak."

My brain said, *That's ridiculous. He's just trying to sleep with you. None of this is real.* But I replied, "That would be awesome!" I left the conversation chuckling to myself. *Me working with the military in Germany? That's the most ridiculous thing I've ever heard.*

The only person I knew at the conference was a VVAA classmate from the Vermont National Guard. Even during our eight-month class, I couldn't figure out why members of the National Guard were there and was always too embarrassed to ask. But since I knew no one else in the sea of thousands, I reached out, and we set up a dinner with the other Vermont National Guard attendees and myself.

The awkwardness of forcing people to have dinner with me wore off, and I leaned into the new friendships and connections I was making from my state. We laughed, and they teased me over my choice of restaurants based solely on my need for scallop crudo. "Next year, we'll pick the place," they said. *Next year—that would be nice,* I thought, a small smile on my face.

Over the days leading up to my session, I would attend other sessions on victims' rights, advocacy services, and prosecution, wanting to learn as much as I could. I sat in the second row as Tarana Burke delivered her keynote address to the thousands of attendees. Tears streaming down my face, I listened to her words of wisdom as she spoke of founding the #metoo movement and the strength of survivors.

I made other friends, including a woman from Ohio with quick wit and fabulous style. Others who recognized my face from the picture on the conference app befriended me over drinks. I also met the woman who helped run VINElink, the app I had used for years, and fangirled over their work. I'm sure they are still laughing years later. I dutifully handed out my business cards and told those I met about my session, mentally pleading for them to attend, fearing no one would show.

Then, I located the room I would speak in and counted about seventy-five seats. *If even half of them fill up, that will be great.*

Torrential rain streamed down my hotel windows the day of my speech. "This Girl Is on Fire" played from my phone as I bowed over the porcelain throne, emptying my stomach contents. Fear and nerves took over as I called Ellen for the seven-thousandth time. I texted with Detective Carver, Mimi, Megan, and others.

When I checked the conference app again to make sure my session hadn't been canceled, I noticed the room I was to present in had been changed. After a quick brush of my teeth, I headed down the elevator and to the help desk. They explained that there were so many people pre-signed up for my training they had to move me to a bigger room, the biggest room they had for a break-out session. Shocked and numb, I returned to my room to continue my friendship with the toilet and take my freak-out to the next level—and, of course, play "Eye of the Tiger."

The three-hundred seats in the room were filled fifteen minutes before I began to speak, and the door monitors had to turn people away. The faces of the few friends I had made were there, but the vast majority were strangers with encouraging looks on their faces, eager to hear what I had to say.

I stood behind the podium, knees buckling, clutching my sweat-stained speech, and began to speak. The next seventy-five minutes roared past me as if it had been seventy-five seconds. I wound down the time with the fact that this was an ongoing case, and legally, I couldn't continue. I finished with this:

"That was a changing point for me because if this is a part of my life, what am I going to do with my life? I could change my name, live in the shadows. But that's not me, and I'm guessing you can tell that isn't part of my personality after this last hour and a half. As I like to say, I'm Anna Fucking Nasset. No one can take that."

People immediately jumped to their feet and clapped. The tidal wave of support knocked me backward, and I leaned on the podium for support, my eyes filled with tears, and the biggest smile spreading across my face.

Their questions to follow were insightful, not picking into my story but instead asking questions about how they could all better work with victims of crime. They were looking to understand how to respond to stalking, commending the response of the multidisciplinary team I had created around me, asking how I found the stamina to continue the fight toward justice knowing it may never be served. Military leaders, university program leaders, state advocates, prosecutors, and more wanted to know my opinion. They had *learned* from me.

Everything changed after that, and over the next few days, I fielded a barrage of questions and comments whenever I left my hotel room. Two women asked for selfies with me in the bathroom, and at the escalators, I was greeted by nervous women sharing their stories of stalking. I hid at the pool with my new friend and celebrated my speech at the rooftop bar with other new friends. Everywhere I went at the hotel, I would hear people say, "That's the woman who did the stalking talk" to their colleagues, or "Way to go—you are a badass." I soaked it in and hated it at the same time. I don't know what I was expecting to come out of the conference; I still hadn't wrapped my head around it other than to hope my story could serve others.

---

I was bartending by night, but during the day, my inbox began to fill with requests to speak at various places around the country, from the University of Toledo to the Connecticut National Guard. My Ohio friend hooked me up with Walsh College, a customer at Tucker Hill connected me with Norwich University, and I explored other opportunities as well. In turn, I Googled, "how to be a public speaker" and did my research at a rapid pace, in real time, as I replied to and accepted invite after invite. I booked a gig in Washington with Joint Base Lewis-McChord for a conference—then called Megan and Ellen screaming! The earth shook under our feet as we jumped for joy in unison thousands of miles apart. And then, yes, Daniel from the bar came through, because not all men have a sexual agenda, and invited me to travel to Germany and speak.

I bought a paper calendar and penciled in the dates of travel, my days filling fast. I also contracted with a few design clients. Mapping out the next months, I began to think, *Could I do this full time?* I mulled over that concept, staring out over the bar as I served drinks. Looking at the smiling faces, it dawned on me—if I hadn't worked in the service industry, if I hadn't bartended, I would have never been able to become a speaker. The skills I had gained in holding court night after night, laughing and talking over drinks and meals served, had taken me to this point of no return. Stick season fast approaching, I eagerly awaited the quietness and barren landscape, knowing it would reveal my next step.

Mullet and I had been messaging, and when he came up for Thanksgiving, I eagerly met him at The Mad Taco. Just as he had entered The Smokehouse years prior, the room erupted with greetings when he walked in—greetings similar to those I had received at NOVA. This man was a legend in the Valley, I quickly realized.

As we settled instantly into deep conversation, the crowded room full of shouts and chats faded around us. I told him about NOVA, and he shared with me about his thesis on police brutality. We would spend the rest of the weekend together, neither of us realizing we had been on a date that first evening at The Mad Taco.

He pursued me with a zeal I had never experienced, and within a week, I made the terrifying drive to his place in Cambridge for the weekend. Did we sneak Dolly in to see the Gutenberg at the Harvard Library? Absolutely! Feast seaside on oysters and rolls? For sure. Walk the historic paths of Harvard campus and enjoy cocktails at fabulous bars? One hundred percent. But by the weekend's end, I found myself backing away, overwhelmed by his excitement of what could be for our relationship.

Back in Waitsfield, I found myself connecting with another man, Jared. He and I had awkwardly run into each other over the years, and I had a hidden crush on him. A loud yet caring curmudgeon, he was someone I didn't know a lot about, but he always smiled when I saw him.

When he called to ask me out, I accepted. I'm not one to date two men at once, and I shared with both my quandary. Did I choose Mullet, who lived in Boston and who, yes, had many shared interests but also had an intensely energetic personality that was far too similar to mine? Or did I choose Jared, the highly intelligent and hilarious man who lived in the Valley yet clearly had a dark side and harbored hidden pain?

I chose Jared. We celebrated Christmas/Hannukah together with champagne, a hot tub, and a rack of lamb. A week later, New Year's Eve, was my last shift at Tucker Hill Inn. I was going to Stand Up full time.

# CHAPTER NINETEEN

# January 2019 – July 2019

Considering that stalking cases pose unique challenges to prosecutors, less is known about the circumstances in which prosecutors do pursue stalking charges. It is important to understand the decisions made by prosecutors, in particular, because of their central role in advancing cases through the criminal justice system via the charging decision.[22]

More than half of states classify stalking as a felony upon the second or subsequent offense or when the crime involves aggravating factors.[23]

During my days of research and learning, I discovered that stalking victims get a whole month. January is Stalking Awareness Month, and I jumped into my new work, eager to participate and learn.

I traced the founding of Stalking Awareness Month back to its origins and the work of Debbie Riddle. January 18, 2003, Debbie's sister, Peggy Klinke, was murdered by a former partner of hers who had stalked her and caused her to relocate across the country. He tracked her down and murdered her. Debbie, in her grief and pain, got to work to raise awareness about stalking and founded National Stalking Awareness Month, which would be signed into law in 2011 by now President Joe Biden and Senator Orrin Hatch (R-UT). On a whim, I reached out to Debbie and thanked her for her work because it very much may have saved my life. We began an email correspondence that continues to this day.

I wondered how I could create more change in my own state and reached out to State Representative Maxine Grad. She assisted me in contacting the governor's office, and in late January, we would have the House and Senate pass a resolution honoring National Stalking Awareness Month as well as have Governor Scott sign a proclamation. I was off and running.

But before that exciting day, I was going home, and with a quiet stillness, I boarded my flight to Seattle. I had not been back to Port Townsend since Jeffrey's messages in 2016, and I was ready to return.

Tears filled my eyes as the city of Seattle came into view. We soared over the Space Needle and the waters of the Puget Sound, my Olympic mountains hanging in the background. Before I could even blink, I was on the ferry once more, not sobbing this time, sporting a wide grin, breathing in my safety and the heavy Pacific Northwest air, lingering over my corn dog (the only time you can eat one is the on the ferry, according to Megan). My old pal Kyle met me at the ferry terminal, and off we went. The looming firs gave way to the clear sign I was back: the Hood Canal Bridge. The hour drive flew by, and he delivered me, suitcase and all, to the Port Townsend Brewery for my friendunion.

Everyone—except Ellen, who was on her way—was there as I entered, and I hugged each person with a clinging embrace. I noted to myself how bright it was in the small pub, wondering if they had changed their bulbs to a higher wattage.

When Ellen burst through the door, the Red Sea parted, everyone knowing better than to stand in our way. Colliding together in laughter and hugs, our quick-paced conversation amplified by our excitement of being together, we had nothing and everything to catch up on. Ellen and I generally spent three hours a week on the phone, so there was no news to report at our in-person meeting, just the tender love of friendship.

With Jeffrey still in jail, I settled into Port Townsend, the first time in eight years I was able to be there safely. I wanted to see and do everything. I popped by the coffee shop at the Northwest Maritime Center the next morning for a cup of coffee with dear friends, and walking in, I thought, *They changed their lighting as well—it's brighter.* Was there some strange community initiative Ellen had neglected to mention about higher wattage bulbs to beat the gray Pacific Northwest away? *That's ridiculous,* I said to myself as I hugged friends and community members tightly.

Stopping to see the fellas at Edensaw, another great reunion, I noticed the lights were once again brighter. Not connecting the dots yet, I pushed the thought aside and began chatting with my guys and former colleagues.

Afterward, safety not at the forefront of my mind for once, I stopped to sit in my beloved boatyard, with emerald waves lapping on the shore and a storm moving overhead, filling the sky with darkness. When the storm passed, a bright sky sparkled on the horizon line, golden against the deep gray clouds. I gasped at the gold and at the brightness as I realized no one had changed their light bulbs—with me safely coming back, everything in Port Townsend physically appeared brighter to me. I took in how dark my years had been and mourned that time. Then, I threw my car in reverse and headed to the courthouse one more time, climbing into the towering building on the hill.

*Prosecutor James Kennedy is a tall, awkward man,* I noted upon meeting him. We had corresponded for over a year about the case but never met in person, and I was grateful for the time he'd carved out to meet with me. James had recently been elected as the lead prosecuting attorney in Jefferson County, and in doing so, he'd moved from the Clallam County Courthouse back to Port Townsend. When he'd initially shared this news with me the year prior, I'd felt deflated until he told me, "I have petitioned the courts to keep this case, and they have allowed it." My case was the only one he kept when he moved on to his new job. That's how seriously he took it and how seen I felt. Another prosecutor from Clallam worked alongside him—Steve Johnson, whom I would not meet until the trial.

James's office was located on the top floor of the courthouse and had the only stairwell that led into the clock tower on top of the building, the tallest lookout point in the town. We sat down at a high table and began to talk. He showed me a large legal book of the Sentencing Reform Act and cautioned me about the possibility of Jeffrey only getting a year or two unless we could file for aggravated felony stalking. He showed me his case files, asked me questions, and never once looked down on me. He met me as an equal.

While in the meeting, my old advocate came in. The sad grin that I had received so many times was replaced with an earnest and encouraging smile. An officer I knew popped in on another matter, and the same happened—there was no pity. It had been replaced with joyful confidence upon seeing me. Each person's reaction to my presence gave me strength and empowerment to keep up with this arduous journey.

After a long meeting and strategy session, James looked at his watch and said, "Do you want to go into the clock? It's about to strike noon."

I replied, "Hell yes, I do." Though this was our first in-person meeting, one of the things I most admired and responded to from James and the rest of the team was how they just let me be me and how their personalities aligned with mine. I didn't need to put on a demure professional act; I could simply be myself.

While climbing the towering staircase inside the clock tower, we chatted. My former advocate joined us too, though they wouldn't be my advocate for the trial (different counties). We three were linked, and it was a perfect bonding exercise.

Below the clock face were a series of windows where you could gaze out over the entirety of the area, its beauty smashing me in the face with each gust of wind, cleansing me of the past and renewing my soul for what lay ahead. Into the clock face, we entered, the clicks and whirls of the old mechanics leading me to believe Julie Andrews and Dick Van Dyke may pop out to perform at any moment, and I marveled with ecstatic glee.

James warned us, "Get ready," as the first BONG sounded. BONG, BONG, BONG, BONG, BONG, BONG, BONG, BONG, BONG, BONG, BONG. The sound filled my cells, reset my nerves, brought tears to my eyes. I looked at the two men before me. They had just taken me to the highest point. Could I soar even higher? I would damn sure try.

A few days later, after all the visits and love had filled my cup—I even went to see my old hair stylist for a fresh do—I headed to Joint Base Lewis-McChord for my first ever on-base speaking engagement. Helicopters flew over, tanks drove down the streets in between vehicles, and I took in every bit of it with awe and wonder. Service to others being my goal in speaking, it dawned on me that I could also serve my country through this work. I spoke to a room full of military advocates and community-based advocates, sharing my story once more, lingering over the moment and experience. *Would this be a typical day for me?* I marveled.

Afterward, I headed toward the Hood Canal in an old Four Runner borrowed from Megan. I was on tour. The drive led me to a small casino for a conference of advocates and law enforcement, and there, I would see a few old friends once more—Officer Corrigan and Judge Landes. Corrigan had agreed to speak with me, and Judge Landes, now retired, had come to support us. We sat at the casino restaurant that night, three unlikely friends, and caught up. Just like in the clock tower, I felt stronger than I ever knew I could feel in their presence.

At the conference, I would also meet, for the first time, Jillian, my victim witness coordinator. She and I had traded countless emails and phone calls, and we finally stood face to face. Just being able to meet this woman who would take me to the finish line, whatever it looked like, settled my soul.

Every time I speak, the time flies by, and that day was no different. I leaned into the support of those in the room who had gone so far with me. When the speech was done, I hopped into the borrowed rig and continued my drive, THE drive I had done with Tom so many times before. I drove right past Tom's road; he was overseas, but I reflected on my fond memories of my unlikely dear friendship. He was delighted by my work with the military and shared stories of his time at Joint Base Lewis-McChord through email. I stopped at Anna's Bay, taking in the coastal pastures and roaring mountains. I treated myself to oysters at the Hama Hama and to a big burger dip and new sweatshirt at The Geoduck, Tom's presence with me even if he wasn't. Finally, I ended my two-day speaking tour at Megan's new house in Brinnon for one last night of laughter and friendship.

---

I was home for only a few days before Jared met me in Montpelier for my day at the capitol. Having no real idea what I was doing, I didn't think to invite the media and instead invited Andrea from the Vermont Center for Crime Victim Services and Karen, the executive director of the Vermont Network, to accompany me to the governor's office and proclamation signing.

As I shook with nerves, Governor Phil Scott walked in and greeted me warmly. Our small group sat at the large table, and he began to talk directly to me. Asking me about the crime committed against me and discussing with me the debilitating effects of stalking, he took time and consideration to let me know I was heard and seen. He signed the proclamation and then handed to me the pen he used. I held tightly to this object. The proclamation, no different than my lifetime protection order, may be just a piece of paper, but to me, it's a symbol of being seen and believed.

● ● ●

*September 1, 2009, I didn't know that Jeffrey lived in the shadows ready to pounce. All I knew was that I would buy my dream that day—my art gallery. Carson and I awoke with excitement for the future that lay before us. With my newly cut hair, severe with straight bangs across my forehead, and a "gallerista" outfit on my body, I was dressed for the confidence I did not have. That day, I would sign the papers, hand over the large check I had procured from a private investor, and in turn, be given the keys to MY gallery. I delighted in my first sale, a pair of earrings to a friend, and as my girlfriend rolled into my new world, we toasted and danced the night away. There is a photo, taken from outside the gallery, that shows us all joyfully dancing in the sparkly gallery.*

*My mind tends to linger over the past trauma and dates marked with pain, the personal anniversaries of grief and abuse. I privately mark those dates each year, moving into the space I need to support myself and grieve. Those painful anniversaries needed to combat the positive moments, the triumphs, the personal wins.*

*Little did I know what or, more aptly, who may have also been outside the gallery that night. Jeffrey may very well have been lurking on the street, watching my new world unfold, but that matters not. Through all the loss, change, and critiques, I can now look back on the evening I accomplished my dream and beam with pride once more.*

●　　●　　●

That afternoon, a friend joined me as the House and Senate passed a resolution to honor National Stalking Awareness Month, and as every voice said, "Aye," chills covered my body. Representative Maxine Grad read the resolution and then spoke of me and asked me to stand. Elected leaders clapped as I rose, and their applause would follow me in the months to come. I tucked their claps away in my mind; I'd remember them when I needed the strength and courage to soldier on. Afterward, we met Detective Carver for a celebratory drink, and I saw the pride and joy in his eyes.

In the span of one week, I had been with my Washington people who had built and supported me to this point and then returned to Vermont surrounded by the people who had unknowingly picked me up and carried me to the next phase. It was profound in its power.

Not all speaking engagements go as planned, I quickly learned. I had a three-part tour in Ohio that I hit the road for, Dolly by my side. We drove the familiar roads once more in the frigid January air. Excited to see my mom and to show her what I could do, I had invited her and her friends to hear me speak at Ohio Wesleyan University, the college in my hometown.

The night of the event, I was a bundle of nerves, knowing the people I knew and loved would hear my story in raw reality. My hosts at the college had hung posters and promoted the event, but the people I knew outnumbered the students, and I felt embarrassed for myself and my mom. If only they could have seen what I had done at other venues. Nonetheless, I gathered my wits and did my best despite the meager audience, omitting certain parts that I knew would be too upsetting to my mom. My speech was met with a great reception, but I walked away feeling deflated.

That feeling would continue when, the next day, both the University of Toledo and Walsh University had to postpone. Temperatures had dipped well below zero, and all classes and events had been canceled for the next few days. While I was delighted to see my mom and friends, the old familiar feeling of failure, the blanket of self-doubt I curled under, surrounded me as I hit the road and journeyed back to Vermont.

Winter began to ebb away, my Ohio speaking engagements were rebooked, and charges were filed against Jeffrey in March, as he had served his time at Jefferson County Jail and was relocated to Clallam County Jail. The fears and unknowns filled my body once more, and I took to my stacks of quilts and *Gilmore Girls*. Or, if I was at Jared's house, I spent countless hours watching *Say Yes to the Dress*, not because I wanted to get married but because I liked to critique and make fun of the brides and their ridiculous choices or cheer for the ones who had endured hardships.

Jared and I journeyed to Portland, Maine, for a concert, and upon entering the venue, I found myself immediately seeking out all emergency exits, unable to enjoy the music, wondering if there was a stalker or mass shooter there. My body pushed into high alert once again, I couldn't find the words to express my fears, and Jared took them to be irrational.

The weeks rolled on, and with them, a tidal wave of hearings out in Clallam County. Thousands of miles away, I would sit staring at my phone in the evening hours, waiting for Jillian, my victim witness coordinator, to call and inform me of what had happened at the latest hearings. This wasn't my first rodeo, but the stakes felt significantly higher with the aggravated felony stalking and felony cyberstalking charges. Jillian would call and inform me of the news: Jeffrey wanted to defend himself, and they were trying to stop that from happening. Or Jeffrey had threatened his court-appointed lawyer, competency evaluations were required, the list went on and on.

After every call, Jillian would email me what she had just told me. She had asked me in the beginning how I wanted to be communicated with, and after years of dealing with these processes, I knew what my brain could compute and couldn't. I was grateful for the extra steps she took and proud that I had finally learned how to fully advocate for myself and my needs.

I visited my sister and her family when I went to speak at my rebooked gigs for the University of Toledo and Walsh College. Her newborn baby snuggled into my arms, and I marveled at her tiny presence, relishing in my auntie role and saddened by the remembrance that I would never be a mother.

That evening, when the phone rang, I slipped out the front door to talk to Jillian privately, not wanting my sister's five children to hear the adult content. Jillian's voice was heavy as she informed me that the court had decided to let Jeffrey defend himself. It was his right to do so, and we had to prepare for the hellscape to come.

After the call, I breathed into the night air, gasping in fear of the face-off we would have, and then brushed the tears away, painted a smile on my face, and walked back inside to the gaggle of little ones eager to play. Carrie and her husband could see through my false smile, and I just shook my head "no" as if to say, "we cannot discuss this right now."

Not having children had given me the gift of processing much of this in whatever way I needed. Seeing the faces of Carrie's kids, I thought of the millions of people who did not have the fortune I did and had to continuously live in debilitating fear while also protecting their children. That moment changed the way I would speak moving forward—changed the data and facts I would share. It would push me to continuously step outside of my story and share my experience from a place of acknowledging the millions of people suffering in silence and fear. My story is not my own; it is a story for any stalking victim.

Another milestone month lay before me—April, Sexual Assault Awareness Month—and with it, I was going big. My pen pal, Sue Russell, and I wrote an op-ed for our local paper, talking about the importance of this month and connecting our two stories from thousands of miles away. A speech for the Connecticut National Guard, a conference in Kansas, a keynote for the Vermont Crime Victims' Rights Week ceremony, and then Germany, because yes, my friend from NOVA had been true to his word.

In preparing for the keynote, I met with my friend Andrea once again. Our journey together had started only eighteen months prior at the coffee shop where she'd asked me if I would ever consider speaking, and now we sat in her office discussing me giving a keynote address. During our conversation, I shared with her the up-to-date news of the trial. Andrea being Andrea, she once again asked the right questions, inquiring whether I had an advocate and support systems in Vermont. I looked at her, confused, saying, "Well, no, the case is all out in Washington. I didn't think anyone from Vermont could work with me." The kind educator that she is, she mentioned Amy Farr, a legendary advocate, and suggested perhaps I should speak with her.

Amy, an advocate for the attorney general's office, had presented on my first day of class at the VVAA the year prior. I don't fangirl over celebrities, but Amy was a rock star in my eyes, and I couldn't believe she would even consider working with me. At the ceremony, shortly before I gave my keynote, we were introduced by Andrea. I shyly said hello, and she gave me her card to set up a meeting. Then, I walked onto the stage and spoke.

Trial dates were set and pushed back a multitude of times. The first trial date had been set for the end of April and thankfully was moved to June, when I would be heading to Germany and then enjoying a five-day layover in Portugal. Until speaking, I had never traveled alone other than to see family, and stepping onto the plane in Boston, a bundle of excitement and nerves, I took off into the unknown.

The trip was incredible—the military bases, the landscape, the language, the food. My hosts were my road trip companions as we drove the German landscape. They kept me laughing and at peace. Even as we sped down the Autobahn, something that would have induced a panic attack just months prior, I felt cared for and safe.

I shared my story and received my first challenge coin from the Army general who attended my session. These coins, given by military leadership, are a symbol of unity, service, and honor to those who receive them, and they are rarely given to civilians. I drank in the once-in-a-lifetime experience before taking off to Portugal.

I chose Portugal because it was cheap, and I had always wanted to walk the cobblestoned streets of Lisbon. I spent hours finding the best lodging for my budget. I wanted to be upstairs so no one could break in, be in a safe neighborhood, and hopefully have a view. My research paid off with a spectacular panoramic view of the city. It was lonely at first, eating alone at a restaurant as a female. One night, the waiter forgot I was there as I sat at an outside table. However, it was also empowering as I mapped out my days. I would quickly meet other women alone in Lisbon, and we would plan activities together, unlikely friendships blossoming.

The trip was a breath of air, perhaps my last. I knew what I'd have to face when I returned, and I took my time in Europe, filled with gratitude for the life I had begun to create on my own terms after living on Jeffrey's terms for so long. I came back to Vermont ready to take on what lay ahead.

With each hearing, each court delay, each day, I waited to find out what would happen to my life. Jeffrey received another misdemeanor charge, as he had been sending letters about me to the prosecutor's office with false claims of our sexual relationship, claiming he'd had celestial sex with me while in prison and that I had participated. The prosecutor on that case never even called me. I found out about it through Steve, the prosecutor assisting James, and when the case was heard, because the assigned prosecutor had done little work to prepare, Jeffrey was sentenced to ninety days with thirty suspended. In all my unluckiness for having Jeffrey choose to stalk me, I count my fortunes for the prosecutors who have walked alongside me and not seen me as a faceless victim.

With summer came more speeches, more design jobs, a sponsorship for a podcast on crime victim services, meetings with advocate Amy about my case, my annual panic attack at the Warren Fourth of July parade, and a trip to Maine where we would gather to celebrate Missy's wedding. All the while, a cloud of uncertainty hung over me.

In July, the court date for the trial was set for August, and everyone felt confident it would stick. With that news, I boarded a plane for Phoenix to speak at my second NOVA conference.

# CHAPTER TWENTY

# August 2019

**Stalking behaviors can arise in a wide range of court cases, including domestic violence, sexual assault, protection orders, custody, divorce, child welfare, employment, human trafficking, and immigration cases as well as other family, civil, or criminal court matters. Many crimes frequently co-occur with stalking, including trespassing, burglary, computer crimes, nonconsensual distribution of intimate images, vandalism, threats of bodily harm, voyeurism, and witness intimidation.**[24]

One year after my first conference, I wasn't sitting alone at the bar eating. Every meal was booked with friends from the previous year. I had the Vermont National Guard dinner to look forward to, VINElink had invited me to dinner, there were countless people who wanted to work with me, and I reconnected the greatest of them all...LEA! She was also there speaking, and we planned our dinner and sleepover with glee. I met nationally known advocate Anne Seymour and sat poolside with friends. I had found my people, the world I was meant to work and walk in, and I needed the connection as the trial loomed a few weeks away.

Lea and I met in a movie montage embrace. We hadn't seen each other in two years, and we had much to discuss. Not only were we dear friends, but we were also now colleagues of sorts in our adjacent fields, and she had postponed her departure by a day to hear me speak.

The day of my speech, I was once again placed in the largest break-out room, and it was filled to capacity, with many being turned away. Taking the knowledge I had learned over the last year, my speech was different, more inclusive. Comparing and contrasting the experiences of domestic violence victims, it went outside of what I had experienced and brought in the countless voices of stalking victims throughout the world. I worked to teach professionals how to empower and understand all victims through their advocacy.

When my talk concluded, so did my time with Lea, as she had to catch her flight. I returned to my room a few hours later and found this note from her:

"Anna, you are a powerhouse of amazing. You hold and share your story with so much clarity, dignity, and poise. I am so fucking proud to call you a friend. I'm probably going to quietly weep the rest of the day, in awe of your resilience and courage. I love you. Love, Lea"

It would be the first of many notes and quotes from friends I would hang on my wall at home to guide me through the coming weeks.

I had extended my trip to Phoenix, and as the conference ended, I was picked up by one of my oldest and dearest friends, Emily. We had just seen each other in Maine at Missy's wedding a few weeks earlier, and I couldn't wait to continue the connection and fun by visiting her and her family, as they now lived in the Phoenix area.

The oppressive heat didn't matter as we sipped our milkshakes and stopped at World Market on our way to the evening's adventure. In the car, I scanned through my emails and saw one from James. I clicked on it as the conversation and laughter flowed around me and read the following words:

"Here we go—I know this will not be easy and I encourage you to have an advocate with you as you go through this, at least the first time.

I apologize if these questions are confusing, this is one of the most complex direct examinations I have ever written, it covers a lot of territory."

My stomach turned as I read the lengthy email and saw the direct examination, the questions James would be asking me, attached at the bottom.

James ended his email with this apology and caveat:

"Ok, now that is out of the way. Take your time, there is a lot here. Please touch base with me next week. I know this is going to be painful and I wouldn't ask you to have to do this if it wasn't absolutely necessary."

I leaned on his compassionate words, followed his instructions to not click on the direct examination, and closed my email. The anticipation of what questions were in there flowed from my mind into my nerve endings. I walked to the restroom in World Market to get sick, then returned to the car quietly. This continued well into the night. I told Emily what I had received and felt the support of her family. Emily and her husband are two of the funniest people I have ever met, and their boys are a reflection of them. The laughter and jokes and quirky quick-witted conversation was the salve I needed.

The next morning, Emily and I took off for Sedona to do a "short hike" to Devil's Bridge. I don't hike, but I was up for the adventure, and she promised it was a half mile in and a half mile out. She's a damn liar! In 105-degree heat, each of us carrying a small plastic water bottle, we took off up the red sand path, climbing in elevation, scrambling over rocks, pulling ourselves up higher and higher. We noted that the trail was clearly longer than her promised half mile and would later discover it was four miles round trip. Red dirt sticking to our sweaty skin, we hiked on, not knowing where the Devil was leading us but continuing with the journey.

Reaching Devil's Bridge, I stood in awe of the expanse filling my vision and of what my body had done, the red mountains surrounding us and the piercing blue sky contrasting against them. In that moment, having done something so out of my comfort zone, I knew I had the strength to climb my highest mountain—the trial—and stand tall.

I returned to Vermont to take on my new full-time job: preparing for trial.

---

Amy had set up several three-hour preparatory meetings with me. She would later share she was certain we wouldn't need such long sessions, but she set the time aside regardless, and we ended up needing every minute. The drive to Montpelier for the first one to go over the direct examination, which I had not opened per James's advice, was terrifying.

Detective Carver had suggested we meet for coffee before, and sitting in the warm sun, I shared with him about NOVA, and he asked me how I was feeling. As coffee wound down and we got up for me to head to my meeting, he offered to escort me to Amy's office. My protector and friend, he did this for me every time I came for trial prep, knowing, more than I did, that I needed to be delivered or I may run for the hills and never return.

Over the next two weeks—that's all the time we had—Amy coached me on where to look, advising me to focus on James, the judge, the jury, and my friends during the trial. She taught me how to pause when there was an objection and to sit in the uncomfortable silence. She educated me on how to respond, to allow emotion in but hold to the clear and concise answer. She encouraged me to think about what I would need in the witness stand, urging me to find a small stone on the beach in Port Townsend to hold onto and describing how to ground myself in the chaos.

We went over the direct examination many times. I even dressed in court clothing for each meeting, wanting to practice what it would feel like to be in the courtroom. I talked to her about how I didn't think I could get on the plane alone. I didn't know how I would physically do it. She suggested making playlists to support and center me and to reach out in a larger way for support from my community and friends.

Taking Amy's words into account, I sat down and, for the first time ever, made a public Facebook post. I wrote that I would be coming to Washington, explaining that it was not for a good reason, and asked people if they saw me around to offer support and not ask too many questions. I shared that I was coming to testify against Jeffrey. The outpouring of support from across the country was staggering, with many people in Port Townsend stating they had no idea I had endured this for all these years. My community in Vermont began to offer smiles and a shoulder squeeze when they saw me in town.

In those moments, it begged the question, *What if I had just shared with my community from the very beginning? Would the outcome be different? Would I still have my gallery and live in Port Townsend?* These questions of the past do not serve us, only shame us, and I worked to hold them at bay.

I asked for songs to create my playlists. I wanted songs to amp me up and songs to center me. The Facebook world didn't disappoint, and creating the playlists was a fun and loving distraction. I named my one to get me fired up, "Power Play," and the one to calm me down "Stacks of Quilts." They continue to be my favorite playlists to this day, cherished gifts of song from countless people.

Closer and closer the date appeared. There were evenings of lengthy phone calls with James, and dinner plans changed as the conversations continued. One evening, Jared and I met Mimi and Colby at The Mad Taco, and while I sat at a picnic table in the afternoon sun, I got a call from Clallam County Prosecuting Attorney's Office. They needed to purchase my plane ticket for the trial. I moved away from our picnic table and to the side of the building, and the person on the other line helped me select my flight and sent me the confirmation. In that moment, all of the preparation, the unknown, the looming fears became a very clear reality, and I returned to the table shaking and afraid. I shared quietly with my friends as others laughed and joked around us.

At the last session with Amy before I left for Washington, she had a lawyer from the attorney general's office set up to run through the entire direct examination with me while she coached. I put on the blue dress I had purchased for the trial, a dark navy button-down dress with a dress shirt collar. It was sleeveless, which I did on purpose to help with sweating, and I paired it with a khaki blazer. The dress, on sale at H&M, felt disposable to me. I knew I would never wear it again after the trial.

White sunglasses hiding my pain and fear, I walked down the sidewalk of Montpelier to meet Detective Carver for one last coffee. The street was busy, and as a young man approached me, I saw his eyes scan my body. When I was within earshot, he said to me, "Damn, you look so good, I want to fuck you." I walked on, shoulders falling in the moment I needed my confidence the most, inaudibly whispering, "Fuck off." I found Detective Carver and told him what had just happened, grateful that I wouldn't have to walk alone again.

At the end of our last training, Amy handed me a note she had written:

"More Grounding Actions:

- Deep Breath (remember: YOUR PACE!)
- Feel your body sitting in the chair. Feel your feet on the floor. Press your back in the back of the chair. Does the chair have arms? How do they feel? Smooth? Rough? Touch the seat of the chair—is it soft? How does it feel?
- Feel Your Back!

Anna—Girl You've got this! I believe in you and am in awe! May the wind be at your back and may you kick ass!"

The night before I flew, Mimi, Colby, and Jared took me to Tucker Hill, where I would be surrounded by the support and care of Kevin and Patti and my old coworkers. The next morning, a Thursday in August,

I listened to Brandi Carlile, and I did put one foot in front of the other and boarded the plane into the unknown.

• • •

*Shortly after moving to Washington in 2006, single and alone, I began to stand up once more. My heels sank into the grass as I left the small cabin in my friend's backyard. Dressed in slacks and a button-up, I was off to work. No one at the office knew I was living in a shed up on the hill in Port Townsend. I had been in town less than a year, had left my relationship with the man I had moved there with from Maine, the one who had sexually assaulted me, and was forging my path on my own. Megan had connected me with her friend who had the small shed. No bathroom or running water, but I didn't mind. It was a cozy spot to lay my head, and the main house was just a short walk through the yard where I could access utilities.*

*There was a resolve in me that summer of 2007, a determination to make Port Townsend work, and I had a great job as the production manager for a screen-printing and embroidery company that worked with young men in recovery. Most of them came from millionaire parents, with them partying away their trust funds until they caused too much trouble and were sent to rehab in Port Townsend. As I managed these young men, teaching them how to sweep a floor, fold shirts, and pack boxes, none of them knew of my housing. I was a shed girl setting out on her own.*

• • •

I wore my white sunglasses the entire flight, needing them to protect me from the journey ahead, to shield me from the showdown. I wondered if I could wear them in the courtroom but quickly laughed to myself, *Of course not. You will go in eyes wide open. You are the shield.* The Seattle skyline didn't hold the beauty it had months prior; it held the sadness I felt. My body moved without my brain, getting me to the ferry, dragging my heavy suitcase and heart behind me.

I needed to use the bathroom and asked the older gentleman reading his paper to watch my belongings. When I returned, he asked me where I was headed, and the words flew out of my mouth as his eyes widened. Poor guy thought I was on vacation, and he muttered his apologies to me.

Kyle greeted me at the ferry terminal on Bainbridge Island, and we discussed the trial during the hour ride to Port Townsend. As he had before, he dropped me at the Port Townsend Brewery to pick up Megan's extra car and delivered me into the arms of my friends. I had only asked a few ladies to meet me there, and I collapsed into the embrace of Ellen, Megan, Emily, and a few others. We talked in low tones, and everyone else at the brewery that day respected our space, knowing I was not there for a joyful reunion.

My plan was to get through the next few days, soak up all the love and support, follow all the notes I had written, study the direct examination questions once more, and just be. Friday, I had what would be my only in-person practice session with James. I didn't even try to climb the stairs of the courthouse. Instead, I took the elevator, riding up to the top floor. My eyes lingered on the holding cell and police in their office, located across from James's office, knowing Jeffrey had been held in that cell multiple times. I turned away and was greeted by James. Then, we settled into a conference room and got to work.

We worked through the direct examination, James standing while I sat, practicing what that would feel like. I cracked jokes during the most disgusting questions, and he allowed me to settle into my discomfort. Both of us were on edge and nervous, as James was still waiting to hear from Steve, the other prosecutor, and the Clallam Superior Courts. Even in this late hour, the final countdown, the trial could be postponed. We were both also eager to know a big piece of information that would factor heavily into the trial.

Jeffrey, defending himself, had the choice of a bench trial (just the judge) or a jury trial. The latter could greatly prolong the process and provide its own complexities. How did the jury view stalking? Would they think I was overreacting? Perhaps one of them had stalked in the past? Although James liked the judge who would preside, a bench trial would also provide its own challenges, with one person making the choice of guilty or not guilty.

During our hours of preparation, we would take breaks and talk strategy. We had both agreed not to flood the courtroom with supporters. I would be bringing four friends, and that was it. The reason for this was that Jeffrey wanted an audience. It fed his ego, and we didn't know how he would act out with a larger group there. Also, because two of his other stalking victims had worked in the court and criminal systems, we didn't want him to try to find new victims in the supportive faces. I shared with James all that Amy had taught me, and he felt confident in my skills.

Our time together was ending when we got the word that Jeffrey had chosen a bench trial. We celebrated this small unanticipated victory, preferring the judge over a jury. Fragile and alone, I walked down the familiar courthouse steps again. My clothes felt sweaty and uncomfortable. Arriving at the Port Townsend Brewery for Friday night with the Edensaw crew and friends, I changed in the bathroom, threw up, and joined everyone for encouragement and distraction.

Tom was overseas working, but I felt his presence and encouragement in the messages he sent, and it amplified the strength I carried in myself. My love for him had faded over the years into a loving friendship, certainly, but the romantic love had gone.

The next few days I spent at Ellen's, comforted by her care. She hosted a small garden dinner for me and a few others, let me sit in my silence, and supported me as I created a large group text message to notify those around the country of the proceedings. Amy had suggested this. She urged me to have one group text thread for friends, to create a separate one for my mom and Carrie, and to assign either Megan or Ellen to give information to the group throughout the trial. That final task completed, there was nothing left to do but wait.

# CHAPTER TWENTY-ONE

# August 12 – 13, 2019

**It can be hard to talk about an experience with sexual violence, and sometimes, it may feel most daunting to bring it up with people you are closest to, such as family, friends, or a romantic partner. Whether you choose to tell others right away or years later—or prefer not to disclose at all—is completely up to you.**[25]

I looked out my window from the hotel in Port Angeles at the Olympic Mountains looming just behind the small town and thought to myself, *In some ways, I hope this is the worst day of my life because at least I know I'm going to get through it. It's going to end—I'm not going to die.* My eyes trailed from the mountains to the Clallam County Courthouse, a squat brick building that stood out against the low Pacific Northwest businesses.

Megan was in an adjoining room. She had sat with me the night before as I pressed my court clothes, the simple navy dress and khaki blazer. Megan and I had met up with friends at a local pub. All through the evening, I had felt small yet strong, as if I were living an out-of-body experience. Everyone chatted as I tried to munch on a slice of pizza. I listened and sat, attempting to stay in the present, but every part of me wanted to scream, "HOW DID I GET HERE?!" After nearly eight years, we were finally going to trial.

That morning, I chugged Imodium AD and Pepto-Bismol and prepared myself for the fact that I was so terrified to testify and be in the same room as Jeffrey that I may need to wear adult diapers.

Texts of encouragement came in. I had my "Power Up" playlist on, and I went through the motions of readying myself for the inevitable with robotic movements. The only person I allowed to call me was my advocate, Amy Farr, reaching out from thousands of miles away. I don't know what she said, but I know I needed to hear it.

Megan gently got me out the door of the hotel and into the car, carrying my bag of snacks, change of clothes, computer, notes, and heart with her. We drove the block and a half to the courthouse because I didn't think my legs would carry me that far. Ellen, Emily, and Kyle met us at the courthouse doors. Even though they had walked this journey for years, I once again found myself cautioning them about what they would hear, protecting them while needing protection.

I had my army, and we walked into the courthouse like we were going to war; I was the weapon. My motley army and I found the district attorney's office where Jillian greeted us. Her calmness, humor, and poise warmed my heart as she escorted us to a conference room she had set up for us. There was water, snacks, and coloring sheets to pass the time and keep me calm, but nothing was going to settle me. As my friends sat and did their best to distract me, I journeyed countless times to the bathroom, out to have a smoke, and back to their cheerful chatter. Opening arguments had begun, and all we could do was sit and wait until it was my turn to take the stand.

I nearly wept when the friendly face of Officer Bill Corrigan appeared. We weren't allowed to talk about anything regarding the case, but I could see his concern for me and also his delight at meeting my friends and support system he'd heard about over the years.

During one of my trips to the bathroom, I walked past the courtroom and could see in for just a moment through the window. I hadn't seen Jeffrey in years. What was it going to be like to face him, to see him, to hear his voice? I saw the back of him sitting at the defense table, balding, dressed in black and white prison clothes. There he was. I was told he would be in shackles and not allowed to approach me. There would be extra security, and the courts had done whatever they could to ensure both of our rights—his right to defend himself and my right not to have the crime recommitted in the courtroom. However, let's be honest, acting as his own defense is, in many ways, recommitting the crime of stalking. As we know, the court system is used by offenders of stalking to continue their behavior.

Regardless, I knew it was a one-in-a-million chance that we were actually here, that prosecutors all the way across the country had decided to pursue this case, to file felony aggravated stalking and felony cyberstalking charges. James and Steve had taken on the impossible, to prove stalking, and the only way we were going to get a conviction was through me. I needed to buck up, stop vomiting and shitting, and get myself in order. I walked back into our conference room, sat down, and quietly picked up my phone. I found the song I needed, turned up the volume, and slammed the phone down on the table. "Eye of the Tiger" by Survivor. *Let's roll, motherfuckers, I've got this.*

All the prep in the world doesn't prepare you for walking into the courtroom. I felt like everything I had trained myself for had just flown out the window. I shakily took the stand, looking around to try to get a sense of my surroundings and gather my nerves.

The Honorable Judge Basden presiding over the court, a man in his mid-fifties wearing the typical robe, seemed firm, and yet there was a hint of kindness. Bailiffs were surrounding the defense table, where Jeffrey and his appointed counsel sat. Though he was defending himself, he had to have an appointed lawyer, even if he didn't want to use the lawyer's advice. James and Steve sat at the state's table with Jillian directly behind. My four friends were scattered throughout the courtroom. Later, I found out Jillian had asked them to do this so that I saw support wherever I looked. Since it was a bench trial, there was no jury, but above the jury booth to the left was a clock. I looked at the box I was in—water, tissues, and yes, a bucket tucked under the side table per my request in case I needed to vomit.

I looked everywhere and at every face except one: Jeffrey's. I had worked on training myself with my advocate to not look at him. He may have stolen my life over all these years, but he wasn't getting anything from me today, not even a look.

Judge Basden swore me in, I took my seat, James stood up, and we began.

QUESTION 1: WHAT IS YOUR NAME?

QUESTION 2: WHAT IS YOUR OCCUPATION?

QUESTION 3: WHERE DO YOU LIVE?

QUESTION 4: HOW LONG HAVE YOU LIVED THERE?

QUESTION 5: WHERE DID YOU LIVE BEFORE THAT?

QUESTION 6: IS THAT IN THE STATE OF WASHINGTON?

QUESTION 7: WHEN DID YOU LEAVE PORT TOWNSEND?

QUESTION 8: WHY DID YOU LEAVE PORT TOWNSEND?

"Objection!" Jeffrey yelled in his strange, drawn-out voice that sometimes squeaked. "Anna is saying my name wrong."

Judge Basden said, "I didn't hear that. What do you think she is saying?"

"She's saying Bradfart," he replied.

Every pair of eyes in the room widened. No one cracked a smile because while the idea of me saying the word "fart" may be funny, it wasn't in that circumstance. We all began to quickly realize how this was going to go—we were in for a long day. I wanted to stand up and scream, "I didn't. I swear I didn't say that. We are in court—I would never do that." But the judge could also see what was starting to unravel and replied, "Denied. Please proceed, Ms. Nasset."

•   •   •

*Sophomore year at the small country school outside Delaware, Ohio, Mr. Samuelson, my homeroom teacher, took notice of me and began commenting on my appearance. I often wonder if predators can sniff out those they victimize and prey on them. If so, I was an easy target.*

*When I was wearing a dress one day, he commented on my legs. Another day, he complimented my bright eyes. He would put a hand on my shoulder and let it slide down to my back. Already violated by my peers, I thought my teachers were there to protect me, not continue the cycle. The days, weeks, and months rolled on in this pattern of harassment. I didn't speak a word; I shrank instead. I ate less, grew quieter. My bright light fell flat.*

*One particular day, Mr. Samuelson cornered me in a room alone. He wanted me to attend a booster event and be his partner in a card game, and I said "no." He grabbed my wrist and wouldn't let me leave, pushing me farther into the room, face close to mine. "If you don't attend, you'll be in trouble," he sneered at me. I shrank smaller and said, "Okay."*

*What is it about men not understanding the word "no"?*

*Scared and defeated, I collapsed into sharing everything with my parents that evening. There were many questions, the kinds of questions parents shouldn't have to ask their daughter. My sweet and kind father's face fell because he couldn't protect me, and Mom, she was downright pissed.*

*Before long, there was a phone call, and an appointment was set with my parents, myself, and Mr. Samuelson in the principal's office. The principal, a friend of Mr. Samuelson, sided with his denial, and we left the meeting with me being assigned to a different homeroom. There were no apologies, there was no punishment, and I would carry the embarrassment to the new room assignment. I had raised my voice, but I was shamed after doing so. I would assume the blame, and I would grow silent. I learned what is done to me is my fault.*

*Mr. Samuelson continued to teach at Buckeye Valley for years. I transferred to a small Christian school the following year after begging my parents not to make me go back.*

•    •    •

I wanted to tug my ear, the sign to Jillian that I needed a break. I thought, *We've been at this for hours*, but when I looked at the clock, I realized it had only been five minutes. Judge Basden may have been presiding over the court, James and Steve may have been questioning me, but Jeffrey set the cadence. Every few questions, Jeffrey would object again, prompting me to pause mid-sentence and wait for the judge to speak, James to ask the question again, and my answer to return. The chaos of this continual process left my brain clattering around.

During each pause, I found a point in the room to rest my eyes—on Judge Basden, James, a bailiff, or Jillian. Occasionally during the objections, I locked eyes with one of my friends, but when doing so, I would see the shock and horror in their eyes, even though they had walked this journey with me. Despite our countless conversations to prepare them, nothing could truly prepare them for this. If I held their gaze, I would crumble, so my eyes would skitter away.

The three hundred questions were asked at a snail's pace due to Jeffrey's constant interruptions. Judge Basden, in his fairness, held and considered each objection before making a decision. Many went in our favor, but sometimes, he ruled with Jeffrey. Judgment is about fairness, and I could sense that in Judge Basden. After an hour, everyone needed a break, including the judge, and I was escorted to the empty jury room, where I collapsed alone into a seat. Jillian encouraged my frail spirit, and soon, we were back for round two.

After a few questions, Jeffrey once again objected, saying I had called him Bradfart. I waited for Judge Basden to finish speaking, holding my tongue, and then quietly said, "Pardon me, Your Honor," into the microphone. "May I please refer to Jeffrey Bradford as the defendant moving forward?"

The entire room exhaled as Judge Basden replied, "Yes, let's continue."

I felt a surge of confidence. I had outsmarted Jeffrey, advocated for myself, and found a solution to at least this issue. As a witness, there are very few moments in a trial when your rights matter, and in a case like this, Jeffrey was very much committing the crime in real time, but in that moment, I won.

By lunch, I felt like I'd gone ten rounds. My body and brain were pummeled, and as my friends headed out to grab a bite to eat, I declined their request to join them. I sat alone in the conference room, attempting to eat a rice cake, giving up after a few meager bites. I laid my head down on the faux wood table and closed my eyes. Before I knew it, my depleted body fell asleep. I am not one to nap and still look back shocked that, in that moment, my body slumbered. The body knows what it needs, and for fifteen minutes, I drifted from reality and into rest.

Having spent weeks studying the direct examination, I knew where James was in the schedule of questions as we proceeded into the afternoon filled with objections, me struggling each time to recollect the specific messages James referenced. I held tight to the truth and spoke with all the clarity I could muster amongst the chaos. Tears slipped down my cheeks and into my words with some questions, and anger filled my veins with others.

I tugged my ear, looking at Jillian. I needed a break after just an hour—I couldn't hold on any longer. She nodded, and once again, I was tucked into the jury room, where I slumped into my seat next to Jillian, a boxer and her trainer. She wiped my brow with her encouragement, bandaged my wounds, and sent me back into the ring.

The cadence of chaos continued. I could linger in the horror of that day for thousands of words, but it was a balance of giving him voice at a time when, even though I was the one speaking from the witness stand, I felt silenced. When court had adjourned for the day, we had only gotten through about two hundred of James's prepared three hundred questions. Day two and Jeffrey's cross-examination loomed, and every face—the bailiff's, prosecutors', friends', hell, even the judge's—looked exhausted. I didn't even look in the mirror; in one day, I had aged a decade.

My friends gathered around me in the afternoon sun, ready to say their goodbyes and head back to Port Townsend for the night. Megan was to go with them. They looked at me, and Megan gently placed her arms around my shoulders.

"We all decided there is no way in hell we are letting you be alone tonight. I'm staying."

My shoulders released their tension for the first time that day in accepting gratitude. "Are you sure?" I protested, knowing she needed to work.

"It's already done, and all the ladies from work send their love."

The others returned to Port Townsend. At a later date, Ellen would share with me the shock they had experienced in the courtroom. They talked on the car ride home, processing what they had witnessed, grappling with what I had experienced all these years, and finally understanding why I'd stayed the course to get us to trial. Returning to town, they would sit in the Port Townsend Brewery beer garden, unable to fully share what they had seen with those who asked about the trial. I know anger was expressed, tears were shed, and none of them were ever the same. Gratitude fills me to this day for them journeying into the depths alongside me.

Megan unpacked her bags again for night two. She splurged for the room with the deck, and we sat sipping shitty wine, smoking cigarettes, and taking in the view that lay before us, its magnitude vast.

The Coast Guard station jutted out on the spit in front of us, giving me comfort. It was there to protect those on the water, and the sinking ship of emotions I felt was calmed by its presence. The view, though different, reminded me of my old apartment in Uptown, and I let it hold me.

In our conversation on the deck and at dinner that night, Megan let me take the lead in my fragile state. Anger flowed from my lips, every other word an expletive about Jeffrey, and I vomited my release in spewed-out hatred. She would bring me back to balance with memories of good times past, keeping me tethered to Earth as she spoke, when all I wanted to do was float far away.

---

Morning brought reality: It would be the showdown. It was the day that Jeffrey would cross-examine me, and nothing could prepare me, not a damn thing. Hours of preparation didn't matter. With his legal right, he would question me, and I would have to answer.

Megan and I both packed our bags, manifesting my testimony to not go a third day. Emily couldn't attend that day, but Kyle and Ellen met us again at the courthouse doors, and as we walked in, my friends were quiet, not knowing how to give encouragement. Everyone appeared worn from the day before. James and I spoke in low tones over the conference room table, bolstering one another for what was to come.

The trial began again, and in my fear for the cross-examination, I lingered over the questions James asked. I wanted to freeze time, skip time, just have my body and brain check out until it was all over. Hours of questions and breaks passed that Tuesday morning. The objections were frequent, and Judge Basden presided with grace and fairness. I knew James was coming to the end of his direct examination as he began his conclusion.

## CONCLUSION

293. WE HAVE COVERED A LOT OF TESTIMONY THAT SPANS EIGHT YEARS. PLEASE TELL THE COURT AGAIN WHEN YOU FIRST MET THE DEFENDANT.

294. BEFORE THAT, YOU HAD NEVER MET HIM?

295. WHAT WAS YOUR LIFE LIKE PRIOR TO 2011?

296. WHAT HAPPENED TO YOUR BUSINESS?

297. HOW HAS YOUR LIFE CHANGED NOW?

298. WHAT STEPS DO YOU TAKE TO PROTECT YOURSELF?

299. WHAT ARE SOME OF THE THINGS YOU HAVE EXPERIENCED?

300. WHAT IS THE CAUSE OF THOSE SYMPTOMS?

301. WHAT IS THE REASON FOR YOUR BUSINESS CLOSING IN PORT TOWNSEND?

302. WHAT IS THE REASON YOU MOVED TO THE OTHER SIDE OF THE COUNTRY, VERMONT?

303. DID WE COVER EVERY SINGLE INCIDENT OR ENCOUNTER YOU HAD WITH THE DEFENDANT?

In my fear of what was to come, I could barely whisper my answers. I forgot the things I had practiced. For question 299, I couldn't even remember I hadn't had a period in two years because of Jeffrey. My brain and body froze, the words came out jumbled, and I felt defeat. I had let James and Steve down. I hadn't done my job. I wanted to go back and answer the questions again. I lingered in the jury room, berating myself for my failure and fearing it would be my undoing when Jeffrey took his turn at me in a few minutes.

With a deep gulp of air, the last real breath I would take until the cross-examination was over, I sat back down in the witness stand. Jeffrey, in shackles, stood and began his cross-examination, the moment he wanted, his glorious time to shine. I focused my eyes on Judge Basden, my body directing my gaze and reminding me to never look at Jeffrey. I answered his questions. Questions about employment at Edensaw, questions about the location of my mom, objections from James. I sat, I listened, and I answered with laser clarity. I broke my gaze from Judge Basden only to look at James during objections and to glance at the clock. *The clock must have broken*, I thought. *There is no way only three minutes have passed.* I already needed a break. But I continued.

Jeffrey pressed on, posing rambling questions. He began to ask about my employment and location in 2008 – 2009, before I had the gallery, before I ever knew he existed in the world. He poked and prodded with his questions. I don't know the language he used—I can't remember it, and I don't want to see it. But as he asked the questions about 2008 – 2009, Megan and I locked eyes, hers bulging with anger and horror, and in that moment, fighting for my freedom with only my voice and truth, it rushed over me.

He had been stalking me long before I knew it. Having your stalker of nearly a decade tell you, while cross-examining you, he has been stalking you since 2008 or 2009 is beyond an emotion I can express. The years of being questioned about my choices in the stalking case, the times I was told I was overreacting or simply reacting to experiences from my past, the instances I was dismissed or made fun of all snapped into clarity. I had been correct all along; my instinct that kicked in November 2011 had been spot on. There would have never been a way to ignore him and hope he went away. He had been stalking me for years before I even knew. The past harassment and violence I had experienced at the hands of various men over the years had shaped me to be hyperaware and seek help in the very early days. Had my past traumas saved my life? The question begged to be asked.

I broke eye contact with Megan's furious protective gaze and focused back on my points. Judge Basden, the bailiff behind Basden, James, clock, repeat, repeat, repeat. I think my mind and body's refusal to cave undid Jeffrey. To this day, I don't know how I did it. I will never know how I soldiered through. To quote a friend, I had "sacred rage." I gave him nothing but my answers, in that moment holding on to what little I still felt was mine. His line of questioning rapidly declined into questions around my involvement with the Catholic Church's child sexual abuse and my access to nuclear codes from Trump. It fell apart fast. Judge Basden gave him an opportunity to get back on track and continue, but he couldn't.

My eyes stayed focused on the clock, watching seconds that took hours to pass, and within an hour of his cross-examination starting, it was called by Judge Basden. Time of death, just before lunch on a sunny Tuesday in August in Port Angeles, Washington.

Jillian ushered me once again to the jury room while they escorted Jeffrey back to the jail. I walked into the room, ripped off my blazer, and collapsed onto the floor, colliding with the stained office carpet. My body released into sobs as I lay curled into the fetal position. James, Steve, and Jillian stood over me whispering their apologies. It was done. I was done. I was guided from the courtroom by Megan, Ellen, and Kyle, my face locked in anger with tears spilling down. I saw Officer Corrigan waiting for his turn to testify. He looked at me as if to ask, "Are you okay?" My face crumpled in fury; all I could do was vigorously shake my head no.

I ripped the rest of my court clothes off in the parking lot of the Port Angeles Courthouse, shielded by friends and using the car door as a dressing room. I threw on cut-offs, yearning for my body to feel the salt air. My heroes tucked me into a car and whisked me off to lunch, where I ate the first full meal I'd had in days and languished over my cocktail. What we had witnessed, what I had endured, needed to turn to laughter fast, and with my part done, I needed to have humor fill my soul.

Megan returned to the table with a round of drinks. Dropping them down, she said, "And that fucking Chatty Kathy (referring to Jeffrey), well, he just loves the sound of his own goddamn voice." I laughed in earnest for the first time in days, Jeffrey's power falling away. Us ladies were about to begin our journey down to Megan's house on the Hood Canal, and as we did, Jillian called. Everyone froze in time, fearing I'd have to go back and testify more. Thankfully, I just needed to sign some paperwork.

I ran back into the courthouse, cut-offs and flip flops on, and signed the paperwork releasing me from my duties, pausing to say hello to Officer Corrigan and Officer Holmes who had also come to testify. I said nothing of my experience in the courtroom but thanked them both for their years of service. As I headed out the door, Officer Corrigan made hand motions of swimming through waves. I smiled knowing that he knew that's exactly what I would soon be doing.

Megan, Ellen, and I drove the hour down the Hood Canal to Megan's house and stormed her beach in Brinnon, all of us diving into the briny water to wash away the filth of what we had walked through. Our sisterhood, our tribe, floated on the party barge Megan had inflated, diving in, sunning, sipping, laughing, salt coating our skin. I'm sure we talked about the trial that night, but what I remember is laughing for the first time in months. Guttural, primal, girlfriend laughter.

The trial continued that day and into Wednesday. I did not attend. I could have, but I didn't want to give Jeffrey anything. He had already taken everything. I went back to Port Townsend and found myself lost in my own town. Not knowing how to proceed, I brought cookies to the Port Townsend Police Department and drove in endless circles. I wanted to talk to no one and everyone. I ran into people, and they hugged me and thanked me for standing up for the safety of the community. I tearfully accepted their hugs.

My body hung in tension when the three other victims, including Erica, testified in order for the aggravated charges to be further proven. Erica and I had communicated only about meeting up, and we had a date at Sirens for when she finished testifying. Luckily, the other victims only had to testify for about thirty minutes each, but it was thirty minutes too long. I had known for years that this was much larger than myself, and the strength those three women summoned to go and testify, the sisterhood of strangers, persists.

Erica and I met at Sirens, her mother and fierce protector with her. We sat down at the bar, elbows on the old wood, locked eyes, and let it all go. We had no fucks left to give. We just both sat shell-shocked. Champagne appeared, we toasted, and we started to talk, and over the next few hours, the community showed up. Everyone knew why Erica and I were together; they approached gingerly with thank yous and receded back like the waves below us, giving us the gift to be. I don't think we paid for a drink over our hours together, our drinks replenished without question, our bills nonexistent. Erica and I dropped down into conversation in a way that we never had before. We let it all go and shared the darkest pits of our pain, fears, and psychological burdens, and our community stood in a silent circle of support around us.

The evening wore on, and though I wanted to blanket myself in the comfort of our community, my weary body and brain needed to rest. I stayed at Emily's that night. She was in the city at a concert, and for the first time since I arrived in Port Townsend, I was alone. I sat at her dining table, chain smoked cigarettes, drank a glass of wine, and stared into the dark night. Dragging my haggard soul to the air mattress, I slept the sleep of the dead, for tomorrow was verdict day, and I was going back to Port Angeles. I wanted Judge Basden to look me in the eye and give the verdict.

# CHAPTER TWENTY-TWO

# Mid-August 2019 – September 2019

Among female victims of attempted and completed intimate partner homicide by male partners, in the twelve months prior to the attack: 85 percent of attempted and 76 percent of completed homicide victims were stalked; 91 percent of attempted and 89 percent of completed homicide victims who had been physically abused during the relationship had also been stalked; and 46 percent of attempted and 54 percent of completed homicide victims reported stalking before the attack, most commonly to police.[26]

Driving around Discovery Bay, I took in the jaw-dropping beauty of the Pacific Northwest, the terrifying beauty of towering firs lining the winding road on one side and the hundred-foot drop to the ocean on the other side. My body and driving skills were not up for the challenge, so I slowly drove, forcing my focus to stay on the road while my brain drove right off the cliff.

I stopped at the old train depot and was greeted by Officer Corrigan with his pristine performance Porsche, ready to escort me to decision day. With us both having testified, we were able to spend the drive together, and I welcomed the company, plus the stylish ride, as we headed back to Port Angeles once again. We nervously chattered on the drive. I shared my day with the gals and my time with Erica, and

I could see kind compassion in his face as he heard about my support systems. He shared with me about taking his Porsche (to the best of my understanding) to the cleanest performance car show with his wife the next week. I thought, *Should I have taken my shoes off? Dear lord, thank god he's never seen my trailer trash of a car.*

We arrived back in Port Angeles, and my body seized as we walked to the courthouse doors, my teeth clenched and muscles filled with ice. Corrigan opened the door, and I walked in. Jillian greeted me, wearing the week on her face. She settled me outside the courtroom and shared with me that in all of her years as a victim witness coordinator, she had never seen prosecutors as exhausted as they were by this trial.

Everyone—James, Steve, Jillian, and even Corrigan—had agreed I would stay in the hallway until Judge Basden delivered his verdict. I would not be present for any closing arguments, as we didn't want to rile Jeffrey up. I needed to stay in the shadows.

Corrigan went in for closing arguments, and I sat alone, staring, eyes boring into the courtroom doors as my life hung in the words being spoken in those walls that lay before me. Still sitting listlessly by myself, I texted my mom and sister and the vast group chat of supporters, I looked at Facebook and Instagram, and I watched people who had been arrested, couples filing for divorce, and those renewing license plates walk past me. I sat alone, I watched, and I waited.

After what seemed to be an eternity but was probably an hour, Jillian came out and said, "It's time. Follow my direction." I, a small frail child, did just that. She led me into the courtroom and sat me in the back row, directly behind Jeffrey. There were probably fifteen rows of seats between us, and she did so in hopes he wouldn't turn around and see me. My very presence in that room needed protection. I sat, clenching my life, looking around, and noticing six or seven police officers in the otherwise sparse audience. I wondered if one of them was Detective Dropp, whom I'd never met in person. I assumed the threats that Jeffrey had made toward killing law enforcement was why they were there. We all nodded at one another, and an older couple who showed up for victims on verdict day moved closer to protect me from Jeffrey if he turned around.

Judge Basden nodded to me from his seat high above us all. My face collapsed into a kind grimace, and I nodded back. As he began to speak, blood rushed to my head, filling my brain with rushing white noise, and I sat and waited to hear what my life would become.

As he spoke, my heart fell. I didn't understand. He explained that he needed to delay his verdict by a week; he wanted to go over the case and the trial again to ensure he made the correct verdict. He went on to say, "I know there are people in this room today who are here to hear my verdict, but I need to do my due diligence, and for that, I need to delay."

My mind collapsed in confusion as Jillian turned to me and said, "This is okay. I'll explain to you outside. Right now, I need you to duck down." Still the obedient child in that moment, I ducked my head down as Jeffrey began to stand to be led back to his cell. She wanted to hide me from his gaze. Others wanted to hide me as well; officers whose names I don't know to this day quickly rose and walked over, forming a standing wall in between me and Jeffrey until he was gone.

That moment of solidarity from the police officers—maybe thirty seconds long—conveyed the seriousness of the situation and provided me with needed support. It turned out one of the officers was Detective Dropp, and I thanked him through tears as Jillian escorted me back to the prosecuting attorney's office. James, Steve, Jillian, and I would stand together in the office, and they would share with me that most likely Judge Basden's delay in verdict was to prevent future appeals or a mistrial. I grasped to understand but accepted that they knew more than me, and with awkward hugs, I said goodbye to my team. I found Officer Corrigan waiting for me in the lobby and headed back down the road in defeated silence. I had waited eight years for an answer.

There was a dark pall over our ride home as Corrigan encouraged me. He dropped me off at my borrowed car in Discovery Bay, and I headed to Megan's for one last night. I stopped for frozen pizzas, wine, beer, anything I could grab to say thank you to this lady who had carried me through. When I arrived at her house, she was at work. I thought I would head to the beach and swim away the day, but instead, I lay on her couch, stared out upon the Hood Canal, and drifted in and out of sleep for several hours until Megan arrived home.

Megan didn't arrive alone; Ellen and our friend Kirstin surprised me by showing up as well. I pulled my weary body off the couch and got my ass into a swimsuit. Then, my gals took me on the swim of my life. As I thrust my body into the salty evening that was collapsing upon us, they cheered me on. I let the salt wash away Jeffrey and his crime against me. All of us were beyond exhausted by the week's events, while Kirstin, who had not been there, was the presence I needed in that moment. Megan and Ellen tucked into bed early, needing a much-deserved reprieve from what they had held, but Kirstin and I sat up talking for several hours.

Kirstin, who had known of the stalking for years, sat me down on the deck at Megan's. We looked out, high above the water, the moon glistening on the waves, and she said to me, "It seems to me that stalking is an endless open wound. It will never heal. It is a wound that no matter how many bandages you put on it, they will always get ripped off, or even if it heals to scar, he will cut it again, and you will begin to bleed all over. It's the wound that won't heal." I have never heard it explained to me so perfectly.

The next morning, I woke to the fog in my brain, and finally, the landscape matched my mind as I looked at the thick gray clouds clinging over the Hood Canal. I headed to Port Townsend one last time, as I would be flying out that night with no firm knowledge of my future. I had a breakfast planned with Ford, the man who had told me to go to the police eight years prior.

To my surprise, the day before and that morning, I had started to note something in my body. I could not stop burping or farting. I mean, it just kept happening, my body embarrassingly releasing the tension I had carried for so long in unfortunate ways.

Sitting down at the patio of the Spruce Goose Cafe, watching small planes soar over the mountains, I greeted Ford, whom I hadn't seen in

years, and immediately burped. My cheeks turned red as I explained
my body's release and that I had lost control of it. He nodded and told
me it was normal and not to be embarrassed. Then, we began to chat.
Other tables of locals gave kind waves, sad smiles on their faces, and I
nodded my head back in gratitude. Ford, the gruff Marine and mentor to my ex-husband, exuded kindness and care, gingerly asking me
questions about the trial and my life. I welcomed the presence and
conversion.

Through our breakfast, I would learn more of my story, contribut-
ing to a continual acceptance that my story was not my own and that I
needed protecting from it. I learned that for the last eight years, Jeffrey
had been sending Ford letters about me. My eyes widened in horror at
this new information, and though I wish he had told me years ago that
this was happening, I understood his protective nature.

We continued to talk, and I shared with Ford that in the months
prior to my gallery closing, I would have someone with a concealed
carry permit at the gallery during gallery walks. He looked me square
in the face and said, "There were others protecting you as well." My
face screwed into a question. He then shared that during gallery walk
nights, he and several other retired military members would be in the
area of the gallery. I began to softly cry, burps coming out as I did. With
this, I came into a deeper acceptance of the community danger and
fully acknowledged that my story is not just mine.

The last stop that day was the Port Townsend Brewery, where I
would meet my friend who would take me to the ferry. Many friends
gathered to bid me farewell, congratulating me on my role in the case.
I sat numb and nervous, returning to Vermont without the answer I'd
come for. Tears filled my eyes as I spoke quietly and thanked people,
and then my friend gently told me, "It's time, Anna. We have to go."

If I'd sobbed when I left Port Townsend to move to Vermont, I
wailed with this departure. Clutching, clawing, gnashing teeth, I
openly wailed. I clung to Megan and Ellen, and through uncontrolla-
ble burps and farts, I let it all out. It was infinitely more painful to say

this goodbye than it had been when I'd moved. Friends and strangers watched. Those who knew me well took in the moment and realized the trauma I had endured in a way I had never shared.

The orcas didn't greet me on my ferry ride this time. The flight home was filled with turbulence, Jared picked me up from the airport, and I went home to bed. Pulling the quilts over my head, I closed my eyes, still weeping, farting, burping. I fell into slumber.

---

During that week of waiting, I swam in the nine circles of Hell. I couldn't leave my apartment. I couldn't speak. I tried to have normalcy and failed greatly. I kept distance from Jared, not allowing him too close—arm's length support was all I wanted.

I went out only once to meet friends at The Hostel, where I had nearly been assaulted years prior. As I walked in, the bartender, knowing what I had endured, clapped and bowed deeply at me. Tears filled my eyes, and I whispered "thank you" as he handed me a glass of wine. I settled into conversation with friends. Vermont felt different and foreign, not like Port Townsend where my community had seen my journey. In Vermont, I had to explain my journey, and I didn't have words.

I hid in my nest, in my blankets, with Dolly snuggles and *Gilmore Girls*. I never took a full breath that week. My body suffocated itself, gasping for air. I continued to uncontrollably burp and fart for days. I woke each morning with my jaw aching from clenching and grinding my teeth. Uncertainty surrounded me and dragged me down into its murky waters.

Because the trial had been postponed a multitude of times, I had continued to accept speaking engagements, and months before, I had been invited to The Dells in Wisconsin to speak to advocates and police. My date of travel fell one week after my return from Port Townsend. I looked over my speech, I added the pieces I could now legally share, and I stopped at the end. My speech, my story, the trial had two very different possible endings, and as I packed my bag for the airport, I didn't know how it would culminate.

The evening before I flew, Jillian informed me that Judge Basden would give his verdict the next morning. Taking into consideration the time difference, I would receive the verdict while boarding my plane.

At gate eleven of the Burlington airport, coffee in hand, white sunglasses glued to my face, I sat in the absurdity of the moment. Obviously, I should have canceled the speaking engagement, but the fact that Jeffrey had already taken years from me pushed me to go. Jillian texted me as she entered the courtroom. The plane began to board, and I sat in my corner seat in the terminal. My body could not board the flight without the verdict. I quivered as groups boarded the flight. They were getting to last call, but my phone stayed silent. The attendants at the gate looked at me as the last people boarded. I sat solid in my chair, and then my phone chimed.

Guilty. Guilty of aggravated felony stalking. Guilty of felony cyberstalking. Sentencing in one month.

My body crumpled over into a puddle of sobs. I gathered myself up, wrapped my shawl around my shoulders, white sunglasses still firmly in place, and boarded my plane. Still sobbing, I sat down next to a man. I sent my group text the news and then turned my phone to silent as the plane took off, the man next to me terrified of the crying woman. I never took off my sunglasses; my security blanket of shade was necessary that day. My body went into autopilot and got me onto my flight to Madison, Wisconsin, and into my rental car, and somehow, I arrived at the Kalahari Resort, where the conference would be held.

The Kalahari Resort was a safari-themed indoor water park and conference center. They played two songs on a loop at all times—Toto's "Africa" and the resort theme song. Bronze elephants, giraffes, and tigers lined the walkway and lobby. Plants and fake jungle sounds filled the foyer to complete the safari feel. This is where I would spend my celebration of the verdict. The absurdity of the situation was palpable, and all I could do was laugh. I also felt the depths of sadness in my aloneness. I wanted and needed my people, but I was in the jungle by myself. I spent the evening talking on the phone with everyone I knew, sipping a martini or two, and finally jumping on my bed in victory.

I had flown in a day early. When I had planned the work trip nearly a year earlier, I had wanted to attend sessions at the conference. However, with all that had transpired, I opted out of the trainings and headed into The Dells for a celebratory lunch and walk along the river. Food was still not my friend, but I ate what I could and then headed to the river path to take a walk alone—a walk of glory, stepping into the unknown and basking in the safety the guilty verdict may provide.

I had spoken with Jillian and James and knew that sentencing could go many different ways, the maximum being ten years. They said we'd be lucky to get five, but there was the risk that Judge Basden would give him the minimum and he could be out of jail in a couple of months. No matter—I'd take the time I got. Jeffrey's sentence was not his own; it was a sentence for all of his victims.

Reaching the path, I noticed an older man staring at me, and as I got to the trailhead, he began to walk toward me. The old terror filled my soul. He started to make comments about my appearance, talking about what he would like to do to me. I brushed past him, defeated in my freedom walk, my shoulders sunk. I tried to continue with my walk but quickly turned around and went back to my car. I drove to the Kalahari for another night in the faux safari, feeling beaten down. I had just wanted one walk. But here's the thing: Walking this world as a female, we never are fully safe.

The next morning, finished speech in hand, I took to the stage. The crowd of strangers would be the first people I celebrated with in person. I shared my case study, my experiences, the evidence, and the horror of Jeffrey, and then, I spoke the words to people, not just into the phone, for the first time. Voice quaking with emotion, I said, "Two days ago, as I boarded the plane for here, he was found guilty on all counts."

The audience members rose to their feet in thunderous applause, and tears rolled down my cheeks.

•    •    •

*That fall of 2018, I had signed up to speak at a fundraiser for the local domestic and sexual violence center. Walking into ArtsRiot in Burlington, Vermont, I was a bundle of nerves. Part of the fundraiser was storytelling by survivors, hosted by a producer for NPR's The Moth. Eager to continue to learn how to craft my words and use my voice, I had agreed to participate. Unlike the other times I had spoken, when using this storytelling format, I could not have notes with me, and I spent the hour drive to the event rehearsing out loud.*

*I didn't know anyone in the room and watched from the shadows as the three-piece band set up. They would play a song after each story was told. I had requested "Eye of the Tiger" but was unsure what they would play.*

*My feet carried me to the stage when it was my turn to speak, and I opened my mouth, letting the rehearsed words tumble out. I tied my story together in a tight container of uncertainty. I didn't have an ending to it yet—I wouldn't for another year. I talked of loss, of finding a new home—a new path—and the unknown of the future.*

*As my words ended and I walked off the stage, the band began to play, and the song they chose caught me with a deep inhale. I had never considered myself a Tom Petty fan until that moment.*

> **You could stand me up at the gates of Hell**
> **But I won't back down**
>
> **(Tom Petty, I Won't Back Down)**

•    •    •

That evening, on my flight home, I welcomed the empty seat next to me. The plane was otherwise full, and I felt a depth of gratitude that I could be alone. I wanted to go home to whatever home was, to see faces I knew, to dive into a Mimi hug, to celebrate this step of the process with those around me. I needed community.

Just as the door was about to shut, a woman burst onto the plane, curls bouncing around her, and collapsed into the seat next to me. Sweating and out of breath, she turned to me. "Holy shit—I just ran a mile to catch this plane. Do you want a drink? Let's get a drink." I nodded dumbly, overtaken by her presence.

Gin and tonics in hand, we began to chat. She introduced herself as Lansie, and within a few minutes, she shared that she was going to Waitsfield and asked if I knew where that was. Five minutes brings bad meetings, and it brings good ones. This was a good one. I laughed and responded, "That's where I live." Our conversation deepened, and by the time we landed in Burlington, gate eleven, the same gate that had delivered my verdict a few days prior, I had offered her a ride back to Waitsfield to visit her grandparents. I knew my mom would be relieved that I wasn't driving home alone in the dark, and I welcomed Lansie's cheery presence.

The hour drive passed in a flash, and I shared with her a bit of my story, the trial and the verdict, not certain how to tell the tale to this new friend. Arriving at town, we both agreed we should stop by The Smokehouse to continue growing our friendship over a cocktail. Stepping onto the old wooden floor, I was greeted with cheers from my friends who were there. Izzy threw herself at me in a bear hug. "YOU DID IT!" she screamed. Others offered hugs and congratulations. Lansie stopped and looked at me. "What you just went through was a very big deal, wasn't it?" she asked. I smiled and nodded my head.

That night, I dragged my suitcase up the old stairs. I opened the door to my apartment and found it filled with flowers, balloons, and cards. Tears slipping down my cheeks once more, I curled up with Dolly under the stacks of quilts that had held my pain and slept deeply.

The next few days were celebratory for certain. Jared would take me to breakfast the next day and confess that it was he who had sweetly filled my apartment with the flowers and balloons. During our drive through the valley and gulf to a favorite café, I found myself gagging when Jared said the word "evil" in a sentence, the term snapping me back to Jeffrey and his years of calling me evil. When we approached the village of Bradton, I recoiled at the sign that stated the town's name and year formed. The word Bradton made me queasy, as it was similar to Jeffrey's last name.

Instead of leaning on Jared for support, I found myself pushing him away and coming to the realization that I had nothing to give him in the form of a relationship. I had only partially allowed him on this journey with me. Yes, he had helped me in the way of basic needs being met and even financially, but he lacked the knowledge and skills to offer the support I needed. He leaned more toward his old-school Boston ways of, "Buck up—you're fine." Within a week of my arrival home, while sitting on his front porch, I would end the relationship. I needed to be alone through this next phase.

All the men from my past—the loves, the relationships, the crushes, the flings—they all wanted to fix me or just have me get over it, to save me in some way or another. Of course, there had been encouragement and support, but the brass tacks of it all was that there seemed to be a desire to fix the unfixable. And in this moment, I needed to be alone. The only one who could fix this was me and my words.

But sometimes, an ex becomes a dear friend, and that was the case with Mullet. He was in town, and as soon as I walked into The Mad Taco to meet him, he practically tossed me across the room in a victory hug. We jumped up and down like schoolchildren, celebrating the verdict. Because he was getting his law degree, I could open up to him in ways that needed no explanation. I celebrated with other friends and meals, taking in the love from my community. Even in this unknown time of what the sentence would be, in my openness, I began to feel the Mad River Valley was the supportive home I needed for this next chapter in my life.

At the same time, it was challenging for me to accept the congratulations and kindness that surrounded me. These people hadn't seen the stalking firsthand as my well-wishers in Washington had. Along with that, the only thing we could celebrate was the verdict. I hung in the gallows of purgatory awaiting the sentencing.

Mimi and I plotted a party for after the sentencing at her new restaurant. The theme would be decided after we knew how much time Jeffrey would be given. If he walked on time served, the theme would be Anna is changing her name and moving away. If he got more than five years, we'd host a "stoked on solidarity" party to support other victims/survivors of crime. Even my party's theme waved in the air uncertainly.

Judge Landes, now retired, reached out to see if she could call me, and one day, when I was lying on my couch, the phone rang. Her conversation with me conveyed her own grief related to Jeffrey stalking me and others. She told me how sad she had felt the first time I had walked into her courtroom. Apparently, she had feared an outcome like this, but she was also grateful that I was alive.

She said to me words that still haunt my cells: "It's not a matter of if he is going to kill—it's when, and I'm so glad you are alive." The couch swallowed me as her statement hit me and reality began to sink in deeper. While I was still processing her words, she applauded my bravery for standing up to Jeffrey's sexual violence. With that message, Judge Landes was the first person who called stalking what it is—it's sexual violence. Overall, it wasn't a pleasant conversation, but a truth conversation, and afterward, I rolled into my quilts with my reality, waves washing over me. I turned on *Gilmore Girls* once more.

Days later, I tucked into my favorite coffee shop, The Sweet Spot, and began to craft my victim impact statement. This is a written or oral statement delivered by the victim or their family after the verdict has been handed down but before sentencing. The judge or, in my case, jury can use the statement to make their decision or recommendation of sentencing.

After writing only a few sentences of my statement, I found myself doubled over the coffee shop's toilet, vomiting. My body continued to turn against me. I headed home and locked myself in with the solitude and proximity to a toilet required to write the statement, and I wrote for my life. Outside of my four walls was premature celebration; inside was solitude and grief.

Amy, my advocate, had warned me before the trial of the fallout, cautioning me that even if we got the outcome we wanted, it would come at a price. She talked to me about how after the trial, everyone who worked on it would move on to other cases, and I wouldn't have their support. We discussed justice and talked about the fact that justice wasn't necessarily found in the sentencing—it was found within.

I clung to that warning as I fell into depression once again, desperate to know what the sentence would be, attempting to make sense of what I had experienced—not just the trial and its darkness but the last eight years. I struggled to find meaning and lost myself in the noise that filled the words of my impact statement.

Once more, I drove to Montpelier to meet Amy and go over my statement. Detective Carver met me for iced coffee, and I felt the support of his knowing smile. There were few people who could understand the complexities of stalking and the trial, and he was one of them. One last time, he delivered me to the attorney general's office, up the elevator and to Amy. The hand-off complete, he gave me a side hug and a wink and left. Then, Amy and I sat together and went through every word I had written. She made recommendations, and I took notes and nodded solemnly. Amy and Detective Carver knew that we were a long way from done, and the outcome of the sentencing may very well hang in the words I wrote.

I continued to rewrite and send the new versions to Amy, and when it was finally where I wanted it, I made a post on Facebook asking if anyone would edit it. I wanted the statement to be as perfectly professional as it could be, and one of my sister's friends from high school volunteered. After the edits were complete, I looked at the statement, a few pieces of paper that could change the course of life—not just for me but for countless others.

# CHAPTER TWENTY-THREE

# September 18, 2019

**One in three women and one in six men will be stalked at some point during their lifetime.**[27]

Dolly snuggled under the stack of worn quilts, nestling into the crook of my back. Each of us were lingering in bed, fearing the day and the future it held. Dolly's neurotic nature soothed me while my body begged my hand to hit snooze. I wanted to stay in this cocoon of safety forever. I didn't want to know what lay ahead in the hours and minutes of the day. My life, my freedom, my future, my choices would be decided by a judge in a courtroom nearly three thousand miles away. All of it would be decided for me in the next few hours—and that seemed an awful lot to get out of bed for.

Texts of encouragement interrupted my misery, each chime of my phone a reminder I was not alone. I stared down the finish line from the horizontal position in bed and chose to believe in those messages I was receiving and not the doubt or fear that filled my brain.

In between getting sick, I dressed as the warrior I wanted to be—fitted black jeans with zippers at the ankle, cheap black feminine combat boots tied with a bow, black and white blouse, and blazer. I teased my hair as big as I could, trying to conjure up the mood I wanted to create. I fastened necklace after necklace around my neck, pinned the cameo my dad had given me years ago at my wedding on my jacket, and stared at the pile of sunglasses. There was only one pair that was worthy of this day—they only come out for special occasions. Vintage and oversized white plastic, rounded at the bottom and cat-eyed at the top, with gold bridge and accents and blue mirrored lenses—they were their own mood. They were the only pair large enough to shield me from my fears. I clothed myself in the strength and boldness I needed, hoping it would seep in and salve the fears parading through my brain.

●　　●　　●

*Tucked in the back seat of a sedan with a group of college classmates, I headed to a political science conference where I would inevitably steal Henry Kissinger's pen. My white sunglasses were perched on my nose as we drove along. I dove into a biography about a female artist, ignoring the conversations around me. Reading the book about one of my favorite artists, I came upon a short paragraph speculating a sexual assault had happened to her. A name appeared in my head. Billy McCowan.*

*Why am I thinking of the neighborhood babysitter I had when I was three years old? I haven't thought of him in years, not since we moved from Pennsylvania. I'm reading a book that mentions molestation, and all I can think about is Billy McCowan. This makes no sense.*

*From behind the white sunglasses, I sat in stillness. The voices of others, the music blaring, all of it went mute. Why the fuck am I reading a book about this artist maybe being molested and thinking about the babysitter I had when I was three years old? I pushed his name as far out of my brain as I possibly could, but it lingered in the dark crevices of my mind.*

*The weekend was a blur of young people eager to create change in the world, to be the leaders of tomorrow. Other than swiping Henry Kissinger's pen after he abandoned it at his book signing table, the only thing I can recall is the name Billy McCowan and how it continued to haunt me as I listened to speaker after speaker. I began to recall muddy memories. I was swimming at the McCowan pool and scared of the person holding me. Billy is jumping over our family's couch to tickle me. The vivid nightmare of someone lurking in the dark bedroom that had stayed with me for sixteen years. My mom is upset that I wet the bed every time they went out for an evening.*

*These memories combined added up to nothing, but in me lingered the question...* Did Billy McCowan do something to me? And if so, why the hell was I just now remembering it? *I needed to know. Returning to campus with a suitcase of questions, I sought out my older sister, Carrie.*

*Finding Carrie on campus was easy. We both were studying art, and I knew she would be in the art department's hallowed halls, creating yet another stunning ceramic piece. We sat on the stairs of a corridor, and I whispered the question I was seeking to know. "Did Billy McCowan do something to me?" I didn't have the words at nineteen years of age to say molest. Her face fell, and tears rolled down her cheeks, giving me the answer before she spoke it: "Yes." We talked for a while, and she didn't remember that much, only that Billy had always favored me and had inappropriately touched me. That was as much as I needed to know as I unpacked the concept that you could repress a memory for sixteen years and have it smack you in the face while reading a book.*

*A few weeks later, carrying my newfound secret with me, I was home to visit my parents in Ohio. I didn't whisper a word of what I now knew and instead dug about in old pictures, searching for answers. I noted the picture on our home's dining room wall. That's odd, I thought because my sunglasses now were white. Then, as I looked through years of my life in old family albums, I discovered a link—almost every picture where I was outside, I wore white sunglasses. Had I unknowingly been wearing my version of a "Scarlet Letter" my whole life, or was this my security blanket and shield, keeping me hidden from the pain I didn't even know I carried? I vowed that day only to wear white sunglasses for the rest of my life.*

●　　　●　　　●

Even on this day of reckoning, I needed to care for others and rushed to The Warren Store to pick up pastries and drinks for the gaggle of warriors who would attend the sentencing hearing with me in Vermont. They would face down Jeffrey with me, and the least I could do was feed them with gratitude and snacks.

Mimi and others scooped me up and drove me to Montpelier. I chose to sit in the back and stare out the window. I didn't hear a word they said as I took in the rushing river and leaves changing colors. Paralyzed and numb, I focused on the river. It took me back to the drives with my dad while he was dying, and his presence was palpable.

The dome of the capitol in Montpelier glistened above us. It was a bluebird day, which felt unfair given the uncertainty it held. I craved gloomy rain to match my mood. Luckily, if there was any luck in this situation, I was able to appear by phone for the sentencing hearing. I had offered my apartment, but Amy, my advocate, wanted me to be in a space I would never have to be in again, and sentencing would take place in a conference room at the attorney general's office.

I sensed a transference of support from Washington to Vermont as I led these women into the office where Amy Farr awaited us, along with my future. Calmly and with certainty, Amy laid out the process to my friends as we sat around a jumble of conference tables brought together to form a rectangle with a phone on the table placed in front of me. Amy sat to the left of me, holding my safety and composure; Mimi was to my right.

Still scratching for control in the process that had never been mine to control in the first place, I broke out the snacks. Just because I couldn't eat didn't mean that others shouldn't. I quietly shared with the ladies that Jeffrey would probably say things about me. I didn't know what he would say, but it wasn't true. I cautioned them about the graphic content they may hear. They each looked at me as if to say, "No shit, Anna. You can lay it all down now. We are here for you." Their small talk swirled around me, trying to distract me in its intent. It sailed over my head. I sat surrounded yet alone. Even "Eye of the Tiger" didn't give me strength.

Amy called into the courtroom in Washington on the phone placed in front of me, and my two worlds separated by thousands of miles came colliding together. The only thread connecting them was me. Staring at the phone in front of me, the pages of my impact statement, the faces of my friends, I know my eyes begged for protection, to stop time in place.

*Let me out of this room. We aren't going to get ten years. We probably won't even get five. This is all for nothing—I'm never going to be free. I need to run and hide.* In the courtroom, I could hear the faint sound of metal, the chains around Jeffrey's ankles. *I am so grateful to appear by phone. I don't think I could do this in person.*

The proceedings began. Judge Basden was going through procedural pieces, and Jeffrey objected every chance he had, his voice filling our conference room. Everyone's eyes focused on me. This was the first time my friends in Vermont had heard his voice, the voice that had haunted my world for longer than I had known. My mind still couldn't accept the reality that he had been stalking me since 2008 or 2009.

James, the prosecution, spoke with clarity and reason while Jeffrey interrupted him, calling him a "bitch," a "liar," and other choices words, then challenging him to a fight outside. James, with measure, continued, stopping only when Judge Basden tried to quiet Jeffrey while upholding the law.

*Put yourself under a stack of quilts. Float away, Anna. Do not hear his voice. Muffle the sounds under the protective fibers.*

James spoke to the fact that the criminal justice system didn't have an answer for a person like Jeffrey. He spoke to my loss and then asked for an exceptional sentence of eight years of incarceration and two years of community custody. I heard the metal of Jeffrey's chains again, and Judge Basden asked Jeffrey to sit down and stop pacing.

*Drift farther away, Anna—it will all be over soon. Bury yourself in white sunglasses.*

James finished speaking, and Judge Basden invited me to read my statement.

With strength birthed out of brokenness, I began. "Honorable Judge Basden, thank you for allowing me time to speak today. I am sitting in the Vermont attorney general's office."

Jeffrey interrupted me, but I didn't hear his words. I sat silently, staring down, waiting for the judge to let me continue. *Fuck you, Jeffrey. NOW I SPEAK.*

Judge Basden reminded Jeffrey that this was my time to speak, and Jeffrey would be able to reply afterward.

I began again. "Honorable Judge Basden, thank you for allowing me time to speak today. I am sitting in the Vermont attorney general's office."

Judge Basden interrupted me. They were having a hard time hearing me in the courtroom, and he requested we call in from another number. I was frozen. I had zero confidence I would make it through my entire statement, let alone start over for the third time with all the interruptions. Amy took over the logistics, and before I knew it, I started again.

"Honorable Judge Basden, thank you for allowing me time to speak today. I am sitting in the Vermont attorney general's office. With me from the attorney general's office is Amy Farr as well as several friends and community members. These people, the state of Vermont, as well as friends and colleagues..."

"You're a moronic jackass," Jeffrey interrupted and started to trail off on a tangent. He threw out insults left and right, trying to undo me, and he was starting to win.

*Please, please, now I speak...*

Judge Basden's voice flowed through the speaker. He was moving Jeffrey to the holding cell where he could listen to my statement but would be on mute so I could speak without interruption. Judge Basden was giving me voice—he was giving me safety while upholding the law to the nth degree.

Minutes ticked by while the courtroom set up the jail camera, transferred Jeffrey, and readied itself. Minutes, hours, seconds. I only know from looking at the court transcripts.

*I am broken, I am beaten, I am frail—now I speak.* And when invited to, I started to speak again.

"Honorable Judge Basden-

"Thank you for allowing me time to speak today. I am sitting in the Vermont Attorney General's Office. With me is from the Attorney General's office Amy Farr, as well as several friends and community members. These people, the state of Vermont, as well as friends and colleagues in the state of Washington stand with me today in solidarity. By doing this, they show their understanding of the seriousness of which they take the crime of stalking and the importance of the safety of each citizen of Vermont and Washington."

"Today, Your Honor, I am going to speak to you, and not the defendant. I am grateful to have my voice heard. After the trial and reflecting on the process, I can without a doubt say how grateful and fortunate I am to be alive to speak. Today I am not here to debate name pronunciations. I will be referring to Mr. Bradford as the defendant moving forward. I am not here to make justifications for my appearance, discuss how I am not an "evil" person, defend the non-existent sexual relationship with my father, or non-existent relationship with the defendant. I cannot speak for the other victims, but I know their journeys and experiences of being stalked by the defendant are just as horrific as mine. Today I will speak to four areas of my life that have been affected, changed, and limited by the defendant. The defendant was a stranger to me, a man who should have had no bearing or impact on my life. His stalking of me has affected my life for eight years, in emotional, physical, community and financial ways. I will close with my request for sentencing."

"The emotional toll of this crime is vast. In many ways the crime of stalking is invisible. It's psychological: It is calculated manipulation to intimidate and cause fear. We can see the piles of physical evidence in communication and behavior – but the effects are long term, invisible and debilitating. From the first week the defendant made himself evident in my life in November 2011 he has been extremely effective at this. He quickly established he was watching me, that he was attracted to me, that he wanted to be with me. The swiftness of his communication promptly placed me into a state of fear. The strong confident woman I was became a small shell, worrying and wondering each moment of the day of what lurked outside and what he was capable of. Because of the defendant's relentless communication about art and wanting to show at my gallery, the emotional toll quickly encroached into my business, placing me in a paralyzing fear when trying to sell a piece at my gallery. I was constantly afraid he would show up and injure me or others. As the years drew on and his stalking continued those fears became larger and more paralyzing. They became permanent scars on my life, leaving me with PTSD, anxiety, social anxiety, and depression. These still and likely always will plague my life. No matter how safe I know I am, such as when I'm at the farmer's market in Vermont and see a man who resembles the defendant, my stomach drops. When a friend says something about "evil people" I want to sob or defend myself, thinking of how many times he called me "evil" and talked about how "evil" people should die. When I'm at a large community gathering, my eyes are always scanning to make sure I'm safe. Sometimes I'm so fearful I just don't go. My friends know to never try to scare me, to not surprise me, not to show up unannounced at my home, the list goes on. I have created a new path and I am navigating my life the best I can, but it is filled with rules for my own safety, both mentally and physically. The crime of stalking is isolating, and you in turn isolate yourself further to find safety and peace in any way possible."

"The emotional effects have turned into physical effects that have plagued my life for eight years. As humiliating as it is to share the physical effects, I feel it is important to do so. Within the first month of the defendant appearing in my world, I have had a very physical response to his communications with me. When his messages arrived, he followed me, and even when I had to appear in court, I found myself running for the toilet to either vomit or because I have diarrhea. This involuntary response has continued for eight years and throughout the trial. Even as I am writing this impact statement, I must be near a bathroom."

"The stress and anxiety I carry in my body means I clench my teeth all night and recently cracked a back molar because of this. I fall asleep on the edge of my queen-size bed, ready to leap up if danger or harm finds its way into my home. It is challenging for me to take a walk on my own. Walking is my favorite mode of exercise, but my fear keeps me indoors. I don't exercise as I should, and joining a gym is impossible due to financial loss."

"The most long-lasting physical effect is the loss of my period. I am 39 years old, and I no longer menstruate. I stopped having my period in the spring of 2017 when the defendant had been harassing me with his vile communication for six years. I thought he was going to come to Vermont and harm me. My body just ceased having a period. This means I can't have children. I envisioned a life in which I would be a mom. My friends in Port Townsend saved their baby clothes for me. I grew up loving to care for children, and I relish my time with my nieces and nephews. Children of my own will not be part of my life's path. I saw a life in front of me: having a baby, owning my gallery, raising my child with a partner in Port Townsend. It was a beautiful dream, and reality turned it into a nightmare. This dream is not to be, and it still daily breaks my heart."

"Port Townsend was and, in many ways, still is my community and home. I miss my community, my friends, the mountains and the ocean daily. If I were to look at my social media I still see and know more about Port Townsend, than I do my community in Vermont. I loved and valued being a community member there. I delighted in having my gallery and that my gallery in turn supported and showcased local artists. It was a big beautiful gift I got to provide every day. In turn my community loved, held and supported me. That feeling of love and support from community is evident to this day, and it speaks volumes to the people who reside there and their care for each other. Because of this, when the defendant began stalking me, I had a duty to keep my community safe."

"During gallery walks, or whenever the door was open, I was constantly on guard, thinking "I need to make sure others are safe." I changed my life patterns. I didn't go out unless accompanied by someone else. I watched my gallery like a hawk during gallery walks and events. I had to do whatever I could to make sure if the defendant's threats of harm came true, no one else would be hurt or killed. Even when I moved to Vermont, when the defendant made threats of injury to law enforcement, it was my duty to immediately pick up the phone and notify the Port Townsend Police Department. To this day I have an obligation to the community of Port Townsend, because the actions and language of the defendant put many people at risk, not only me. I have had this echoed back to me countless times by community members. It's not a role I wanted to take on, none of this is. The loss of Port Townsend is heart-breaking. Someday, if I can know for sure that I am safe, I want to return to my home in Port Townsend. In the future I look forward to spending more and more time there and being able to immerse myself back into the community, the people and life that I love so much, for as long as I safely can."

"That life and reality that wasn't to be has not only cost me emotionally and physically, it has gutted me financially. My former business, Artisans on Taylor Gallery, closed in October 2013 due in majority part (75%) to the defendant stalking me and the debilitating fear that came along with this. When you are being stalked the last place you want to be is where the stalker knows you are. I was a sitting duck in my gallery. Compounding matters, there was a community of people who would visit regularly. My greatest fear was injury to others, even more so than myself. The effects were staggering, on my ability to even complete the simplest of transactions, to hold regular business hours, to be present when engaging with buyers. From November 2010 to November 2011 I did $250,000 in sales at my gallery, which means I personally made approximately $60,000 during that year. If I had continued with that success and my gallery had not closed due to the emotional and physical effects of the defendant stalking me, I would have made an income of $480,000 over the last eight years. I have not recouped this amount, and I never will. I am still paying off my gallery to this day. I relocated across the country which is not a cheap thing to do. I have spent thousands of dollars in therapy. I took a job and then had my hours cut when I had to make my employer aware of the defendant after he said he was going to come to Waitsfield, VT to be with me. I live off an income that is well below poverty. My credit is wrecked. I doubt I will ever be able to buy a house. The defendant's stalking of me has destroyed me financially – there is no other way to state it."

"The emotional, physical and financial effects, combined, have created the life I have now. I live in a studio apartment, in an old falling-apart farmhouse. It has two exits so I can safely flee if he were to break in and attack me. I work from home because I feel safer there than in the community. I occasionally waitress to make ends meet, something I hadn't done since my 20s. I've tried to date but I have had several relationships end when they found out why I moved to Vermont. Suddenly my dates feel I am not safe. It has been the same with jobs: When I tell them of my situation, my employer cuts my hours. So I only do this if there is a chance of threat to my employer."

"I look in the mirror and see the woman I once was, and I mourn the loss of her. This loss is because the defendant, a man I do not know, I have never known, with whom I have never had a relationship of any kind, wreaked havoc on me and others. His actions have made others feel unsafe to be around me, when I have done nothing but try to protect myself and those around me. I mourn the life I thought I would have: the business, the community, the children, the family. I work each day to figure out the life that's been forced upon me."

"The crime of stalking doesn't end. It has been an open wound that cannot heal. Through these eight years, through court hearings, losing my business, moving myself across the country, I thought I might begin to bandage the wound and start to heal, but it never stops and thus the healing can't begin. During the last several years, even while incarcerated, the defendant has continued to stalk me, through letters, through the court system, through the not knowing for myself what the outcome would be. The feelings of fear and danger he conveys through many different modes are always there. Even during trial, he continued to harass me while testifying and being cross-examined. So the wound got still larger. The defendant has not shown remorse or any indication that he will discontinue his behavior."

"The sentence you hand down today could allow a clean bandage to be put on this gaping wound and for healing and closure to begin."

"Judge Basden, today I ask you to consider the maximum penalty of 10 years for the defendant. This is not only a sentence for the defendant, it is a sentence for each of his victims. It is our sentence to freedom. My freedom has been gone for nearly eight years, and perhaps longer than that. During the trial and questioning I realized the defendant was likely stalking me before I was aware of it. The financial, personal and emotional loss is immeasurable, but my sense of freedom and safety trump even those things. What you do today, Your Honor, does not end this crime, but it gives me and the other victims a reprieve, before we return to that daily fear. You are sentencing all of us today. I urge you to give us the longest sentence you see fit, so we may enjoy our lives of freedom and safety for as long we possibly can."

"If I could turn back time, the defendant would never become an uninvited guest who unraveled my future. I would still be happily open-ing my gallery and sharing my love of art with my community. But I can't turn back time, and I can't undo the last eight years. I can only hope the last eight years and your actions today protect others from becoming victims and give a reprieve to the victims we know about. I am asking for rest for the other brave women who testified and for myself. I believe there is safety in this sentencing for those victims we may not know about. It will keep others and their communities safe. It will allow law enforcement and elected officials to do their jobs without fear of death or injury. And for me, personally, if the young woman working in her shop, just trying to live out her dreams, can continue to do so, if she gets to grow her life in every way I won't, if she never has to know the fear and pain, the trauma and agony of the defendant's vile behavior, then I will walk away with the satisfaction that justice was served. I may have lost almost everything over the past eight years, but today I would like to begin again and build my future for as long as I possibly can."

"Thank you, Judge Basden, for hearing my words today and taking them into consideration as you make your decision."

---

Tears filled my eyes, my body so fragile I feared it would turn to dust, as those around the table soothed me and encouraged me. "You've done it—you did great," they echoed one another. But I was hollow, every pair of white sunglasses I'd ever worn piling onto my head and burying me under the weight I was carrying.

Jeffrey was brought back into the courtroom. He spoke as his own defense, but I didn't hear a damn thing he said. As he spoke, my warriors around the table kept checking in with me. I could no longer hear Jeffrey's voice—it was now meaningless to me, its power sucked out of my brain. He closed his long-winded diatribe, and Judge Basden began to speak.

The countdown to my future started.

5.

"Ms. Nasset, thank you for your statement. It is an accurate summary of crimes of this nature's impact on victims of these types of crimes. We respond to the damages that are most visible when sometimes those least visible are the worst," said Judge Basden. I listened intently.

*Wait, what? This judge actually heard me...*

290 NOW I SPEAK

4.

Judge Basden continued. "Thank you for your courage, the most personal details of your life to allow the courts to better understand."

*Get to it, Judge Basden. Come on, is it two years, five years, eight years—please get to it.*

3.

"The state calculated the accurate standard sentencing range," stated Judge Basden. "However,

in this case, it is clear to the court that it is anything but typical and compel to sentence outside of reasonable range." I clawed at the table in front of me.

*What does he mean outside reasonable range?!!!!!!!!*

2.

"It's clear that the best description may be the reign of terror that you imposed upon Ms. Nasset as well as others should not continue. And despite repeated efforts to stop that, nothing has worked because you seem bound and determined to stalk, to harass, or to disrupt the very essence of life for these victims," Judge Basden said directly to Jeffrey, who, at this point, had been speaking the entire time, throwing insults about me, James, and Judge Basden into the wind.

*Say it, say it, say it. Please just say it. I can't do this for one more second. I need to know my life. I need to know I matter. I need to know I'm seen. I need to know even if it is just for a day that I am safe and free, that I did the right thing. Please, please, please just say it.*

1.

While Jeffrey continued to speak, Judge Basden continued. "The court is going to impose the maximum penalty of ten years in this matter."

I never heard Jeffrey's voice the entire time the judge was speaking—I only heard Judge Basden's voice. I only know Jeffrey kept talking because people in the room informed me. I remember only two words when Judge Basden said, "ten years." I clung to Amy's arm, asking her to repeat what he had said. She nodded and stated, "Ten years." I then collapsed to the floor in what my friend would later tell me was the "rawest emotional moment she had ever witnessed." I didn't cry—I gasped for air as Mimi sat on the floor next to me, holding me. Everyone else sat, shaken by what they had just witnessed. In my greatest moment, that is all I can recall. It was too much for my brain to hold that level of release and joy.

Eventually, like a newborn deer, I wobbled back into my seat at the table. The goofiest, happiest, most dumbfounded smile slowly slid across my face, replacing the years of grief and pain. I reached into my purse and put on a T-shirt I had tucked inside "just in case" we won. It simply said, "She Came. She Saw. She Fucked Shit Up." I put on the shirt, knowing that celebrations would start shortly from Vermont to Washington.

There were three people I wanted to break the news to. My first text was to Debbie Riddle, who started Stalking Awareness Month to honor her late sister. The second went to Erica—we were safe now. The last was to my mother.

I walked out of the attorney general's office that day with my stone-cold clan of women, into the bluebird sky day that I finally, finally felt like I deserved. I walked a few steps ahead of my friends, taking in my own strength. I had been supported by countless people over the years, but for the first time, I saw and felt the strength in myself. No one had saved me—I had saved myself. The sun shone fully with its warmth on my face, and I lingered for a minute before lovingly placing my white sunglasses on my face and walking into my decade of freedom.

# CHAPTER TWENTY-FOUR

# WHY ME?

**In a recent meta-analysis of seventeen studies of intimate partner homicide (Spencer & Stith, 2020), stalking produced a three-fold increase in the odds of the abuse escalating to a homicide. In other words, victims who are stalked by an intimate partner are 300 percent more likely to be murdered at the hands of the same intimate partner.[28]**

Each night, a face scratches at the glass of my window. The wind blows it back and forth, smashing dried petals with a rustle against the pane. Startled by the dried mopheads clinging to life on the hydrangea bush, I jump, anxiety tingling my skin. I know it is a cluster of dried and fluffy flowers; my brain knows, my body knows it. Yet each night, as the darkness falls and moonlight rises, the flowers turn into a floating face, clawing to get in. I, in turn, go to battle against them and myself.

The first few months in my new apartment, they beat me nightly in our shared game. Turning the corner into my living room, my breath tightly in the air, I would release an exhale when I remembered, *It's simply dead flowers—no one is looking in your window.* Checking all the locks on my doors, looking out the windows onto the dirt lane lit only by the moon and stars, I'd find peace again in myself. I could have cut the flowers down so they could not attack my nerve system again, yet I needed to win, and I let them stay.

Night after night would pass in this same tournament: hydrangeas – 52, Anna – 0. They took over the dark evenings in the fall and winter of Vermont in 2020; they stalked me, hurling their petaled faces against my window. They took on the persona of every man who had ever injured me, a thin pane of glass that separated us.

Next to the window where the dead ones haunted my dreams was my writing desk. For the first few months, I could barely sit at the desk, terrified of the flowers that stood one foot from me and what they had come to represent, more terrified still of the words that would come out if I sat and put fingers to keys.

I hung a few postcards and one quote on the wall next to the flowers without thought. I had toted these prized scraps of paper around this country for years.

On an envelope, scrawled in black ink, reads:

"I've been absolutely terrified every moment of my life, and I've never let it keep me from doing a single thing I want to do." —Georgia O'Keeffe

Slowly, as the days grew longer, I began to fill the wall around my desk with more notes and words I had received during the trial. The ones from Lea and Amy were joined by others:

"Courageous people can also be terrified in the midst of their courage." —Officer Corrigan

"With all the time you had to be outside of who you are, I hope justice is served." —Anonymous

"Walk yourself in the grace of allowing yourself to unpack it." —Ellen

And finally: "Anna, that's never been a part of your life you've gotten to control." —Megan

I began to write, and I began to take back control of my existence.

Jeffrey's sentence is one of the longest sentences in the United States of America's history for the crime of stalking. That's right—I, Anna Nasset, the woman sitting in her apartment at the end of a dirt lane, up the side of a mountain in Vermont, did the impossible and received this landmark victory. This fact alone begs the question...WHY ME?

Why are Peggy Klinke and Sharon Wiggs dead? Or Karyme Barreto-Sabalza, Tysiona Crawford, Hollie Gazzard, Jenny Gamez, and Laura Simonson? We will never understand the totality of loss, homicide, sexual assault that has happened at the hands of stalkers. If we did know the number, we would be unable to process the magnitude.

I can tell you why stalking is a forgotten and ignored crime. It is brushed off when reported to law enforcement or advocates because it is nearly impossible to prove, and as victims, we are told we are overreacting. Additionally, the majority of stalking victims know their stalkers—it's often a former intimate partner, a friend, even a family member. Cases such as mine make up for only 19 percent of the 13.5 million stalking cases in the United States each year. Because of the lack of education to victim service providers regarding the danger of stalking, it is a major precursor in homicides. Knowledge of stalking will save lives if taken seriously.[29]

Only a small percentage of stalking victims ever report to law enforcement, compounding the danger even further. With the societal view and voyeurism of stalking, portrayed in everything from Valentine's Day greeting cards to hit shows like *You*, victims of stalking often don't even realize the danger or know how to give a name to the crime until it's too late. If it were not for calling Ford in the early days, I could have fallen into this same line of thinking. Even after calling Ford, it took me months to use the word "stalking" and years to use the term "victim of crime" when referring to this part of my life.

The very nature of the crime of stalking is to rip the victim apart psychologically, to have a continual assault on our minds. When that is the reality of every moment you live in, depression, fear, and anxiety take over, and it becomes even harder to step outside of that and make a choice to access help and services. And IF you are one of the people who reports the crime and are met with empathy, what are your next steps? There is no choice but to become your own advocate and investigator in hopes that you can achieve getting a piece of paper in the form of a protection order—a piece of paper that you may very well have to stand next to the stalker to receive.

With the freedom I have been sentenced to for the next decade, I made a decision, I will not be the exception. I will work to make sentences like mine the standard.

It is a horrific uphill battle that appears never to end. I may be the woman who has received one of the longest sentences to freedom in our nation's history, but it took me eight years (known to me—and eleven in reality) to see that justice. And do I think for one second that Jeffrey is going to stop his reign of terror against me when he is released? May my voice echo off the mountaintops as I stand and scream, "NOOOOOOOOO!" I live in the reality that my voice and work will likely one day be silenced—I safety plan for my future upon his release. I will never truly be free of his hold on my life until one of us is dead. Here I sit, working in stalking awareness and prevention, the gold standard of prosecuting a stalker, yet one day, I will have to shelve all of it and descend back into the shadows from which I broke free. I may be your waitress, your marketing manager, your gardener. I don't know where or what I will be, but I know I will slip away again.

I work to create a quiet and simple life with beauty and comfort around me in the form of plants, quilts, macrame, mountaintop views, my safe house. I can look back at it all and see how brave and bold I was to never give up in my quest for freedom for myself and others, but it all comes at a cost. I go days at a time without leaving my home. I navigate in a small circle of comfort. I still sit where I can view the door when eating out, carry a knife when walking, have an app to inform me what mail is arriving in my PO box (in case I receive a semen-filled letter from Jeffrey), and know my security drills inside and out. That is the world in which I live. I have healed the wounds of the other atrocities done to me in my life, but when it comes to stalking, I fear it will be an open wound that will never heal over.

Imagine, then, if I am one of the few who has seen successful prosecution and is alive, how do the other millions of stalking victims feel, having no justice, no privilege, no protection, and no freedom? What choices are they making on a moment-by-moment basis to keep not only themselves but their children, loved ones, and community safe? They make impossible choices, changing names, relocating, quitting jobs, living in constant fear and trauma—often without any resources or support to make these changes. Do you know what happens next? Without intervention and safety, all too often, they are murdered.

It has to stop. I am so damn angry every time I receive an email from a victim needing help. I see their world crumbling around them, and how can I help them? It took eight fucking years for me to have a grasp on freedom. What hope or answer can I give them? I can't wave a magic wand and make it stop. The only people who can stop this crime and save lives are each of you. Take the crime of stalking seriously— don't brush it off, tell us we are overreacting, or make jokes. Start by believing, walk your friend into the advocacy center or the police station, make sure their voice is heard because all they may have is a whisper. Hold people accountable if you see them displaying signs of stalking. Don't look the other way. Stalking is a societal problem that we have a responsibility to change as a society.

And to you, my dear friend, who are experiencing stalking, I see you, and I know you. Wherever you are in your journey to healing, whether you report the incident or not, I see you, and I see your resilience. I know there is a team of people that will be there for you whether you realize it or not. It's hard to see the light in our darkest moments, but I see the light in you, and I know you will go on to do incredible things. These crimes that are done to us do NOT define us. I know that's hard because it seems like the pain fills every cell of our bodies. But YOU are so much more than a victim; you are even more than a survivor. You are quite simply just YOU. And no matter what is done to you, NO ONE can take that from you.

There are still a few straggling mopheads on the hydrangea bush. It will be months before it begins to bloom, but they don't taunt me anymore. I won, I didn't chop them down, I accepted them for what they are. They are outside of me, and I can't control them, not how they grow, nor how they appear. What I have come to realize in the three years since the trial and the two years of living with the hydrangea bush is that I can't control what has happened to me, but it's no longer running me. I'm running my future now, no matter what it holds. Because I am alive, I am one of the few who has won, and I certainly can't let a bunch of dead flowers be what takes me down. It will be spring soon.

# Closing Thoughts

**A**s I finished *Now I Speak* and approved the last of the edits, the Supreme Court of the United States delivered their ruling in an important case regarding stalking. This information shared by Stalking Prevention, Awareness, and Resource Center (SPARC) sheds light on this unsettling event:

**What's the SCOTUS Counterman v. Colorado case?**
The First Amendment protects free speech. However, true threats are not protected speech.

In 2017, Colorado found Counterman guilty of stalking for communicating threats to the victim. Counterman argued that case was wrongly decided because he didn't intend his communication to be threatening; the prosecution never proved he intended it to be threatening; and, therefore, his communication was protected under the First Amendment as free speech. Colorado disagreed, arguing that Counterman's speech would cause a reasonable person to feel fear and was therefore a "true threat" – which is not protected.

**So did the Supreme Court "side with" Counterman?**
The Supreme Court ruled that Colorado needed to prove that Counterman knew or should have known his communication

would be threatening. Rather than focusing on if a reasonable person would feel fear, this new decision specifies that the State must establish the defendant understood their communications would be threatening. SCOTUS said the prosecution must at least show the defendant disregarded a substantial risk that their communications would be viewed as a threat.

SCOTUS sent the case back down to Colorado for them to apply the correct test – that of Counterman's mental state when he made the communication. There needs to be proof that a reasonable person in Counterman's position would understand his statements to be threats.

**What does this change?**
Colorado (and now, all jurisdictions) must show that offenders understood the threatening nature of their communication. A prosecution must show that an offender was at least reckless in making a communication that would be taken as threatening, i.e., a conscious disregard of a substantial risk that a statement would be viewed as threatening.

Many stalking statutes already explicitly or implicitly require that the State prove that offenders acted recklessly, knowingly, or intentionally in making a communication that would be viewed as threatening, so prosecutions in those states do not appear to be impacted by the Counterman decision."[30]

What does this mean for me and the millions of other stalking victims? Only time will tell. When the news of this ruling came in, I found myself gasping for air, physically sick, confused, and thrust back onto the rollercoaster of unknowns I have been trapped on for over a decade. Over the following week, I heard from my prosecutors, who feel optimistic that my verdict will be upheld due to nuances in Washington state stalking laws, yet there are no guarantees.

Remember that I, one of the few "lucky" stalking victims in the United States of America, as my case turned out with the maximum sentence, is sitting in the uncertainty and fear once again... How do the millions of others who have not been able to access services, who were not believed, and who have countless barriers placed on them feel?

In the end, I know nothing is certain. I don't know how this could affect parole hearings or ability to prosecute in the future, and I once again stare down the path of the fearful unknown. But I know I am not alone, and I know that for however long I am able, I will use my voice to push for change and safety for all stalking victims. For now, I speak.

# Acknowledgments

This book is my story and my life, and it represents the lives of millions of other victims and survivors—faceless and nameless. It is a book for all who have experienced gender-based violence. To anyone who sees themselves in my words, I sit in gratitude and support with you.

On my wall hangs a framed piece of printer paper. There are over one hundred names I hand wrote on the page in between the trial and sentencing—he names of everyone who walked the path to justice with me. When I began writing my book, I wanted to include every one of them and, of course, learned how confusing that would be to the reader. If you think your name is on that paper, it is, and I thank you for all you have done for me and with me. I told our story to the best of my ability and memory with care to share my failings and triumphs. It was a brutal undertaking, and I know each of you were with me.

To my parents, the great Deb and the late, great Mark. I have walked a path different from what you would have wanted for me, I am sure, and I thank you for loving me though this journey. You have protected me and championed me every step of the way, which I can imagine is not always easy. You are shining stars of parents, and I am forever grateful to have been born into our family.

To my sister, Carrie, never judging, gently listening, always steady, and her husband, Paul, for your support and understanding.

To Maw Maw, my grandma, for teaching me to sew, encouraging my business since day one, and having my business card on hand in case you meet a victim in need.

To the rest of my extended family, aunts, uncles, cousins, thank you for the connected kindness.

To the people who first taught me to use my voice back in college—Kathy, Darah, Julie, Katie, Kay, and Professor Knapp. We aren't the best at staying in touch, but our formative time and experiences of growth during our younger years walked me through this journey.

To the ladies of Maine—Missy and Emily, Joe's Angels. We have grown up together in our adulthood. I was absent for a while, but in gratitude for the laughter, friendship, conversations, encouragement, and texts that make me spit out my coffee with laughter, I love you.

To Elisabeth, my original business partner and dear friend, you have taught me to make life a little more beautiful, to look closely at the tiny treasures, and to face myself head on.

To Port Townend—in the sadness and triumph of this book, I was transported back to my favorite place. This book is a love letter to my old home and to each of you.

Ellen, my bestie out westie, I love you. We have fought hard for our friendship, faced its challenges, and talked for more hours on the phone over the last years than I could even begin to imagine, and you are with me for life.

Megan, you shining human. You have shown up and quietly carried me through the toughest moments of my life. Your joy, curiosity, and presence have made my life completer and taught me countless lessons.

Christel, Kirsten, Sara, Corrine, Eric, Emily, Kyle, Caroline, Joe, Rachel, and Gerda, thank you for your support, love, laughter, and encouragement.

Jason, my friend, supporter, and advisor, thank you for the presence you have had in my life, even in those complex moments.

Kiwi, the late Jimmy, the late Ted, and the rest of the Edensaw crew— ya'll may be a little gruff on the outside, but you have been the kindest bonus dads I could have ever received, and I thank you for letting me be part of your family.

My weird quirky community, Port Townsend, I love you and thank you.

To Vermont, I fell in love with you more and more as I wrote. I've always liked you, but as I sat lingering over my story and how I came to this state, I realized I'd always been resentful. Walking into my years here, I began to see the beauty of the people and place here more clearly, and it has changed me to be more present in these Green Mountains I call home.

Mimi, I adore you. You have helped me dream again, to throw on a pair of rose-colored glasses and explore the world with curiosity. You've also taught me that sometimes it's not about asking the questions—it's about simply hanging the curtains.

Grace, our friendship began as I started the process of writing nearly three years ago and has blossomed into the most beautiful mutually supportive and connected gift I could have ever asked for.

Ana, your ability to quietly radiate peace and understanding has inspired me and challenged me more than you will ever know. Thank you for our friendship.

Mullet, thank you for the numerous conversations, reminding me of parts of my story my trauma-filled brain forgot, and all of the encouragement.

Kevin, Patti, Audrey, Jean, both the Jacks, Karin, Lorien, Lansie, Rebecca, Sasha, the numerous ladies of the valley, and countless others in the Mad River Valley, thank you for welcoming me to this, my home.

To Ballast Books—Savannah, Andy, Kayleigh, Breanne, Lauren, and the rest of the team. My journey to you was long and filled with rejections. I was told countless times, "She's a good writer, but...," "She doesn't have enough social media followers," or "Jeffrey didn't sexually assault her, so it's not that bad." After that path of failure, I found you, and you believed in me. Your encouragement, excitement, and willingness to answer all my questions have shaped me into the writer I now am.

Kevin, thank you for all the work you put into the early phases and for teaching me that "sometimes a chicken is not a chicken."

Erika, my editor and neighbor, in meeting you, I didn't just find a "writer friend"—I found a lifelong friend and confidante. Looking out at night while I wrote and seeing your lights, I knew I was not alone. Thank you.

To Lea, you are a damn land mermaid of equality, fighting for the rights of others. In you, I began to learn how I could use my voice for change. Thank you, my cherished friend.

To Sue Russell, my pen pal, whose legacy I work every day to carry on, inspired by your encouragement, strength, and legendary work in victims' rights. I am honored to know you and call you a friend.

Andrea, you saw in me something I would never have begun to grasp—my voice—and asked me one simple question that would change the course of my life forever.

Debbie Riddle, the first person I texted after the sentencing, the work you did after the tragic loss of your sister changed the way the nation sees stalking. I am alive because of your work.

The Center for Crime Victim Services, Vermont Network Against Domestic and Sexual Violence, Detective Sawyer, Maxine Grad, Dr. Patrick Brady, Lenora Claire, 2018 cohort of the VVAA, EVAWI, NOVA,

VINElink, SPARC, and every organization and individual who has brought me in to speak and share, thank you. I work to serve you as you serve others.

To everyone who worked on the trial, thank you—you saved my life.

Officer Corrigan, thank you for believing me the day I walked into the PTPD and for your unwavering support. Thank you for fighting for me.

Dee Boughton, thank you for taking on the case in 2012. Your foundational work led us to this victory.

Retired Honorable Judge Landes, for many years until you retired, I saw you as the gatekeeper of fairness to my safety. Since your retirement, I now see you as a historic supporter of safety for victims of crime, a champion, a friend, and a stand-up comedian. I am honored to know you.

Detective Dropp, your investigation and kind communication led to this trial and to me be willing to continue the process.

Judge Basden, thank you for your fairness and judgment.

Jillian, through countless phone calls, emails, texts, and more, you never stopped keeping me informed and bringing any peace you could into the years leading to the trial.

Steve Johnson, the hundreds of hours of research you did in building this case, working away behind the scenes, is work that often goes unnoticed, but I noticed, and I carry it with me each day.

Amy Farr, you didn't need to take me on in the advocacy role, but you did. You set aside hour after hour to prepare me, meet with me, and encourage me. You are what advocacy looks like.

James Kennedy, you took on the impossible. You fought for safety and freedom for me and others, but more notable is how you did it.

You peeled back the layers of my victimhood, saw me as a full human, and treated me as such—with dignity and honesty. I was able to stand in my strength, to go the distance, to speak my truth because of you. Thank you.

Additionally, Ford; The Dove House; Vermont Attorney General's Office; Port Townsend Police Department; Port Angeles Police Department; every bailiff, advocate, court clerk, and therapist; Clallam and Jefferson County; Washington courts; and countless others working to protect, I thank you.

To Erica and all the other victims, we are survivors in arms. We share an experience that no one will ever fully understand, and we are linked forever to that. Thank you for standing up.

# Endnotes

1 https://www.nyc.gov/site/ocdv/services/introduction-to-domestic-violence-and-gender-based-violence.page

2 https://www.stalkingawareness.org/wp-content/uploads/2019/01/SPARC_StalkngFactSheet_2018_FINAL.pdf

3 https://bjs.ojp.gov/content/pub/pdf/sv19.pdf

4 https://www.leagle.com/decision/inwaco20110907b30 (name changed in legal document above)

5 https://www.stalkingawareness.org/wp-content/uploads/2019/01/SPARC_StalkngFactSheet_2018_FINAL.pdf

6 https://www.stalkingawareness.org/wp-content/uploads/2019/01/SPARC_StalkngFactSheet_2018_FINAL.pdf

7 https://bjs.ojp.gov/content/pub/pdf/sv19.pdf

8 https://www.stalkingawareness.org/wp-content/uploads/2019/01/SPARC_StalkngFactSheet_2018_FINAL.pdf

9 https://www.stalkingawareness.org/wp-content/uploads/2020/01/SPA-19.005-Prosecutors-Guide-to-Stalking-00000002-revised.pdf

10 https://bjs.ojp.gov/content/pub/pdf/sv19.pdf

11 Medical News Today, August 2017, Kanna Ingelson

12 https://www.stalkingawareness.org/wp-content/uploads/2018/11/Stalking-IPV-Fact-Sheet.pdf

13  https://www.stalkingawareness.org/wp-content/uploads/2023/01/
    SPARC-FUTURES-Workplace-Stalking-Fact-Sheet.pdf

14  https://www.stalkingawareness.org/wp-content/uploads/2019/01/
    SPARC_StalkngFactSheet_2018_FINAL.pdf

15  https://www.stalkingawareness.org/wp-content/uploads/2019/01/
    SPARC_StalkngFactSheet_2018_FINAL.pdf

16  https://www.intuitivehealingnyc.com/blog/2021/12/27/how-rewatch-
    ing-shows-can-help-ease-your-anxiety#:~:text=Ultimately%2C%20
    rewatching%20your%20favorite%20shows,security%2C%20
    familiarity%2C%20and%20comfort

17  https://www.stalkingawareness.org/wp-content/uploads/2018/08/
    Stalking_Effective_Strategies_for_Prosecutors.pdf

18  https://www.stalkingawareness.org/wp-content/uploads/2018/12/
    Response-Tips-for-Law-Enforcement.pdf

19  https://www.stalkingawareness.org/wp-content/uploads/2023/01/
    SPARC-FUTURES-Workplace-Stalking-Fact-Sheet.pdf

20  https://startbybelieving.org/what-to-say/

21  https://www.stalkingawareness.org/wp-content/uploads/2020/07/
    SupportingLovedOnesExperiencingStalking.pdf

22  A Focal Concerns Perspective on Prosecutorial Decision Making in
    Cases of Intimate Partner Stalking Patrick Q. Brady University of
    West Georgia Bradford W. Reyns Weber State University

23  https://www.stalkingawareness.org/wp-content/uploads/2019/01/
    SPARC_StalkngFactSheet_2018_FINAL.pdf

24  https://www.stalkingawareness.org/wp-content/
    uploads/2022/06/Judicial-Guide-For-Stalking.pdf

25  https://www.rainn.org/articles/telling-loved-ones-
    about-sexual-assault

26  https://www.stalkingawareness.org/wp-content/uploads/2018/11/
    Stalking-IPV-Fact-Sheet.pdf

27 https://www.cdc.gov/violenceprevention/pdf/nisvs/nisvsStalk-ingReport.pdf

28 Brady, P. Q., &; Hayes, B. E. (2018). The intersection of stalking and the severity of intimate partner abuse. Violence and victims, 33(2), 218-238.

Spencer, C. M., &; Stith, S. M. (2020). Risk factors for male perpetration and female victimization of intimate partner homicide: A meta-analysis. Trauma, Violence, & Abuse, 21(3), 527-540.

29 https://www.stalkingawareness.org/wp-content/uploads/2022/04/General-Stalking-Infographic.pdf

30 SPARC https://www.facebook.com/photo/?fbid=261063099902834&set=pcb.261063149902829